HARRY L. MILLER

MARJORIE B. SMILEY

Education in

the Metropolis

THE FREE PRESS, *New York*
COLLIER-MACMILLAN LIMITED, *London*

Preface

This collection of readings results from a project under Grant Number 62201 of the United States Office of Juvenile Delinquency and Youth Development. The Project, entitled TRUE, or *Teachers and Resources for Urban Education,* has been conducted at the Hunter College Curriculum Center since 1962.

The book of readings, of which this volume constitutes the first section, has been used experimentally in a number of classes at Hunter College and other institutions providing special courses for teachers of disadvantaged youth. The second section of the original work, to be published in the Fall of 1967 as a separate volume, *Policy Issues in Urban Education,* contains selections which contribute to an understanding of the specific public and professional policy decisions arising out of the social and economic problems described here.

H.L.M.

M.B.S.

Acknowledgments

Mrs. Helen Randolph, Miss Joan Roberts, and Mr. Steven Zuckerman assisted in the research and the selection of materials.

Mr. Mark Feldstein is responsible for the fine photographs used to illustrate the text.

A number of people were involved in the production of this collection. We wish to express our appreciation to Miss Elaine Paul, typist, for her willingness to undertake the laborious task of typing charts and graphs as well as text; Miss Carol Ratner for art work and layout; Miss Carol Gibbons and Mr. Richard Meyer for performing a variety of tasks among which were layout and reproduction; Mrs. Susan Stein for general supervision of production; and Dr. Stuart A. Selby and Mr. Feldstein for their coordination of all these efforts to produce the experimental edition.

Special thanks are due to faculty members of the Hunter College Education Department for testing the readings in their classes and for providing constructive suggestions for revision.

Contents

vii

PART I

The Situation and The Problems

During the past decade the attention of public-school educators has focused with such increasing intensity and sharpness on the problem of the big-city schools that a special term, *urban education*, has come to stand for the special adjustments made by schools attempting to prepare the city slum child for an overwhelmingly technical society in a state of rapid change. Whatever set of terms we apply to these children—"the disadvantaged," "the underprivileged," "the socially handicapped," or others even more blandly elevated for public relations purposes—we are talking about those who, in the midst of affluence, grow up in the rotten depths of the city, in despairing poverty, with little hope for the future, and often bearing the special stigma, in this society, of color.

Although these children are predominantly Negro, and the educational problems related to them are consequently often considered "Negro problems," it is well to realize that this is far from true. Other disadvantaged ethnic minorities in various cities of the United States—Mexicans, Puerto Ricans, American Indians—face similar difficulties in schooling, where they are part of the "hard core poverty" culture. And the child of the economically better-off working-class family, as many of the following readings demonstrate, seldom gets an even break from our middle-class oriented schools.

The first section of these readings, whose general purpose is to help the future teacher understand the problems of urban education, deliberately emphasizes, perhaps overemphasizes, the underlying social correlates of those problems. Teachers who enter the classrooms in the city slums are, by the ordinary course of their training, prepared to interpret the behavior of the children who sit before them, and to seek solutions for the discipline and learning problems they encounter, within the framework of an individual psychology. The largely psychological orientation of most teacher education quite properly stresses attention to the individual child, to his special needs and problems and to the unique nature of the troubles he may have. But, although the slum classroom is often full of troubled children, we mislead ourselves and blunt our efforts to help them if we assume that the significant problems can be dealt with individually.

The difference, and it is a very important one for teachers to consider, lies in the contrast between personal troubles and what the sociologists call institutional structures. C. Wright Mills puts it this way:

> When, in a city of 100,000, only one man is unemployed, that is his personal trouble, and for its relief we properly look to the character of the man, his skills, and his immediate opportunities. But when in a nation of 50 million employees, 15 million men are unemployed, that is an issue, and we may not hope to find its solution within the range of opportunities open to any one individual. The very structure of opportunities has collapsed. . . . Consider marriage. Inside a marriage a man and a woman may experience personal troubles, but when the divorce rate during the first four years of marriage is 250 out of every 1,000 attempts, this is an indication of a structural issue

having to do with the institutions of marriage and the family and other institutions that bear upon them.[1]

So, in a normal classroom in a suburban school, when one child is unruly, or another is not working up to his capacity, or a third is failing to read on grade level, we look to individual circumstances, to special problems of adjustment, in order to fashion a solution. But when children in the big-city schools are, *on the average*, reading one or two grades below the norm, when half or more of them drop out of high school before graduating, we must look for explanation to fundamental structural problems in the school as an institution and in the society at large.

In this sense, a teacher puzzled by the behavior of her pupils might well find a better explanation for them by noting the latest statistics on national employment trends of differences in income than by probing the psyches of her children. This section, then, documents the underlying social structures relevant to the behavior and achievement levels of children in the slum school.

One way of looking at discussions of basic social situations is to concentrate on differences. A society in which people do not move about from one kind of life to other kinds of radically different circumstances, where everyone lives at essentially the same level, may have problems, but they are unlikely to be the same sort of problems that we face. The sharp differences in the human condition for different members of our society generate those problems we see as social issues, as something we need to fashion strategies for. Thus, an East Indian visitor to the slums of Harlem might find conditions vastly superior to those endured by the people at the bottom of the social heap in his culture; the Harlem resident, however, is comparing his status not to that of the Indian masses but to that of the American middle class, whose life is pictured for him on every side in glossy splendor and, indeed, is flung in his face whether he likes it or not by the industrious and omnipresent mass media.

1. C. Wright Mills, *The Sociological Imagination*, New York: Oxford University Press, 1959, p. 9.

The significant differences among the groups in our population that have some bearing on the problems of metropolitan education are shown in a number of perspectives in the readings that make up this section.

1. One major source of difference arises from the dislocations related to movements of large numbers of people to alien places —modern migrations that resemble in some respects the major waves of European immigration that once swept into the United States, but that differ from them in other ways. For the eastern half of the country perhaps the most influential migration has been the movement from the rural South to the urban North, which Charles Silberman's article, "The City and the Negro," describes very well. Those who are part of that movement face tremendous problems of adjustment: alien life styles and value patterns, linguistic differences which confront them with what amounts to the task of learning a new language, the need for a totally different set of economic skills, and others.

A second migration stream has moved from Puerto Rico to the large cities of the United States, about 60 per cent of the stream in recent years[2] to New York. The often paradoxical differences between the nature of the migration and the adjustment of the Puerto Rican as compared to that of the southern Negro are worth close study and discussion; Glazer's piece, "The Puerto Ricans," suggests some, but far from all of the answers. Why are Puerto Rican incomes below the level of Negro incomes, although as a group the Puerto Ricans seem to show far more signs of upward mobility into business and other middle-class occupations? How important to the differences between the groups are the factors of language, history, and family structure? How influential is the ease with which the Puerto Rican can reverse his movement by returning to the island? Such questions suggest that despite the consistencies in the "culture of poverty," which the next section emphasizes, the city school must develop somewhat different strategies to deal with various ethnic groups.

2. *Facts and Figures,* New York: Commonwealth of Puerto Rico, Migration Division, Department of Labor, 1963, p. 15.

The third migration of interest, a much more subtle one, takes place within the boundaries of the metropolitan regions themselves, consisting of movements into and away from the inner city. It is the sometimes gradual, but often very rapid shift of middle-class people to suburban areas and the consequent stratification of areas within the region into single class sections, leaving the core of the city to deterioration and blight on the one hand, to pyramiding affluence on the other. In New York, at any rate, the rich share Manhattan with the poor; in other cities, such as Chicago, with a considerably greater degree of urban sprawl, one must travel almost to exurbia to find the wealthy. The economic consequences for the schools are disastrous, as Sexton's data on the Detroit situation show. The rich can support their children's private schooling, and do so; the mass of the middle class support good suburban public schools and work to make them better; the harassed and alienated poor in the central city leave the problem of the schools to an army of civil servants who are already caught in the tax squeeze resulting from the flight of industry and the middle class to suburbia, and from the historic fiscal conflicts between metropolitan and state governments. If money helps make education better, at least part of the differences in school achievement between the slum child and middle-class suburban one can be explained by the disparity of the sums spent per child in their schools.

Some specific data from several of the large metropolitan areas may serve to make these generalizations more concrete. Sexton's study of the Detroit schools, for example, divides them into four groups by the income level of their neighborhoods. The average age of elementary-school buildings in the two lowest groups is about forty-five years, of the two highest about twenty-five years. Almost half of the schools in areas whose income level is below $7000 have substandard science facilities, 90 per cent of them have substandard music and speech facilities, 66 per cent lack adequate toilet facilities, 91 per cent have inadequate auditorium space. Examining the number of schools with serious building deficiencies, she found that in all categories, including those representing safety hazards, schools in the low-income neighborhoods far exceeded those in the higher income areas. Examples: dangerous traffic hazards—25 to 7; need for safety fence—10 to 4; building combustible—34 to 3.[3]

Without regard to the unprovable questions of what is cause and what is effect, it is hardly surprising to find lower levels of academic achievement in the poorer schools. Sexton found that fourth graders in 96 per cent of the Detroit schools in the lowest income areas were below grade level on the Iowa Achievement Test, compared with none at all in the highest group. In confirmation of what educators now recognize as a general state of things, children in the lowest income level schools lose ground as they proceed through the grades; fourth graders in Detroit's lowest economic level are only a half grade behind standard, but by the eighth grade they are over a full grade below.[4] In New York City, a study of sixth graders who were not born in the city showed reading levels as much as two grades below the standard in schools with a high proportion of in-migrant pupils.[5]

Havighurst's study of Chicago schools reports similar data on achievement for schools divided into social-class groupings. With few exceptions, reading readiness scores at the first grade and both reading and arithmetic achievement at the sixth grade are lower in less favored area schools. In more favored schools, three fourths of the children come to school with average or better readiness to read; in low socioeconomic area schools, more than half of the children entering first grade are below average in reading readiness. Grade 6 reading and arithmetic scores range from 7.5 in the school with the highest socioeconomic rating to average scores of 5.5 in least affluent school districts.[6]

In New York City, data on pupil transiency in 1960 for

3. Patricia C. Sexton, *Education and Income*, New York: Viking, 1961, p. 30.

4. *Ibid.*, p. 26.

5. L. Moribur, *School Functioning of Pupils Born in Other Areas and in New York City*, New York Board of Education, Publication #168, May, 1961, Tables 42, 43.

6. Robert J. Havighurst, *The Public Schools of Chicago*, The Board of Education of the City of Chicago, Chicago 1964, p. 39.

Manhattan, the core of the city, indicate that well over one out of two of the elementary schools had transiency rates of over 50 per cent and that one out of five had transiency rates of over 80 per cent.[7] In Detroit, elementary schools in districts where annual income levels are below $3000 show a transiency rate of 49 per cent compared to a rate of 17 per cent in districts of $9000 and over.[8]

Schools in districts under the $7000 income level in Detroit have faculties on which almost 20 per cent of the teachers are emergency substitutes holding regular positions; the comparable proportion among faculties of the higher-income schools is 5.5 per cent.[9] In the elementary schools of New York City, if one compares those with high proportions of Negro and Puerto Rican children to those with very low proportions of these minority children, almost the same difference in substitute teachers is revealed.[10] Sheldon and Glazier report that only 2 per cent of the junior high schools serving comparable school populations had as many as 65 per cent of their teachers permanently licensed, as compared with 34 per cent of more favored junior high schools.[11]

In Chicago, the percentage of regularly assigned teachers ranges from 94 per cent in "high status" to 64 per cent in "inner city" schools. Conversely, the proportion of substitutes ranges from 6 to 36 per cent in these two ends of Havighurst's four-way classification. Median years of teaching experience range is from nineteen years to four years. Havighurst also reports a high rate of transiency among inner-city school principals in Chicago.[12]

Furthermore, all of these movements together confront cen-

---

7. From Blanche Robins Kasindorf, *Pupil Transiency in the Elementary and Junior High Schools, School Year 1959–60,* prepared for the Board of Education of the City of New York, Bureau of Educational Research and Statistics, Publication #166, March, 1961.

8. Sexton, *op. cit.,* p. 96.

9. *Ibid.,* p. 120.

10. *The Status of the Public School Education,* The Public Education Association and New York University Research Center, October, 1955.

11. E. P. Sheldon and R. A. Glazier, *Pupils and Schools in New York City,* New York: Russell Sage Foundation, 1965, p. 58.

12. Havighurst, *op. cit.,* p. 175.

tral-city schools with an almost insuperable difficulty, seldom stressed, perhaps because no one has suggested a solution for it: pupil turnover. In some slum schools a teacher may face, toward the end of the year, a group of children among whom is not one who was in her class at the beginning of the school year. Such a situation provides a rather ironic commentary on the current efforts of many parent's groups in the big cities to preserve the traditional "neighborhood school" concept, if the model of that concept includes a stable neighborhood, consistent attendance at school over a long period, and close ties between the school and parents. In the central city, the neighborhood school is a myth.

2. Another set of differences arises from income disparities, measured by a series of arbitrary levels which the Department of Labor designates as poverty, deprivation, comfort, and affluence. In a period in which programs for the elimination of poverty have become political issues, it is inevitable that we should be embroiled in arguments over where we should draw the lines between these statuses; some argue that one is not really poor unless he earns under $2000 a year, others that the poverty level should be set at $3000. Obviously, where one draws the line considerably affects one's perception of the gravity of the problem, but it is hard to deny that wherever one draws it there is an embarrassingly large number of very poor people for a society that likes to consider itself affluent.

The Department of Labor estimates very carefully the income necessary to cover a "modest but adequate" budget for city families at about $6,200, which is close to the median income for the country as a whole. The 1960 Census indicates that there are about ten and a half million multiple-person families living on incomes below $4000 (the poverty level suggested by the Conference on Economic Progress).[13] Even if one uses the more sophisticated income level of $3,130 which the Office of Economic Opportunity employs to qualify a four-

13. Conference on Economic Progress, *Poverty and Deprivation in the United States,* Washington, D.C.: Conference on Economic Progress, 1962, p. 17.

person nonfarm family for poverty aid, this is a considerable number of people.

The inequality of the poverty burden may be seen by considering the income levels of different groups in New York City. Fifteen per cent of New York's Negroes and Puerto Ricans earn incomes under $2000, against 8 per cent of whites; 37 per cent of the Puerto Ricans and 29 per cent of the Negroes earn between $2000 and $4000, compared to only 14 per cent of the whites.[14] Nor, for the country as a whole, has this income gap between white and nonwhite diminished over the past decade. In 1962, average Negro incomes were only 63 per cent of average white incomes, exactly the same proportion as in 1957, with variations of only a few percentage points during the intervening years.[15] Although a larger number of whites live in poverty than Negroes, a considerably greater proportion of Negroes than whites are poor.

Poverty means much more than children appearing in school poorly dressed and lacking a decent breakfast, which is what teachers notice and mention most often as examples of their pupils' poverty. Our culture has encouraged the development of an image of the "respectable poor," decent, hard-working, sober unfortunates, doing the best they can, working for the betterment of their children, trying quietly to improve their situation through industry and frugality. This tradition, which helps create our middle class indignation at those poor who are surly, brutal, or addicted to drink, is compounded of bits and pieces of the American past, memories of immigrant family and neighborhood life, Jefferson's sturdy yeomanry, the genteel poverty of some declassed small-town aristocracy, all of them consonant with the powerful American ideal of egalitarianism.

Such a concept is a poor tool for understanding the meaning of real poverty in the big city during a period of the disappearance of unskilled jobs, and of a poor which lacks the

14. *U.S. Censuses of Population and Housing: 1960,* Census Tract Report for New York City, Table VI–7.

15. U.S. Bureau of the Census, *Current Population Reports-Consumer Income,* Series P-60, annual issues, Table IV–I.

binding elements of a common, traditional culture. If, indeed, the image was at any time little more than a comforting, middle-class dream of reality. Poverty means, to take Detroit as an example, four times the death rate from pneumonia, twice the accident death rate, twice the rate of infant deaths, greater maternal mortality and general death rate.[16] It means an enervating struggle with overcrowded and substandard housing and children in trouble. As Harrington's chapter points out graphically, it means a terrifying insecurity about basic survival, and if the way out is blocked by special handicaps of ethnic identity, it means the frustrated and desperate bitterness that, as Baldwin tells us, destroys the self and leaves one alienated from society.

In *Major Barbara*, Shaw's devastating dissection of poverty and power, Undershaft, the munitions king, indicts the romance of poverty and poverty itself in words that apply to New York and Chicago today as well as they did to London a half century ago:

Have you ever been in love with Poverty, like St. Francis? Have you ever been in love with Dirt, like St. Simeon? Have you ever been in love with disease and suffering, like our nurses and philanthropists? Such passions are not virtues, but the most unnatural of all the vices. The love of the common people may please an earl's granddaughter and a university professor; but I have been a common man and a poor man; and it has no romance for me. Leave it to the poor to pretend that poverty is a blessing: leave it to the coward to make a religion of his cowardice by preaching humility: we know better than that. . . . [Poverty is] the worst of crimes. Poverty blights whole cities; spreads terrible pestilences; strikes dead the very souls of all who come within sight, sound, or smell of it. What you call crime is nothing: a murder here and a theft there, a blow now and a curse then: what do they matter? they are only the accidents and illnesses of life: there are not fifty genuine professional criminals in London. But there are millions of poor people, abject people, dirty people, sick people, ignorant people, ill-fed, ill-clothed people, poisoning us, forcing us to organize

16. Sexton, *op, cit.,* p. 105.

unnatural cruelties for fear they should rise against us and drag us down into their abyss. Only fools fear crime: we all fear poverty.[17]

3. A third difference, and perhaps the one most directly related to schooling, is what the German sociologist Weber called "the life chance." In every organized society, we can estimate the probability for a given individual of achieving security and status, an interesting life, and self-realization, the basic human goals at all times. Clearly, as the extremes illustrate, the life chance of a child born of white, upper-middle-class professional parents on Manhattan's East Side is infinitely superior to that of one born to Negro lower-class parents perhaps no farther than thirty or forty blocks to the north.

One has only to examine the data to spell out the details. Negro men fill only 2.5 per cent of professional and technical jobs, only 6 per cent of clerical jobs, only 4 per cent of craftsmen and foremen positions, and only 10 per cent of semiskilled jobs. They make up instead 44 per cent of private household workers, 20 per cent of low-paid service workers, and about 25 per cent of both farm and nonfarm unskilled labor. In whatever category they work, their median earnings for that job are less than whites' in the same category (for example, median earnings of Negro professional and technical workers are $4,563 vs. $6,691 for whites).[18]

Education presumably means better jobs, but in 1960 almost 50 per cent of white high-school graduates, but only 20 per cent of Negro graduates, were in clerical jobs. Only 10 per cent of white graduates, but 25 per cent of Negroes, were employed in service occupations.[19] The percentage of the Negro work force unemployed is about double that of the white work force, and

17. Bernard Shaw, *Major Barbara*, Baltimore: Penguin Books, 1951, pp. 85, 149. Reprinted with permission of The Public Trustee and The Society of Authors.

18. *U.S. Census of Population: 1960, Detailed Characteristics*, United States Summary, Tables 205, 208.

19. *Hearings Before the Subcommittee on Employment and Manpower of the Committee on Labor and Public Welfare*, p. 434.

recent declines in over-all unemployment rate (in 1965, particularly) has left the Negro rate virtually undisturbed.[20]

There is a positive and high correlation in this country between level of education and income, but if one considers only the group in the upper quarter of intellectual ability, 75 per cent of upper-middle- and upper-class youth finish four years of college, in contrast to 25 per cent of working-class and lower-lower youngsters.[21] In 1960, only 6 per cent of the boys from the lower-lower-class level entered college, as compared with 40 per cent of their total age group.[22]

Thus, in summarizing the life chance of the Negro child one can point to the following probabilities: He will be far more likely to drop out of school before high-school graduation (see the selections in this section on school dropouts); no matter how intellectually competent, he is far less likely to go on to college; in the job market, he will be the last hired and first fired; it is unlikely that he will attain occupational status of a high order; and in whatever job, he will be relatively less well paid. In what is becoming an unbroken circle of deep poverty and social dependency, for many families into the third generation, his own children may face the same limited life chance that he did.

Obviously, the school cannot be held accountable for structural flaws in the economic and social institutions which surround its young charges. In several of the introductions to the selections in this section the question of how much can realistically be expected of education in solving a problem that has so many historical and structural roots is raised. Those who demand that the school provide the levers for social mobility, for instance, are probably asking too much; recent analyses of mobility from one generation to another in highly industrialized societies suggest that schooling has far less to do with it than we have thought. The school can do little about the ques-

20. *Employment and Earnings*, Bureau of Labor Statistics monthly bulletin, February dates for each year, 1953–63.
21. Robert J. Havighurst and Bernice L. Neugarten, *Society and Education*, 2nd ed., Boston: Allyn and Bacon, 1962, p. 234.
22. *Ibid.*, p. 252.

tionable social morality of permitting the process of automation to proceed at full speed with no regard for the human costs involved in the inevitable shifts in demand for skills and in functional unemployment. It can do even less about changing deeply rooted employer and labor union prejudices and traditions regarding the hiring of members of minority groups, or about strengthening the family structure so that children will come to school motivated to learn.

But the school, as an institution, is in the business of training children to the best of their individual capacities to live in the real world and to make as good a life as they can in it. Whether or not an individual child has the competence or ambition to climb into the middle class, school is an essential means for all children in obtaining stable employment above the subsistence level. To blame the substantial failure of big-city schools to train employable youngsters on the failure of the society to provide the right kinds of jobs, or on the failure of the family to provide the right human material, although both charges are certainly true, evades the issue.

Teachers and educators are supposed to know how to motivate children to learn. They are presumed to have the skills to formulate a body of materials and methods that will be effective for particular groups of children. They are part of a larger institution charged with developing the knowledge and skills necessary to predict the probable shape of economic circumstances affecting job markets and technical skills. And even the most staunchly loyal professional educator with a knowledge of the urban situation would hesitate to claim that big-city schools are adequately performing the task that is squarely and particularly theirs to do.

". . . the welfare state benefits least those who need help the most."

THE REJECTS *
Michael Harrington

This is the second chapter of Harrington's *The Other America,* the book on poverty that many regard as the first major intellectual salvo in the current war on poverty. In this chapter, the author presents a number of reasons why, in an affluent sociey, we have so many families living at the level of poverty, and suggests a crucial distinction between the structure of poverty during the thirties depression and today. His descriptions of the unemployed and underpaid convey graphically the human meaning that lies behind income statistics, and raise a number of important issues. For educators the most important of them, perhaps, is:

> *Are we relying too much on education and training as an answer to poverty arising from these multiple causes, or does the solution depend on our willingness, as a society, to develop such inventions as negative income tax and created jobs?*

* From Michael Harrington, *The Other America,* New York: Macmillan, 1963, pp. 19–30. Copyright © 1963, reprinted by permission of The Macmillan Company, Publishers.

... IN NEW YORK CITY, some of my friends call 80 Warren Street "the slave market."

It is a big building in downtown Manhattan. Its corridors have the littered, trampled air of a courthouse. They are lined with employment-agency offices. Some of these places list good-paying and highly skilled jobs. But many of them provide the work force for the economic underworld in the big city: the dishwashers and day workers, the fly-by-night jobs.

Early every morning, there is a great press of human beings in 80 Warren Street. It is made up of Puerto Ricans and Negroes, alcoholics, drifters, and disturbed people. Some of them will pay a flat fee (usually around 10 per cent) for a day's work. They pay $0.50 for a $5.00 job and they are given the address of a luncheonette. If all goes well, they will make their wage. If not, they have a legal right to come back and get their half-dollar. But many of them don't know that, for they are people that are not familiar with laws and rights.

But perhaps the most depressing time at 80 Warren Street is in the afternoon. The jobs have all been handed out, yet the people still mill around. Some of them sit on benches in the larger offices. There is no real point to their waiting, yet they have nothing else to do. For some, it is probably a point of pride to be here, a feeling that they are somehow still looking for a job even if they know that there is no chance to get one until early in the morning.

Most of the people at 80 Warren Street were born poor. (The alcoholics are an exception.) They are incompetent as far as American society is concerned, lacking the education and the skills to get decent work. If they find steady employment, it will be in a sweatshop or a kitchen.

In a Chicago factory, another group of people are working. A year or so ago, they were in a union shop making good wages, with sick leave, pension rights, and vacations. Now they are making artificial Christmas trees at less than half the pay they had been receiving. They have no contract rights, and the foreman is absolute monarch. Permission is required if a worker wants to go to the bathroom. A few are fired every day for insubordination.

These are people who have become poor. They possess skills, and they once moved upward with the rest of the society. But now their jobs have been destroyed, and their skills have been rendered useless. In the process, they have been pushed down toward the poverty from whence they came. This particular group is Negro, and the chances of ever breaking through, of returning to the old conditions, are very slim. Yet their plight is not exclusively racial, for it is shared by all the semiskilled and unskilled workers who are the victims of technological unemployment in the mass-production industries. They are involved in an interracial misery.

These people are the rejects of the affluent society. They never had the right skills in the first place, or they lost them when the rest of the economy advanced. They are the ones who make up a huge portion of the culture of poverty in the cities of America. They are to be counted in the millions.

I

Each big city in the United States has an economic underworld. And often enough this phrase is a literal description: it refers to the kitchens and furnace rooms that are under the city; it tells of the place where tens of thousands of hidden people labor at impossible wages. Like the underworld of crime, the economic underworld is out of sight, clandestine.

The workers in the economic underworld are concentrated among the urban section of the more than 16,000,000 Americans denied coverage by the Minimum-Wage Law of 1961. They are domestic workers, hotel employees, bus boys, and dishwashers, and some of the people working in small retail stores. In the most recent Government figures, for example, hotel workers averaged $47.44 a week, laundry workers $46.45, general-merchandise employees $48.37, and workers in factories making work clothing $45.58.

This sector of the American economy has proved itself immune to progress. And one of the main reasons is that it is almost impossible to organize the workers of the economic

underworld in their self-defense. They are at the mercy of un-
scrupulous employers (and, in the case of hospital workers, management might well be a board composed of the "best" people
of the city who, in pursuing a charitable bent, participate in a
conspiracy to exploit the most helpless citizens). They are
cheated by crooked unions; they are used by racketeers.

In the late fifties I talked to some hospital workers in Chicago. They were walking a picket line, seeking union recognition. (They lost.) Most of them made about $30 a week and were
the main support of their families. The hospital deducted
several dollars a week for food that they ate on the job. But then,
they had no choice in this matter. If they didn't take the food,
they had to pay for it anyway.

When the union came, it found a work force at the point of
desperation. A majority of them had signed up as soon as they
had the chance. But, like most of the workers in the economic
underworld, these women were hard to keep organized. Their
dues were miniscule, and in effect they were being subsidized
by the better-paid workers in the union. Their skills were so
low that supervisory personnel could take over many of their
functions during a strike. It required an enormous effort to
reach them and to help them, and in this case it failed.

An extreme instance of this institutional poverty took place
in Atlanta, Georgia, among hospital workers in mid-1960. Men
who worked the dishwashing machines received $0.68 an hour;
women kitchen helpers got $0.56; and the maids $0.55 an hour.
If these people all put in the regular two thousand hours of
work a year, they would receive just over $1,000 for their
services.

The restaurants of the economic underworld are somewhat
like the hospitals. The "hidden help" in the kitchen are an
unstable group. They shift jobs rapidly. As a result, a union
will sign up all the employees in a place, but before a union
certification election can occur half of those who had joined
will have moved on to other work. This means that it is extremely expensive for the labor movement to try to organize
these workers: they are dispersed in small groups; they cannot

pay for themselves; and they require constant servicing, checking, and rechecking to be sure that the new workers are brought into the union structure.

The fact that the economic underworld is so hard to organize makes it a perfect place for two types of racketeers to operate: labor racketeers and their constant companions the management racketeers. In the mid-fifties, some of the locals of the Hotel and Restaurant Employees Union in Chicago were under racket domination. (The crooks have since been cleaned out.) The deal was very simple. The dishonest union man would demand a payoff from the dishonest restaurateur. Sometimes it was figured as a percentage tax on the number of place settings in an establishment. In return for this money, the "unionist" would allow management to pay well below the prevailing union wage. This meant that waitresses were brought into the economic underworld along with the kitchen help.

In New York, a city that specializes in sweatshops, this crooked unionism was even more blatant. There are Puerto Ricans who are "members" of unions they never even heard of. Their rights in these labor organizations are confined to the payment of dues. The businessman, who is so essential to racketeering unionism, makes his payment to the union leader. In return he gets immunity from organization and the right to pay starvation wages. The contracts that come out of these deals are "black and white." All the standard provisions of an honest union contract providing for wage rates, fringe benefits, and the protection of working conditions in the shop are x'ed out. The only agreement is that the place is unionized, which is to say that it is protected from honest unionism.

Indeed, one of the paradoxical consequences of the AFL-CIO "No Raiding" agreement is that it helps to keep some of these lowest-paid workers in the grip of labor racketeers. As long as the racket local manages to keep a charter in a recognized international (and, in the late fifties, this was becoming more difficult, but not impossible), then the honest unions are stopped from going in and decertifying the crooks. Many unionists who see the positive value in the No Raiding procedure have argued for an amendment: "Raiding" will be permitted if an honest union can show that the local in a given situation is a racket outfit creating substandard conditions.

Finally, the economic underworld is made up of small shops, of handfuls of workers, but that does not mean that its total population is insignificant. When the hotels, the restaurants, the hospitals, and the sweatshops are added up, one confronts a section of the economy that employs millions and millions of workers. In retailing alone, there are 6,000,000 or 7,000,000 employees who are unorganized, and many of them are not covered by minimum wage. For instance, in 1961 the general-merchandise stores (with an average weekly wage of $48.37) counted over 1,250,000 employees. Those who made work clothes, averaging just over $45.00 a week, totaled some 300,000 citizens, most of them living in the other America of the poor.

Thus, in the society of abundance and high standards of living there is an economically backward sector which is incredibly capable of being exploited; it is unorganized, and in many cases without the protection of Federal law. It is in this area that the disabled, the retarded, and the minorities toil. In Los Angeles they might be Mexican-Americans, in the runaway shops of West Virginia or Pennsylvania, white Anglo-Saxon Protestants. All of them are poor; regardless of race, creed, or color, all of them are victims.

In the spring of 1961, American society faced up to the problem of the economic underworld. It decided that it was not worth solving. Since these workers cannot organize the help themselves, their only real hope for aid must be directed toward intervention of the Federal Government. After the election of President Kennedy, this issue was joined in terms of a minimum-wage bill. The AFL-CIO proposed that minimum-wage coverage should be extended to about 6,500,000 new workers; the Administration proposed new coverage for a little better than 3,000,000 workers; the conservatives of the Dixiecrat-Republican coalition wanted to hold the figure down to about 1,000,000.

There was tremendous logrolling in Congress over the issue. In order to win support for the Administration approach, concessions were made. It does not take much political acumen to guess which human beings were conceded: the poor. The laundry workers (there are over 300,000 of them, and according to the most recent Bureau of Labor statistics figures they averaged $47.72 a week) and the hospital workers were dropped from the extension of coverage. The papers announced that over 3,000,000 new workers had been granted coverage—but they failed to note that a good number of them were already in well-paid industries and didn't need help.

In power politics, organized strength tells. So it was that America turned its back on the rejects in the economic underworld. As one reporter put it, "We've got the people who make $26 a day safely covered; it's the people making $26 a week who are left out." Once again, there is the irony that the welfare state benefits least those who need help most.

II

The men and women in the economic underworld were, for the most part, born poor. But there is another, and perhaps more tragic, type of industrial poverty: the experience of those who become poor.

This is what happens to them.

On a cold evening in Chicago (winter is a most bitter enemy of the poor) I talked to a group of Negro workers. Until a short time before our meeting, they had worked in the meat-packing industry and were members of the Packinghouse Workers Union. They had been making around $2.25 an hour, with fringe benefits and various guarantees for sick leave, vacation, and the like. More than that, they had found a certain dignity for themselves in that they belonged to one of the most integrated unions in the United States. (The industry had traditionally employed many Negroes; one factor was that much of the work was regarded as "dirty," that is, Negro, tasks.)

A number of these people had found jobs in a plant making artificial Christmas trees. They received $1 an hour and no fringe benefits. The shop was, of course, nonunion. Several workers were fired every day, and crowds gathered on Monday morning to compete for their places.

The $1 an hour was bad enough, but there was an even more important aspect to this impoverishment. When they worked at Armour, these employees knew a certain job security; they had rights in the shop because of the union. It was not only that their wages had been cut by more than half when the plant closed; it was also that they had been humiliated. This was particularly true of these Negroes. As members of a minority group, they had been fortunate to get such good jobs and to belong to a union that took civil rights seriously. Now that they had been thrust into the economic underworld, that racial gain was wiped out. The Christmas tree shop hired Negroes only. That was because they were available cheap; that was because they could be "kept in their place."

One of the workers I talked to was a woman in her thirties. When she spoke, the bitterness was not so much directed against the low pay: what concerned her most was the "slavery" of her working conditions. She had to ask the supervisor permission to go to the bathroom. At any moment she could be fired for insubordination, and there was no grievance procedure or arbitration to protect her rights. She was vivacious and articulate, a born leader. So she tried to organize the shop. A majority of the workers had signed cards asking for a union election, but the National Labor Relations Board had postponed the date. The election will never take place. The Christmas-tree season is over, and these people are out on the streets again.

Yet the workers in the sweatshop considered themselves lucky. They were making $1 an hour, which was something. Two men I talked to were in a different classification: they had passed the line of human obsolescence in this industrial society. They were over forty years of age. They had been laid off at Armour in the summer of 1959. Eighteen months later, neither of them had found a steady job of any kind. "When I come to the hiring window," one of them said, "the man just looks at me; he doesn't even ask questions; he says, 'You're too old.'"

Other men talked of how racial discrimination worked against them when the plant closed. One technique is simplicity itself. A job is rated by a plant well over its actual skill level. Training and educational qualifications are specified in great detail. When the white worker applies, these criteria are waived. When the Negro worker shows up in the hiring line, the letter of the law is enforced. Technically, there has been no discrimination. The Negro was turned down for lack of skill, not because of race. But that, of course, is the most obvious and palpable evasion.

What happens to the man who goes eighteen months without a steady job? The men told me. First, the "luxuries" go: the car, the house, everything that has been purchased on installment but not yet paid for. Then comes doubling up with relatives (and one of the persistent problems in becoming poor is that marriages are often wrecked in the process). Finally—and this is particularly true of the "older" worker—there is relief, formal admission into the other America.

The Armour workers who became poor were, to a considerable extent, Negro. In attitudes toward poverty, there is a curious double standard. America more or less expects the Negro to be poor (and is convinced that things are getting better, a point to be dealt with in a later chapter). There is no emotional shock when people hear of the experience of these human beings in Chicago. The mind and the feelings, even of good-willed individuals, are so suffused with an unconscious racism that misery is overlooked.

But what happened at Armour is not primarily racial, even though the situation is compounded and intensified by the fact that Negroes are involved. The same basic process is at work in Pennsylvania and in Detroit.

In a brilliant report, Harvey Swados wrote of his first impression of Saint Michael, Pennsylvania: "It is a strange thing to come to a town and find it full of grown men. They stroll the narrow, shabby streets, chat at the corners, lean against the peeling pillars of the town saloon, the St. Michael Hotel & Restaurant, and they look more like movie actors than real human beings, because something is wrong."

That "something" happened on April 24, 1958, when Maryland Shaft Number 1 closed down. Since then some of the miners have been able to get jobs elsewhere. But for most of them, there are idleness and a profound change in the way of life. What, after all, do you do with a man who is a skilled coal miner? When the mine closes down, what industry do you put him into? He is physically strong; he has lived his life in a tight community of coal miners; and he has intense loyalties to his fellow workers and to his little town in the mountains. But he has a skill that is hardly transferable.

Some of the men from Maryland Shaft Number 1 got jobs in the steel industry, but they have already been hit by layoffs there. The automation process that destroyed the work in coal is spreading to steel: their problem is following after them. Others are working, for a fraction of their previous wage, as orderlies in hospitals and institutions, as janitors and stockmen in big stores.

But, again, the most humiliating part of this experience maims the spirit. As Swados puts it, "It is truly ironic that a substantial portion of these men, who pride themselves on their ability to live with danger, to work hard, fight hard, drink hard, love hard, are now learning housework and taking over the woman's role in the family."

For the miners have always been an almost legendary section of the work force. Their towns are as isolated as ships, and they have had the pride of metier, the elan of seamen. Their union battles were long and bloody, sometimes approaching the dimensions of civil war, as in the fabled Harlan County struggles. They had a tough life, but part of the compensation was the knowledge that they were equal to it. Now the job has been taken away, and the pride with it.

In many of these mining areas, there are small garment shops that are running away from union labor in New York and other established centers. Their pay is miserable, and they look for the wives of the unemployed. So the miners do the housework and hang around the saloon, and the wife has become the breadwinner.

In Detroit one can see still another part of this process: it is not minority poverty as with the Armour workers, nor is it depressed-area poverty as in the case of the coal miners. It is the slide backward, the becoming poor, that takes place in the midst of a huge American industrial city.

In 1956 Packard closed out a Detroit factory and destroyed some 4,000 jobs. What happened to the men and women involved has been carefully described in a special study of the Senate Committee on Unemployment Problems. The report is entitled "Too Old to Work, Too Young to Retire."

When the Packard plant closed, the world fell in on some of the men. There were those who cried. They had worked in the shop for years, and they had developed a personal identification with the car they built. Some of them were particularly bitter because they felt the company had blundered by lowering standards and turning out an inferior product. They were laid off in 1956, but many of them had still not found regular work when the recession hit in 1958 and again in 1960.

The workers in the best position were those who were both young and skilled. Their unemployment averaged "only" a little better than five and a half months. The young and semiskilled were out on the street for an average of seven and a half months, the old, skilled workers for eight and a half months. Finally, the "old" semiskilled workers (say, machine operators over forty-five) averaged better than a year of unemployment. The old and unskilled were out for fourteen months.

For almost every one of these human beings, there was a horrible sinking experience. Of those who were able to find jobs, almost 40 per cent took a position inferior to the one they had held. Skilled workers took semiskilled or even common-laborer jobs. Most of these did not become poor. They were humiliated and downgraded, but not dragged below the subsistence level. But some of the old, the unskilled, and the Negroes entered the other America in the late fifties. They came from a well-organized and relatively high-paying industry. They ended by becoming impoverished.

So it was in Detroit, Michigan, and the story is substantially the same as in Saint Michael, Pennsylvania or Chicago, Illinois. In the fifties and early sixties, a society with an enormous technology and the ability to provide a standard of living for every citizen saw millions of people move back. Some of them retrogressed all the way, and ended where they had been before the gains of the welfare state were made. Many of them slid back but did not become impoverished . . .

III

The human rejects who have become poor are a particular, and striking, case of the invisibility of poverty in the other America.

In the thirties, as noted before, unemployment was a general problem of the society. A quarter of the work force was in the streets, and everyone was affected. Big business was hit by the stock crash; small business failed because of the general climate; white-collar workers were laid off like everyone else. From out of this experience, there came a definition of "good times": if the statistics announced that more people were working than ever before, that was prosperity; if there was a dip in employment, with 4,000,000 to 6,000,000 temporarily laid off, that was a recession.

But the definitions of the thirties blind us to a new reality. It is now possible (or rather it is the reality) to have an increase in the number of employed, an expansion of consumption, a boom in production and, at the same time, localized depressions. In the midst of general prosperity, there will be types of jobs, entire areas, and huge industries in which misery is on the increase. The familiar America of high living standards moves upward, the other America of poverty continues to move downward.

Professor John Dunlop, of Harvard, has made an illuminating distinction to describe this process. In the thirties, he notes, there was mass unemployment; in the postwar period there has been class unemployment. Special groups will be singled out by the working of the economy to suffer, while all others will experience prosperity.

When class unemployment takes place, the peculiar law that it is better to be miserable when everyone else is miserable goes into effect. It is possible for conservatives and other opponents of Federal action to point to figures showing production and total unemployment at record highs. The average citizen assumes that this means that good times are general; the class hit by depression conditions is forgotten or ignored.

". . . now I began to wake up at night to find hunger standing by my bedside, staring at me gauntly."

BLACK BOY*
Richard Wright

The despair and loss of self-respect that Harrington describes among adults in poverty has a special impact on the child, for whom Housman's famous lines take on a contemporary poignancy—"a stranger, and afraid, in a world I never made." The world he sees has been explored, with insight and anger, by two generations of American novelists, white and Negro, and autobiographically by those who managed to pull themselves out of whatever kind of ghetto they grew up in. As the war on poverty and the role of the school in that war increasingly loses itself in tactical in-fighting about the meaning of statistics and research findings, local political power, and organizational errors, it becomes more urgent that those who have never experienced it know what poverty feels like to the child. This brief excerpt from Wright's autobiography tells how it feels as well as any piece of writing can.

* From Richard Wright, *Black Boy*, New York: Harper and Brothers, 1945, pp. 13–16. Copyright © 1937 by Richard Wright, reprinted by permission of the publishers.

HUNGER stole upon me so slowly that at first I was not aware of what hunger really meant. Hunger had always been more or less at my elbow when I played, but now I began to wake up at night to find hunger standing at my bedside, staring at me gauntly. The hunger I had known before this had been no grim, hostile stranger; it had been a normal hunger that had made me beg constantly for bread, and when I ate a crust or two I was satisfied. But this new hunger baffled me, scared me, made me angry and insistent. Whenever I begged for food now my mother would pour me a cup of tea which would still the clamor in my stomach for a moment or two; but a little later I would feel hunger nudging my ribs, twisting my empty guts until they ached. I would grow dizzy and my vision would dim. I became less active in my play, and for the first time in my life I had to pause and think of what was happening to me.

"Mama, I'm hungry," I complained one afternoon.

"Jump up and catch a kungry," she said, trying to make me laugh and forget.

"What's a kungry?"

"It's what little boys eat when they get hungry," she said.

"What does it taste like?"

"I don't know."

"Then why do you tell me to catch one?"

"Because you said that you were hungry," she said, smiling.

I sensed that she was teasing me and it made me angry.

"But I'm hungry. I want to eat."

"You'll have to wait."

"But I want to eat now."

"But there's nothing to eat," she told me.

"Why?"

"Just because there's none," she explained.

"But I want to eat," I said, beginning to cry.

"You'll just have to wait," she said again.

"But why?"

"For God to send some food."

"When is He going to send it?"

"I don't know."

"But I'm hungry!"

She was ironing and she paused and looked at me with tears in her eyes.

"Where's your father?" she asked me.

I stared in bewilderment. Yes, it was true that my father had not come home to sleep for many days now and I could make as much noise as I wanted. Though I had not known why he was absent, I had been glad that he was not there to shout his restrictions at me. But it had never occurred to me that his absence would mean that there would be no food.

"I don't know," I said.

"Who brings food into the house?" my mother asked me.

"Papa," I said. "He always brought food."

"Well, your father isn't here now," she said.

"Where is he?"

"I don't know," she said.

"But I'm hungry," I whimpered, stomping my feet.

"You'll have to wait until I get a job and buy food," she said.

As the days slid past the image of my father became associated with my pangs of hunger, and whenever I felt hunger I thought of him with a deep biological bitterness.

My mother finally went to work as a cook and left me and my brother alone in the flat each day with a loaf of bread and a pot of tea. When she returned at evening she would be tired and dispirited and would cry a lot. Sometimes, when she was in despair, she would call us to her and talk to us for hours, telling us that we now had no father, that our lives would be different from those of other children, that we must learn as soon as possible to take care of ourselves, to dress ourselves, to prepare our own food; that we must take upon ourselves the responsibility of the flat while she worked. Half frightened, we would promise solemnly. We did not understand what had happened between our father and our mother and the most that these long talks did to us was to make us feel a vague dread. Whenever we asked why father had left, she would tell us that we were too young to know.

One evening my mother told me that thereafter I would have to do the shopping for food. She took me to the corner

store to show me the way. I was proud; I felt like a grownup.
The next afternoon I looped the basket over my arm and went
down the pavement toward the store. When I reached the corner, a gang of boys grabbed me, knocked me down, snatched
the basket, took the money, and sent me running home in
panic. That evening I told my mother what had happened,
but she made no comment; she sat down at once, wrote another
note, gave me more money, and sent me out to the grocery
again. I crept down the steps and saw the same gang of boys
playing down the street. I ran back into the house.

"What's the matter?" my mother asked.

"It's those same boys," I said. "They'll beat me."

"You've got to get over that," she said. "Now, go on."

"I'm scared," I said.

"Go on and don't pay any attention to them," she said.

I went out of the door and walked briskly down the sidewalk, praying that the gang would not molest me. But when
I came abreast of them someone shouted.

"There he is!"

They came toward me and I broke into a wild run toward
home. They overtook me and flung me to the pavement. I
yelled, pleaded, kicked, but they wrenched the money out of
my hand. They yanked me to my feet, gave me a few slaps,
and sent me home sobbing. My mother met me at the door.

"They b-beat m-me," I gasped. "They t-t-took the m-
money."

I started up the steps, seeking the shelter of the house.

"Don't you come in here," my mother warned me.

I froze in my tracks and stared at her.

"But they're coming after me," I said.

"You just stay right where you are," she said in a deadly
tone. "I'm going to teach you this night to stand up and fight
for yourself."

She went into the house and I waited, terrified, wondering
what she was about. Presently she returned with more money
and another note; she also had a long heavy stick.

"Take this money, this note, and this stick," she said. "Go

to the store and buy those groceries. If those boys bother you, then fight."

I was baffled. My mother was telling me to fight, a thing that she had never done before.

"But I'm scared," I said.

"Don't you come into this house until you've gotten those groceries," she said.

"They'll beat me; they'll beat me," I said.

"Then stay in the streets; don't come back here!"

I ran up the steps and tried to force my way past her into the house. A stinging slap came on my jaw. I stood on the sidewalk, crying.

"Please, let me wait until tomorrow," I begged.

"No," she said. "Go now! If you come back into this house without those groceries, I'll whip you!"

She slammed the door and I heard the key turn in the lock. I shook with fright. I was alone upon the dark, hostile streets and gangs were after me. I had the choice of being beaten at home or away from home. I clutched the stick, crying, trying to reason. If I were beaten at home, there was absolutely nothing that I could do about it; but if I were beaten in the streets, I had a chance to fight and defend myself. I walked slowly down the sidewalk, coming closer to the gang of boys, holding the stick tightly. I was so full of fear that I could scarcely breathe. I was almost upon them now.

"There he is again!" the cry went up.

They surrounded me quickly and began to grab for my hand.

"I'll kill you!" I threatened.

They closed in. In blind fear I let the stick fly, feeling it crack against a boy's skull. I swung again, lamming another skull, then another. Realizing that they would retaliate if I let up for but a second, I fought to lay them low, to knock them cold, to kill them so that they could not strike back at me. I flayed with tears in my eyes, teeth clenched, stark fear making me throw every ounce of my strength behind each blow. I hit again and again, dropping the money and the grocery list. The boys scattered, yelling, nursing their heads, staring at me in utter disbelief. They had never seen such frenzy. I stood panting, egging them on, taunting them to come on and fight. When they refused, I ran after them and they tore out for their homes, screaming. The parents of the boys rushed into the streets and threatened me, and for the first time in my life I shouted at grownups, telling them that I would give them the same if they bothered me. I finally found my grocery list and the money and went to the store. On my way back I kept my stick poised for instant use, but there was not a single boy in sight. That night I won the right to the streets of Memphis.

"... in the face of one's victim, one sees oneself."

A LETTER FROM HARLEM *
James Baldwin

Although Wright's autobiographical fragment is
written by a Negro, it might describe as well the life
of many a white child in deep poverty. But when
one adds a black skin to the fact of poverty, one does
more than quantitatively add to the human misery;
one makes it, as Baldwin clearly is saying, intoler-
able. As an essayist, Baldwin much resembles the
Old Testament prophets, who spared no one's feelings as they denounced the sins to the sinful, and,
like the prophets, he is often not very popular with
the sinners he addresses. The well-meaning white
liberal may well find it difficult to read the following chapter from *Nobody Knows My Name* without
getting angry, not at himself, but at Baldwin. But it
is important to recognize that the feelings Baldwin
expresses with such biting articulateness are the same
that the citizens of Watts acted out in a holocaust

* From James Baldwin, *Nobody Knows My Name,* New York: Dial
Press, 1961, pp. 56–71. Copyright © 1961 by James Baldwin, reprinted by
permission of Dial Press, Inc.

that shocked the nation. Educators, in particular, need to face up to the bitter indictment of the last paragraphs.

To what extent is Baldwin correct in charging that we treat the Negro in the North as either a ward or a victim? To the extent that the problems of urban education are the problems of educating children of the Negro ghetto, does the school participate in this kind of treatment, and if you believe it does, in what ways?

THERE is a housing project standing now where the house in which we grew up once stood, and one of those stunted city trees is snarling where our doorway used to be. This is on the rehabilitated side of the avenue. The other side of the avenue —for progress takes time—has not been rehabilitated yet and it looks exactly as it looked in the days when we sat with our noses pressed against the windowpane, longing to be allowed to go "across the street." The grocery store which gave us credit is still there, and there can be no doubt that it is still giving credit. The people in the project certainly need it—far more, indeed, than they ever needed the project. The last time I passed by, the Jewish proprietor was still standing among his shelves, looking sadder and heavier but scarcely any older. Farther down the block stands the shoe-repair store in which our shoes were repaired until reparation became impossible and in which, then, we bought all our "new" ones. The Negro proprietor is still in the window, head down, working at the leather.

These two, I imagine, could tell a long tale if they would (perhaps they would be glad to if they could), having watched so many, for so long, struggling in the fishhooks, the barbed wire, of this avenue.

The avenue is elsewhere the renowned and elegant Fifth. The area I am describing, which, in today's gang parlance, would be called "the turf," is bounded by Lenox Avenue on the west, the Harlem River on the east, 135th Street on the north, and 130th Street on the south. We never lived beyond these boundaries; this is where we grew up. Walking along 145th Street—for example—familiar as it is, and similar, does not have the same impact because I do not know any of the people on the block. But when I turn east on 131st Street and Lenox Avenue, there is first a soda-pop joint, then a shoeshine "parlor," then a grocery store, then a dry cleaners', then the houses. All along the street there are people who watched me grow up, people who grew up with me, people I watched grow up along with my brothers and sisters; and, sometimes in my arms, sometimes underfoot, sometimes at my shoulder—or on it—their children, a riot, a forest of children, who include my nieces and nephews.

When we reach the end of this long block, we find ourselves on wide, filthy, hostile Fifth Avenue, facing that project which hangs over the avenue like a monument to the folly, and the cowardice, of good intentions. All along the block, for anyone who knows it, are immense human gaps, like craters. These gaps are not created merely by those who have moved away, inevitably into some other ghetto; or by those who have risen, almost always into a greater capacity for self-loathing and self-delusion; or yet by those who, by whatever means— War II, the Korean war, a policeman's gun or billy, a gang war, a brawl, madness, an overdose of heroin, or, simply unnatural exhaustion—are dead. I am talking about those who are left, and I am talking principally about the young. What are they doing? Well, some, a minority, are fanatical churchgoers, members of the more extreme of the Holy Roller sects. Many, many more are "moslem" by affiliation or sympathy, that is to say that they are united by nothing more—and nothing less— than a hatred of the white world and all its works. They are present, for example, at every Buy Black street-corner meeting —meetings in which the speaker urges his hearers to cease trading with white men and establish a separate economy. Neither the speaker nor his hearers can possibly do this, of course, since Negroes do not own General Motors or RCA or the A & P, nor, indeed, do they own more than a wholly insufficient fraction of anything else in Harlem (those who do own anything are more interested in their profits than in their fellows). But these meetings nevertheless keep alive in the participators a certain pride of bitterness without which, however futile this bitterness may be, they could scarcely remain alive at all. Many have given up. They stay home and watch the TV screen, living on the earnings of their parents, cousins, brothers, or uncles, and only leave the house to go to the movies or to the nearest bar. "How're you making it?" one may ask, running into them along the block, or in the bar. "Oh, I'm TV-ing it"; with the saddest, sweetest, most shamefaced of smiles, and from a great distance. This distance

one is compelled to respect; anyone who has traveled so far
will not easily be dragged again into the world. There are
further retreats, of course, than the TV screen or the bar. There
are those who are simply sitting on their stoops, "stoned," ani-
mated for a moment only, and hideously, by the approach of
someone who may lend them the money for a "fix." Or by the
approach of someone from whom they can purchase it, one of
the shrewd ones, on the way to prison or just coming out.

And the others, who have avoided all of these deaths, get
up in the morning and go downtown to meet "the man." They
work in the white man's world all day and come home in the
evening to this fetid block. They struggle to instill in their
children some private sense of honor or dignity which will help
the child to survive. This means, of course, they must struggle,
stolidly, incessantly, to keep this sense alive in themselves, in
spite of the insults, the indifference, and the cruelty they are
certain to encounter in their working day. They patiently
browbeat the landlord into fixing the heat, the plaster, the
plumbing; this demands prodigious patience; nor is patience
usually enough. In trying to make their hovels habitable, they
are perpetually throwing good money after bad. Such frustration, so long endured, is driving many strong, admirable men
and women whose only crime is color to the very gates of
paranoia.

One remembers them from another time—playing handball
in the playground, going to church, wondering if they were
going to be promoted at school. One remembers them going
off to war—gladly, to escape this block. One remembers their
return. Perhaps one remembers their wedding day. And one
sees where the girl is now—vainly looking for salvation from
some other embittered, trussed, and struggling boy—and sees
the all-but-abandoned children in the streets.

Now I am perfectly aware that there are other slums in
which white men are fighting for their lives, and mainly losing.
I know that blood is also flowing through those streets and
that the human damage there is incalculable. People are con-
tinually pointing out to me the wretchedness of white people
in order to console me for the wretchedness of blacks. But an

itemized account of the American failure does not console
me and it should not console anyone else. That hundreds of
thousands of white people are living, in effect, no better than
the "niggers" is not a fact to be regarded with complacency.
The social and moral bankruptcy suggested by this fact is
of the bitterest, most terrifying kind.

The people, however, who believe that this democratic anguish has some consoling value are always pointing out that
So-and-So, white, and So-and-So, black, rose from the slums
into the big time. The existence—the public existence—of, say,
Frank Sinatra and Sammy Davis, Jr. proves to them that America is still the land of opportunity and that inequalities vanish
before the determined will. It proves nothing of the sort. The
determined will is rare—at the moment, in this country, it is
unspeakably rare—and the inequalities suffered by the many
are in no way justified by the rise of a few. A few have always
risen—in every country, every era, and in the teeth of regimes
which can by no stretch of the imagination be thought of as
free. Not all of these people, it is worth remembering, left the
world better than they found it. The determined will is rare,
but it is not invariably benevolent. Furthermore, the American
equation of success with the big times reveals an awful disrespect for human life and human achievement. This equation
has placed our cities among the most dangerous in the world
and has placed our youth among the most empty and most
bewildered. The situation of our youth is not mysterious. Children have never been very good at listening to their elders,
but they have never failed to imitate them. They must, they
have no other models. That is exactly what our children are
doing. They are imitating our immorality, our disrespect for
the pain of others.

All other slum dwellers, when the bank account permits
it, can move out of the slum and vanish altogether from the
eye of persecution. No Negro in this country has ever made
that much money and it will be a long time before any Negro
does. The Negroes in Harlem, who have no money, spend
what they have on such gimcracks as they are sold. These
include "wider" TV screens, more "faithful" hi-fi sets, more

"powerful" cars, all of which, of course, are obsolete long before they are paid for. Anyone who has ever struggled with poverty knows how extremely expensive it is to be poor; and if one is a member of a captive population, economically speaking, one's feet have simply been placed on the treadmill forever. One is victimized, economically, in a thousand ways—rent, for example, or car insurance. Go shopping one day in Harlem— for anything—and compare Harlem prices and quality with those downtown.

The people who have managed to get off this block have only got as far as a more respectable ghetto. This respectable ghetto does not even have the advantages of the disreputable one—friends, neighbors, a familiar church, and friendly trades- men; and it is not, moreover, in the nature of any ghetto to remain respectable long. Every Sunday, people who have left the block take the lonely ride back, dragging their increasingly discontented children with them. They spend the day talking, not always with words, about the trouble they've seen and the trouble—one must watch their eyes as they watch their children —they are only too likely to see. For children do not like ghettos. It takes them nearly no time to discover exactly why they are there.

The projects in Harlem are hated. They are hated almost as much as policemen, and this is saying a great deal. And they are hated for the same reason: both reveal, unbearably, the real attitude of the white world, no matter how many liberal speeches are made, no matter how many lofty editorials are written, no matter how many civil-rights commissions are set up.

The projects are hideous, of course, there being a law, ap- parently respected throughout the world, that popular housing shall be as cheerless as a prison. They are lumped all over Harlem, colorless, bleak, high, and revolting. The wide windows look out on Harlem's invincible and indescribable squalor: the Park Avenue railroad tracks, around which, about forty years ago, the present dark community began; the unrehabili- tated houses, bowed down, it would seem, under the great weight of frustration and bitterness they contain; the dark, the ominous schoolhouses from which the child may emerge maimed, blinded, hooked, or enraged for life; and the churches, churches, block upon block of churches, niched in the walls like cannon in the walls of a fortress. Even if the administration of the projects were not so insanely humiliating (for example: one must report raises in salary to the management, which will then eat up the profit by raising one's rent; the management has the right to know who is staying in your apartment; the management can ask you to leave, at their discretion), the projects would still be hated because they are an insult to the meanest intelligence.

Harlem got its first private project, Riverton[1]—which is now, naturally, a slum—about twelve years ago because at that time Negroes were not allowed to live in Stuyvesant Town. Harlem watched Riverton go up, therefore, in the most violent bitterness of spirit, and hated it long before the builders arrived. They began hating it at about the time people began moving out of their condemned houses to make room for this additional proof of how thoroughly the white world despised them. And they had scarcely moved in, naturally, before they began smashing windows, defacing walls, urinating in the elevators, and fornicating in the playgrounds. Liberals, both white and black, were appalled at the spectacle. I was appalled by the liberal innocence—or cynicism, which comes out in practice as much the same thing. Other people were delighted to be able to point to proof positive that nothing could be done to better the lot of the colored people. They were, and are, right in one respect: that nothing can be done as long as they are treated like colored people. The people in

1. The inhabitants of Riverton were much embittered by this description; they have, apparently, forgotten how their project came into being; and have repeatedly informed me that I cannot possibly be referring to Riverton, but to another housing project which is directly across the street. It is quite clear, I think, that I have no interest in accusing any individuals or families of the depredations herein described: but neither can I deny the evidence of my own eyes. Nor do I blame anyone in Harlem for making the best of a dreadful bargain. But anyone who lives in Harlem and imagines that he has not struck this bargain, or that what he takes to be his status (in whose eyes?) protects him against the common pain, demoralization, and danger, is simply self-deluded.

Harlem know they are living there because white people do
not think they are good enough to live anywhere else. No
amount of "improvement" can sweeten this fact. Whatever
money is now being earmarked to improve this, or any other
ghetto, might as well be burnt. A ghetto can be improved in
one way only: out of existence.

Similarly, the only way to police a ghetto is to be oppressive.
None of the Police Commissioner's men, even with the best will
in the world, have any way of understanding the lives led by
the people they swagger about in twos and threes controlling.
Their very presence is an insult, and it would be, even if
they spent their entire day feeding gumdrops to children. They
represent the force of the white world, and that world's real
intentions are, simply, for that world's criminal profit and ease,
to keep the black man corraled up here, in his place. The
badge, the gun in the holster, and the swinging club make
vivid what will happen should his rebellion become overt.
Rare, indeed, is the Harlem citizen, from the most circumspect
church member to the most shiftless adolescent, who does not
have a long tale to tell of police incompetence, injustice, or
brutality. I myself have witnessed and endured it more than
once. The businessmen and racketeers also have a story. And
so do the prostitutes. (And this is not, perhaps, the place to
discuss Harlem's very complex attitude toward black policemen, nor the reasons, according to Harlem, that they are
nearly all downtown.)

It is hard, on the other hand, to blame the policeman, blank,
good-natured, thoughtless, and insuperably innocent, for being
such a perfect representative of the people he serves. He, too,
believes in good intentions and is astounded and offended
when they are not taken for the deed. He has never, himself,
done anything for which to be hated—which of us has?—and
yet he is facing, daily and nightly, people who would gladly
see him dead, and he knows it. There is no way for him not
to know it: there are few things under heaven more unnerving
than the silent, accumulating contempt and hatred of a people.
He moves through Harlem, therefore, like an occupying soldier
in a bitterly hostile country; which is precisely what, and where,

he is, and is the reason he walks in twos and threes. And he is not the only one who knows why he is always in company: the people who are watching him know why, too. Any street meeting, sacred or secular, which he and his colleagues uneasily cover has as its explicit or implicit burden the cruelty and injustice of the white domination. And these days, of course, in terms increasingly vivid and jubilant, it speaks of the end of that domination. The white policeman standing on a Harlem street corner finds himself at the very center of the revolution now occurring in the world. He is not prepared for it—naturally, nobody is—and, what is possibly much more to the point, he is exposed, as few white people are, to the anguish of the black people around him. Even if he is gifted with the merest mustard grain of imagination, something must seep in. He cannot avoid observing that some of the children, in spite of their color, remind him of children he has known and loved, perhaps even of his own children. He knows that he certainly does not want his children living this way. He can retreat from his uneasiness in only one direction: into a callousness which very shortly becomes second nature. He becomes more callous, the population becomes more hostile, the situation grows more tense, and the police force is increased. One day, to everyone's astonishment, someone drops a match in the powder keg and everything blows up. Before the dust has settled or the blood congealed, editorials, speeches, and civil-rights commissions are loud in the land, demanding to know what happened. What happened is that Negroes want to be treated like men.

Negroes want to be treated like men: a perfectly straightforward statement, containing only seven words. People who have mastered Kant, Hegel, Shakespeare, Marx, Freud, and the Bible find this statement utterly impenetrable. The idea seems to threaten profound, barely conscious assumptions. A kind of panic paralyzes their features, as though they found themselves trapped on the edge of a steep place. I once tried to describe to a very well-known American intellectual the conditions among Negroes in the South. My recital disturbed him and made him indignant; and he asked me in perfect innocence, "Why don't all the Negroes in the South move North?" I tried to explain what has happened, unfailingly, whenever a significant body of Negroes move North. They do not escape Jim Crow: they merely encounter another, not-less-deadly variety. They do not move to Chicago, they move to the South Side; they do not move to New York, they move to Harlem. The pressure within the ghetto causes the ghetto walls to expand, and this expansion is always violent. White people hold the line as long as they can, and in as many ways as they can, from verbal intimidation to physical violence. But inevitably the border which has divided the ghetto from the rest of the world falls into the hands of the ghetto. The white people fall back bitterly before the black horde; the landlords make a tidy profit by raising the rent, chopping up the rooms, and all but dispensing with the upkeep; and what has once been a neighborhood turns into a "turf." This is precisely what happened when the Puerto Ricans arrived in their thousands—and the bitterness thus caused is, as I write, being fought out all up and down those streets.

Northerners indulge in an extremely dangerous luxury. They seem to feel that because they fought on the right side during the Civil War, and won, they have earned the right merely to deplore what is going on in the South, without taking any responsibility for it; and that they can ignore what is happening in Northern cities because what is happening in Little Rock or Birmingham is worse. Well, in the first place, it is not possible for anyone who has not endured both to know which is "worse." I know Negroes who prefer the South and white Southerners, because "At least there, you haven't got to play any guessing games!" The guessing games referred to have driven more than one Negro into the narcotics ward, the madhouse, or the river. I know another Negro, a man very dear to me, who says, with conviction and with truth, "The spirit of the South is the spirit of America." He was born in the North and did his military training in the South. He did not, as far as I can gather, find the South "worse"; he found it, if anything, all too familiar. In the second place, though, even if Birmingham *is* worse, no doubt Johannesburg, South Africa, beats it by several miles, and Buchenwald was one of the worst things that ever happened in the entire history of the world. The world has never lacked for horrifying examples; but I do not believe that these examples are meant to be used as justification for our own crimes. This perpetual justification empties the heart of all human feeling. The emptier our hearts become, the greater will be our crimes. Thirdly, the South is not merely an embarrassingly backward region, but a part of this country, and what happens there concerns every one of us.

As far as the color problem is concerned, there is but one great difference between the Southern white and the Northerner: the Southerner remembers, historically and in his own psyche, a kind of Eden in which he loved black people and they loved him. Historically, the flaming sword laid across this Eden is the Civil War. Personally, it is the Southerner's sexual coming of age, when, without any warning, unbreakable taboos are set up between himself and his past. Everything, thereafter, is permitted him except the love he remembers and has never ceased to need. The resulting, indescribable torment affects every Southern mind and is the basis of the Southern hysteria.

None of this is true for the Northerner. Negroes represent nothing to him personally, except, perhaps, the dangers of carnality. He never sees Negroes. Southerners see them all the time. Northerners never think about them whereas Southerners are never really thinking of anything else. Negroes are, therefore, ignored in the North and are under surveillance in the South, and suffer hideously in both places. Neither the Southerner nor the Northerner is able to look on the Negro simply as a man. It seems to be indispensable to the national self-esteem that the Negro be considered either as a kind of ward (in which case we are told how many Negroes, comparatively, bought Cadillacs last year and how few, comparatively, were lynched), or as a victim (in which case we are promised that he will never vote in our assemblies or go to school with our kids). They are two sides of the same coin and the South will not change—*cannot* change—until the North changes. The country will not change until it re-examines itself and discovers what it really means by freedom. In the meantime, generations keep being born, bitterness is increased by incompetence, pride, and folly, and the world shrinks around us.

It is a terrible, an inexorable, law that one cannot deny the humanity of another without diminishing one's own: in the face of one's victim, one sees oneself. Walk through the streets of Harlem and see what we, this nation, have become.

". . . modern technology and automation are here to stay."

TECHNOLOGICAL CHANGE AND AUTOMATION*

John K. Norton

The following selection on the need for educational change to meet the demands of technological change must be read with an understanding of the fact that the urgency it communicates about the rapidity of occupational shifts in the economy is not shared by all economists. The effect on the economy of automation, however it may alarm the general public, is a subject of lively controversy among the experts, many of whom point out that the industrial examples such as Norton cites here do not show up in general figures for the yearly rise in productivity in the entire economy, an increase rate which is not today greater than the average over the past half century.

* From John K. Norton, *Changing Demands on Education and Their Fiscal Implications,* a report prepared for the National Committee for the Support of Public Schools, Washington, D.C.: National Committee for the Support of Public Schools, 1963, pp. 3–18. Copyright © 1963, by the National Committee. All rights reserved.

In industrial societies in which production rapidly expands to the point where it nears the actual capacity of the economy, unskilled workers are rapidly absorbed into the economic mainstream and are, indeed, imported, as in many European countries today. Although educators are seldom equipped to discuss very fruitfully such technical questions, they need to be aware that they live in a society which traditionally regards most large-scale problems as ones that formal schooling ought somehow to solve, whether or not they are really problems the school *can* solve. One might usefully read this article with the following questions in mind:

> *If automation does mainly produce local crises in the economy, can a school system geared to long-range effort respond rapidly enough to be of much use? If automation presents the kind of immediate and large-scale threat that some think it does, does it require drastic reformation of curriculum and school organization, and if so, what changes would this entail?*

RESEARCH, the application of new knowledge to industrial processes, and automation are remaking the economy of the United States. The scope and rapidity of this change are bringing about what some have called the Second Industrial Revolution. The impacts of this revolution are profound for education. It is imperative that schools and colleges respond to the new and changing demands being made upon them.

OCCUPATIONAL TRENDS

Professional and Technical Workers

One of the most persistent occupational trends in the United States is the growing demand for workers with increased general education and advanced technical and professional training. A college degree is required even for admission to training for a mounting number of callings.[1] Many business concerns look upon a college degree as the minimum requirement for employment in positions that lead to the more attractive types of work.

The fastest growing occupations are those that require larger amounts of general education and advanced technical and professional training.

The 1960 U.S. Census Report states that "professional and technical personnel, the most highly educated of all workers, are increasing fastest." The following are figures for 1950–70:

1950—5 million   1960—7.5 million   1970—10 million (est.)

Professional and technical workers in 1950 were 8 per cent of the employed population. By 1970, this percentage will be well over 12.5.[2]

Skilled and Semiskilled Workers

Below the professional and technical occupations in amount

1. U.S. Department of Labor, Bureau of Labor Statistics, *Occupational Outlook Handbook,* Washington, D.C.: Government Printing Office, 1961, p. 29.
2. *Ibid.,* p. 24.

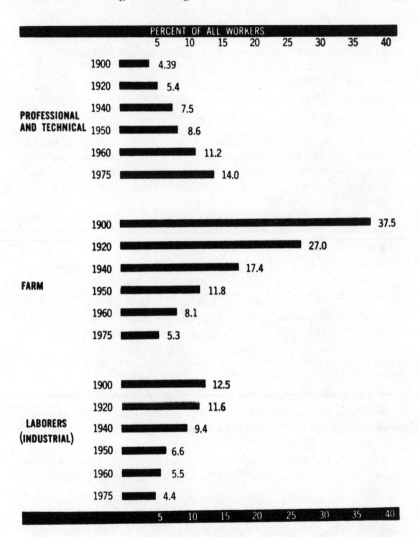

Figure 1. Occupational Distribution of Workers (actual 1900—60 and estimated 1975). *Sources:* Data for 1900—50 from David L. Kaplan and M. Claire Casey. *Occupational Trends in the United States, 1900 to 1950.* U.S. Department of Commerce, Bureau of the Census, Working Paper No. 5. Washington, D.C.: Government Printing Office, 1958. Table 2, p. 7. Data for 1960 and 1975 from the U. S. Department of Labor, Bureau of Labor Statistics.

of training required are those designated as skilled and semi-skilled. Both are growing in number, but the skilled occupations are growing more rapidly than the semiskilled.[3]

Unskilled Workers

The per cent of the employed population now classified as unskilled will continue to decline.

The least skilled of all workers do the hardest physical work, except perhaps farm laborers, and are usually the lowest paid. Over the past half century their place in the labor force has dropped from 12.5 per cent to less than 6 per cent in 1960. In numbers, the need for unskilled workers will remain about the same during the coming decade, but their proportion in the labor force will continue to drop—to less than 5 per cent by 1970.[4]

Figure 1 shows the trend for three occupational groups from 1900 to 1960 and estimates the trend to 1975. The group with the highest training (professional and technical workers) composes a rapidly rising percentage of the work force. The percentages of the work force classified as farm workers and industrial laborers are rapidly declining.

Farm Workers

Farm workers made up 53 per cent of the total labor force in 1870: by 1970 they will represent only about 6 per cent. The greatest technological revolution in the United States has taken place in agriculture.

In 1870, the number of farmers and farm workers was about 7 million. It reached a peak of 11.5 million around 1910.

By 1950, the number of farm workers had declined to 7 million (12 per cent of the labor force), the same number as 80 years before, even though the nation's population had increased almost fourfold and the quantity of farm products by 4.5 times.

This downward trend in the number of farm workers con-

3. *Ibid.*, pp. 22–25.
4. *Ibid.*, p. 26.

tinued during the 1950–60 decade. In 1960, only 5.9 million farmers and farm laborers were in the labor force; by 1970, the total will have dropped still further, to about 5 million, only 6 per cent of the labor force, a ninefold drop in 100 years.[5]

The impact of the reduction in the number of farm workers is far greater in some states than in others. This is how it is in Mississippi:

> The 1960 Census shows that over half the farm population of Mississippi has moved to urban centers in the last 10 years, and also about 75 per cent of the population lives in urban centers, so we need fewer and fewer farmers, and industrialization is demanding more education. To just get out there and plow a mule, you know, like it has been in Mississippi up until a few years ago, could be done without being able to read and write. But, now we have come to the time that something is going to have to be done about this thing because it requires skills and education that haven't been required before. And it is an emergency.[6]

Industrial Workers

The following examples are illustrative of the present condition of industrial workers:

> Because of technological change, about 200,000 production jobs have been eliminated in recent years in the aircraft industry alone.

> Productivity (or output per man-hour) in the soft coal industry rose 96 per cent since World War II, but employment fell by 262,700.

> Steel production in 1960 was almost the same as in 1950, but employment declined by 80,000, or 14 per cent.

> Employment in the manufacture of refrigerators and washing

5. *Ibid.*, pp. 16–17.
6. W. E. Williams, supervisor of adult education, Mississippi State Department of Education. Testimony before U.S. 87th Congress, House of Representatives Committee on Education and Labor, 1962.

machines has fallen 18 per cent, and employment in instrument production has fallen 15 per cent in the last 7 years.[7]

In the highly automated chemical industry, the number of production jobs has fallen 3 per cent since 1956, while output has soared 27 per cent. Though steel capacity has increased 20 per cent since 1955, the number of men needed to operate the industry's plants—even at full capacity—has dropped 17,000. Auto employment slid from a peak of 746,000 in boom 1955 to 614,000 in November 1961.

Since the meat industry's 1956 employment peak, 28,000 workers have lost their jobs, despite a production increase of 3 per cent. Bakery jobs have been in a steady decline from 174,000 in 1954 to 163,000 in 1960.[8]

Employment in railroad jobs fell from a total of 1,400,000 in 1947 to 730,000 in 1961—a drop of 670,000. Technological shifts (the diesel displacement of steam was a large factor) and dwindling business in the postwar period are what worked this occupational upheaval in the Nation's railroads.[9]

CHANGING COMPOSITION OF THE LABOR FORCE

White-Collar and Blue-Collar Jobs

The growing demand for highly trained and skilled personnel and the declining demand for unskilled workers have brought about a major transition in the composition of the labor force.

In 1956, for the first time in the Nation's history, professional, managerial, office, and sales workers outnumbered craftsmen, operatives, and laborers. The startling import of this continu-

7. U.S. 87th Congress, First Session, House of Representatives Committee on Education and Labor, Subcommittee on Unemployment and the Impact of Automation. *Impact of Automation on Employment*. Washington, D.C.: Government Printing Office, 1961, 23 pp.

8. "The Automation Jobless—Not Fired, Just Not Hired." *Time*, 77: 69 (February 24, 1961).

For further data see U.S. 87th Congress, *op. cit.*

9. From a study by the U.S. Department of Labor, Bureau of Labor Statistics, October, 1962.

ing trend can be fully realized only when we remember that in 1910 the number of white-collar jobs was less than half the blue-collar jobs; now they have left the blue-collars behind, and by 1970 they will be 25 per cent greater than blue-collars.[10]

Employment of Women

Another major occupational change concerns the employment of women. It is estimated that during the 1960's the number of women working for salaries and wages will rise at nearly twice the rate for men. By 1970, women-workers will number 30 million and will constitute one-third of the labor force. At least two of every five women aged 20–65 will be gainfully employed in 1970.[11]

The growing demand for skilled, semiprofessional, and professional workers can be met in part by capitalizing the potential talents of our woman power. The considerable percentage of women who lack training required for better-paid jobs are the last untapped reservoir of unspecialized brain power.

GAINS AND PROBLEMS OF TECHNOLOGICAL CHANGE

Technological change has brought highly significant gains and has also created serious problems, as illustrated below.

Hours and Character of Work

On the gain side is a sharp decline in the number of hours per workweek. The hours in the average workweek declined from 70 in 1850 to 60 in 1900 and to just under 40 in 1960.

There has also been a marked change in the nature of work. Fewer and fewer workers are engaged in hard manual labor. Gerard Piel describes this change as follows:

During the past twenty-five years our technology entered upon the era of automatic production. The real work of extracting nature's bounty from soil and rock and transforming it into

10. U.S. Department of Labor, *op. cit.,* p. 23.
11. U.S. Department of Labor. *Manpower Challenge of the 1960's.* Washington, D.C.: Government Printing Office, 1961. p. 7.

goods is no longer done by human muscles, and less and less by human nervous systems. It is done by mechanical energy, by machines under control of artificial nervous systems, by chemicals, and by such subtle arts as applied genetics. While the impact of these developments upon industry has attracted most of the attention, their impact upon agriculture has amounted to a revolution.[12]

Per Capita Production

The length of the average workweek has sharply declined. Hard manual work is the lot of a decreasing minority of our labor force. Nevertheless, productivity per capita has sharply increased in the United States.

Between 1929 and 1962, our population grew 53 per cent, while our gross national product, in constant (1954) dollars, grew 159 per cent. The result is the high standard of living of our affluent society and the economic power that is a major deterrent to foreign aggression.

Technology has brought great gains and also has given rise to serious problems. A major problem is the imbalance between the type of labor force our new technology increasingly requires and the skills and qualifications of large numbers of workers in our present labor force. Far too many receive inadequate education and meager training, while the demand grows for broader education and more specialized skills.

School Dropouts and Elderly Workers

A great variety of unskilled jobs, which youngsters formerly filled at least as stepping stones to something better,[13] or which

12. Gerard Piel, "Can Our Economy Stand Disarmament?" *Atlantic Monthly,* 210: 37 (September, 1962).

13. President Kennedy, speaking in 1962 on behalf of the Youth Employment Opportunity Bill stated that "we have in this country 1 million boys and girls who are out of school and out of work. In the next eight years of this decade, according to some predictions, we are going to have 8 million boys and girls who are going to leave school before they finish, and they are going to be looking for work. They are going to be unskilled, and they may have trouble finding jobs."

elderly workers filled, are now disappearing. For example, in New York City alone, there are 40,000 fewer elevator operators as a result of the use of automatic elevators. Each year there will be proportionately fewer openings for the unskilled worker.

Unfilled New Jobs

At the same time that thousands of jobs are being wiped out, new ones are being created in areas unknown only a few years ago. Many of these jobs are unfilled for lack of qualified workers. It is not that there are not jobs to be filled but that there are not enough people with the training required to fill them.[14]

Costs of Unemployment

These conditions add up to a hard core of unemployed workers. The insidious growth of unemployment is one of the most critical problems confronting our economic system.

Economic losses from unemployment are never regained. The social costs of unemployment are even greater than the economic losses. The discouragement and frustration of able-bodied men and women, eager to work but unable to find employment, cannot be measured in dollars any more than can the distress of their families. Prolonged unemployment contributes to further unemployment, since human capital deteriorates when it is idle. Unemployment impairs the skills that workers have acquired. It also contributes to family disintegration, crime, and other social ills.[15]

The evils of unemployment afflict all age groups in our labor force. Unemployment is especially high among out-of-school teenagers. This is undoubtedly one of the factors responsible for juvenile delinquency. Unemployment among men from age 20 to age 60 or 65 afflicts both the unemployed man and the other members of his family. Many qualified persons aged 60 and older are ready and able to work, but are denied employment.

14. Walter Buckingham, *The Impending Educational Revolution.* Occasional Paper No. 1. Washington, D.C.: Project on the Educational Implications of Automation, National Education Association, 1961, p. 3.

15. U.S. 87th Congress, *op. cit.,* p. 14.

PROPOSED CURES FOR UNEMPLOYMENT

There appears to be general agreement that a greatly expanded program for training and retraining the work force is essential if unemployment is to be lessened. There is disagreement about whether such a program is enough. William Glazier states that there is a persistent hard core of unemployed workers, which grew from fewer than 500,000 persons in 1953 to about 2 million at the beginning of 1960. He writes:

> The number has continued to grow. Technological change, decline in some industries and growth in others, shifts in the geographical locations of plants, and changes in consumer demand have caused these many millions of workers to be unemployed and have kept them that way. They are the victims of growth and progress in the American economy.
>
> The consequential shifts in the structure of industry have left behind a growing pool of unskilled and semiskilled workers handicapped by the limits of a grade school education, equipped with years of routine production-work experience, and burdened with families to support. Many are members of minority groups. In addition, there are the young people, under twenty-two years of age, who have the highest unemployment rate of any group in the nation today; half of them have still to get their first jobs. They are largely untrained for employment.
>
> The paradox . . . is that all over the nation jobs go unfilled. . . . There seems to be no lack of people on the one hand or unfilled jobs on the other; what appears to be lacking is people with sufficient training and the right skills. The jobless worker in the wrong place with the wrong skills and aptitudes, has become the fall guy. . . .
>
> As a social objective, training or retraining employed and unemployed persons is much to be desired. It would improve the employability of workers, open up more attractive and higher-paid job opportunities, and raise the productive level of the entire nation. The debatable issue is the appropriateness of retraining as a remedy for the current chronic unemployment.[16]

16. William Glazier, "Automation and Joblessness." *Atlantic Monthly,* 210: 44–45 (August, 1962).

Positive Measures

Various measures have been suggested so that automation can increase productivity without creating serious unemployment. Some would slow down the pace of automation to a rate that would decrease the amount of labor displacement and joblessness. In some industries, featherbedding is defended as preferable to unemployment.

There is disagreement about how far retraining of those dispossessed of their jobs can be accepted as a solution for technological unemployment.

Regardless of one's point of view on these problems, modern technology and automation are here to stay. They are a stepped-up stage of the industrial revolution through which the output from an hour of labor has constantly been increased. If the United States should attempt to turn back or to stop the clock in this regard, it would lose its paramount economic position in today's competitive world.

The problem is not a new one. At a faster pace than in the past, we must discover the means whereby the rising productivity and standard of living, which are the fruits of technological progress, may be enjoyed without suffering the evil of unemployment and the ills that it breeds.[17]

Government Action

Various types of governmental action to alleviate unemployment are being considered, and some are being put into effect. Among the steps that have been suggested for government to take in dealing with chronic unemployment are these:

1. Objective and thorough study to determine the extent, location, and underlying causes of chronic unemployment.
2. Strengthened programs of vocational and technical train-

17. See the following collection of 20 articles reprinted from *Monthly Labor Review:* U.S. Department of Labor, Bureau of Labor Statistics. *Impact of Automation.* Bulletin No. 1287. Washington, D.C.: Government Printing Office, 1960. 114 pp.

ing to help the untrained become proficient and to retrain those whose original skills are no longer needed.

3. Better information about employment opportunities in other areas of a given state or elsewhere in the country.

4. Industrial development programs on local and regional bases.

The first large-scale effort of the federal government to meet the problems posed by automation and unemployment is the $430 million Manpower Development Training Bill which became a law on March 15, 1962. It authorized $100 million in federal funds for the fiscal year beginning July 1, 1962, and $165 million in each of the two succeeding years, with states matching the federal funds in the third year. More than 1 million persons are expected to benefit during the three-year program. Priority is to go to unemployed persons and to farm families having net incomes of less than $1,200 per year.[18]

It is outside the scope of this report to appraise the many proposals that have been made and the actions that are being taken to alleviate unemployment. The important fact is that there is general agreement that education has a major role to play in working toward this end.

MODERN ECONOMY

Ours is an economy that would be unable to operate without a growing percentage of educated workers. Schools, colleges, and graduate schools, by responding to the demands for an ever more highly educated labor force, make a major and indispensable contribution to economic growth.

This, to be sure, is only one of the purposes of education, but it is an important one. *Occupational Outlook Handbook* states the situation as follows:

The nature of one's job determines in large measure the nature of one's life. Young people who have acquired a skill or a good basic education will have a better chance at interesting work, good wages, steady employment, and greater satisfaction in life

18. "News and Trends." *NEA Journal,* 15: 4 (April, 1962).

in general. Getting as much education and training as one's ability and circumstances permit should, therefore, be high on the list of things to be done by today's youth.[19]

Current conditions indicate that the educated are most in demand and least likely to be unemployed in periods of either high or low economic activity. Under present trends, there appears to be little danger of "overeducating" our population, especially if effective guidance results in as close a matching as foresight will permit of the number trained and the number needed in each field.

One answer to the obsolescence of skills caused by technological change is reeducation and retraining of displaced workers.

Youth out of school and out of work present a different problem. The need is for cooperative work-training programs between schools and industry, which postpone the entry of these youths into the labor market until they are equipped with marketable skills.

Report of the Twenty-First American Assembly

The final report of the Twenty-First American Assembly on Automation and Technological Change states that to prepare our labor force for the needs of the new technology, we must further improve our educational standards generally and

1. Increase substantially the number of scientists, engineers, teachers, doctors, and others in the professions.
2. Develop management personnel equipped with the background needed to understand the social and economic consequences of the new technology and with the capacity to adapt technology to the achievement of greater productivity.
3. Expand training programs for technicians and assistants to engineers, scientists, and other professional personnel.
4. Upgrade and modernize the skills of craftsmen and other workers.
5. Improve the quality of the elementary and secondary educational systems, giving particular attention to he basic skills

19. U.S. Department of Labor, *Occupational Outlook Handbook*, p. 28.

of reading and mathematics, which provide the foundation for all later education and training, and increase the productivity of our education through new techniques.[20]

Range of New Demands

The followng points from several sources suggest new demands which schools and colleges must meet:

1. The work force must be both broadly educated as citizens and highly trained as workers if they are to comprehend and adjust to current and future technological change. People must learn to face the necessity for geographical and occupational transfers; low levels of education and training limit mobility and increase insecurity.
2. An adequate supply of professional and technical people must be trained to meet the growing needs. In recent years practically every field has been hampered by a shortage of scientists and engineers, of managers and competent administrators, of trained researchers, teachers, skilled craftsmen, and technicians.[21]
3. Vocational education must be geared to visible and continuing changes. Vocational education has been slow in adapting to changing needs, operating too much within the boundaries of concepts formulated around the time of World War I.
4. There should be much more careful planning of women's education to take account of the thousands who enter upon lifelong careers and the rising proportion of women who enter gainful employment before marriage and again after their children are in school or are past school age. To permit more and more women to enter the labor market without adequate training would be disadvantageous to them and to the economy.
5. How leisure time is used will determine whether technological progress and the shorter workday and week serve cultural, moral, and spiritual values as well as material ends. This calls for greater emphasis on education aimed at wise use of leisure time.

20. Reported in *Congressional Record,* June 6, 1962.
21. Frank H. Cassell, "Changing Manpower Needs." *NEA Journal,* 51: 55 (April, 1962).

6. More adequate educational and vocational guidance must be offered part-time and full-time junior- and senior-high-school students and community college, junior college, and four-year college students.

7. Education must be a lifelong process. Lifelong learning is a new imperative. To survive as productive members of our society and even to enjoy the opportunities offered by the promise of additional leisure will require additional knowledge and lifelong learning.

"It should be made clear to every worker in the land that the price of holding a job will increasingly depend on continuing education throughout the entire working life of the individual."[22]

How to deal with technological unemployment is a controversial issue. It is clear, however, that there is need for a labor force with constantly rising levels of general education and occupational training.

Schools will be involved in varying degrees in dealing with technological unemployment. In some cases, such as the elimination of illiteracy, the primary responsibility will rest on a system of public education that makes it impossible for a normal child to reach maturity lacking the ability to read and write. On the other hand, the retraining of adult workers, unemployed because of automation and other factors beyond the control of the individual, will require the involvement of schools to a lesser extent. Doubtless this retraining will require the cooperation of management and labor, certain types of governmental action, and understanding on the part of the community as a whole. Such cooperative action will not be easy to accomplish. But to permit the full impact of automation and other elements in the technological revolution to fall upon the individual worker without appropriate response would be folly with the gravest social consequences.

FISCAL IMPLICATIONS

Substantial increases will be required in the financial sup-

22. Harold Clark, "Education in Our Complex Society." *NEA Journal,* 51: 52 (April, 1962).

port of education if it is to play its role in meeting our economy's rising demand for workers with more and better education and training and its role in providing certain types of education to reduce unemployment resulting from automation and technological change.

Whether this additional cost can and will be met will to a considerable degree depend upon the public's conception of the economic significance of education.

". . . but unemployment among youth under twenty is about 20 per cent, or nearly three times greater than the nation-wide rate for all workers."

SCHOOL DROPOUTS *

John K. Norton

Although one can argue about whether economy-wide automation is primarily a school problem, there is little question that, whatever the *rate* of technological change, we are a highly developed economy that demands high levels of technical compctcnce or skill and that the school provides at least the basic skills necessary to their acquisition. Although it is a problem that consequently can fairly be located in the area of formal education, if it were *only* the school's problem solutions for it would not be so difficult to find. Norton's article, for example, implies that youngsters who finish high school have a better chance for a job than those who drop out, and although this is generally so, it is not true for the Negro

boy in particular, who constitutes one of the toughest
of dropout problems. The growing concern at this
time over the whole problem, moreover, clearly reflects the spectacular rise in the number of youth
under twenty-five entering the labor force in the
sixties; in the decade of the fifties less than a million
of these young people were seeking jobs, compared
with almost seven million in this decade. Yet, whether
it is a problem for this generation only, to become less
pressing with a lower birth rate, we must do something about it.

*One of Norton's major proposals is for greatly
expanded guidance facilities for high-school youth.
Conant, in* Slums and Suburbs, *suggests that such
guidance should go as far as finding jobs for young
people and remaining in touch with them for several years. Should this be a function of the high
school? How much of the problem should the proposal take care of, if it were workable?*

THE AMOUNT of schooling of different individuals varies enormously. Some children do not continue in school even to the fifth grade. In succeeding grades, the attrition is higher than most people realize.

According to the U.S. Office of Education, the high school graduating class of 1954 contained only 553 of each 1,000 pupils who had reached the fifth grade seven years earlier.

Just how long each child should continue in school is a matter of opinion. There is wide agreement, however, that the many pupils who drop out of school at 16, or at whatever earlier age the law or circumstances permit, constitute a major problem. One study concludes that school dropouts create an explosive situation and are a serious threat to our society.

School Dropout Rate

For example, the number of high-school graduates in 1962, as a per cent of eighth-grade enrollment in 1957-58, varied from

1962 High-School Graduates As Per Cent of 1957–58 Eighth-Grade Enrollment

1. 92.3%	Wisconsin	18. 74.1%	New York	35. 62.9%	Florida
2. 88.2	Minnesota	19. 73.3	Montana	36. 62.2	New Mexico
3. 86.4	California	20. 73.3	Rhode Island	37. 61.0	Maine
4. 84.8	Nebraska	21. 73.1	Connecticut	38. 60.6	Texas
5. 84.5	Illinois	22. 73.1	Wyoming	39. 57.8	Arkansas
6. 84.2	Washington	23. 73.0	Missouri	40. 57.8	Louisiana
7. 80.6	Hawaii	24. 72.9	Colorado	41. 57.8	Mississippi
8. 78.8	New Jersey	25. 72.5	Idaho	42. 57.4	North Carolina
9. 78.6	Iowa	26. 72.4	Ohio	43. 56.4	Vermont
10. 78.4	Michigan	27. 72.0	Delaware	44. 55.5	West Virginia
11. 78.1	Kansas	28. 71.1	Arizona	45. 55.1	Tennessee
12. 78.1	South Dakota	29. 70.1	Alaska	46. 55.0	Alabama
13. 78.0	Pennsylvania	30. 69.3	New Hampshire	47. 54.2	South Carolina
14. 77.9	Oregon	31. 68.2	Massachusetts	48. 52.6	Kentucky
15. 77.2	Utah	32. 67.9	Oklahoma	49. 51.9	Virginia
16. 76.8	North Dakota	33. 67.5	Maryland	50. 51.8	Georgia
17. 74.1	Indiana	34. 63.7	Nevada	70.6	50 states and D.C.

Source: National Education Association, Research Division. *Rankings of the States, 1963*. Research Report 1963-R1. Washington, D.C.: The Association, 1963. Table 47.

92.3 per cent in Wisconsin to 51.8 per cent in Georgia. The median for 50 states and the District of Columbia was 70.6 per cent.[1] (See table for data on all states.) The average dropout rate between eighth-grade and high-school graduation is approximately 32 per cent.

It should not be assumed that these 32 per cent who quit school in the ninth, tenth, eleventh, or twelfth grades are incapable of learning. Many are the victims of inadequate schooling in one form or another.

Age of School Dropouts

The greatest percentage of withdrawal occurs at about the age when attendance is no longer compulsory, which is sixteen years in most states. In October of 1959, 929,000, or 17.1 per cent of youths aged sixteen and seventeen years were not enrolled in schools.[2]

Grade Reached by School Dropouts

Less than 60 per cent of the boys and girls who reach the fifth grade stay in school through high school. Out of every three reaching the ninth grade, one fails to get a high-school diploma.[3]

The first major drop occurs between the ninth and tenth grades when many pupils are making the transition from junior to senior high school. . . . Another significant drop occurs between the tenth and eleventh grades. Many of these pupils have ob-

1. National Education Association, Research Division. *Rankings of the States, 1963.* Research Report 1963-R1. Washington, D.C.: the Association, 1963, Table 47.

2. U.S. Department of Commerce, Bureau of the Census. *School Enrollment: October 1959.* Current Population Reports, Population Characteristics, Series P-20, No. 101. Washington, D.C.: Government Printing Office, 1960, p. 8.

3. Sam M. Lambert, Director of Research, National Education Association. Testimony before U.S. 87th Congress, 1st Session, House of Representatives Committee on Education and Labor, March, 1961, p. 173.

viously tried the secondary school and found it wanting for their needs.[4]

Current trends indicate that about 7.5 million of the young people entering the labor force during the 1960's will not have completed high school, and that 2.5 million will not have completed even the eighth grade.[5]

Reasons for Dropping out of School

According to the U.S. Department of Labor, Bureau of Labor Statistics,

> Pupils who drop out from the eighth, ninth, and tenth grades most often do so for reasons closely related to their school experiences, such as grade retardation, academic difficulties, and failure to participate in pupil activities. Dropouts from the later grades, however, are chiefly accounted for by other well-defined reasons such as marriage, or the need to work.[6]

Lack of guidance counselors and courses of study to meet the widely varying capacities and goals of high-school pupils today are among the major factors causing pupils to quit school. Parental and community attitudes are also influential. After visiting public schools in "two totally different neighborhoods," Conant concludes:

> One lesson to be drawn from visiting and contrasting a well-to-do suburb and a slum is all important for understanding American public education. This lesson is that to a considerable degree what a school should do and can do is determined by the status and ambitions of the families being served.[7]

4. National Education Association, Research Division and Department of Classroom Teachers. *High-School Dropouts*. Discussion Pamphlet No. 3. Washington, D.C.: the Association, 1959, p. 6.

5. U.S. Department of Labor, Bureau of Labor Statistics. *From School to Work*. Washington, D.C.: Government Printing Office, 1960, p. 1.

6. National Education Association, Research Division and Department of Classroom Teachers, *op. cit.*, p. 7.

7. James B. Conant, *Slums and Suburbs: A Commentary on Schools in Metropolitan Areas*. New York: McGraw-Hill Book Co., 1961, p. 1.

Children of Migrant Workers

It is estimated that 400,000 migrant workers, accompanied by more than 100,000 children, travel from community to community and from state to state each year in search of agricultural employment.

Educationally, these children are the most deprived group in the nation. Frequent moves force them to fall further and further behind in their studies. When they drop out of school for good, their average achievement is below the fourth-grade level.[8] A few states are attempting to deal with this problem, but it is an extremely difficult one.

CHARACTERISTICS OF SCHOOL DROPOUTS

The National Education Association Project on School Dropouts is studying intensively the characteristics of school dropouts.[9] The following are some of the findings:

1. The average dropout is not uneducable. He does tend to score lower on IQ tests than his in-school counterpart, but a nation-wide study conducted by the U.S. Department of Labor showed that 70 per cent of the dropouts surveyed had registered IQ scores above 90, clearly in the educable group. An intensive six-year study in the State of New York revealed that 13 per cent of the dropouts had IQ scores above 110.[10] This rating should permit high-school graduation and some post-high-school training.

2. The average dropout is at least two years retarded in reading ability by the time he quits school. Reading remains the fundamental educational skill; without it no student can perform adequately in school. The consequences of retardation in reading are obvious: dropouts fail three times as many courses

8. Donald Janson, "Migrant Pupils Miss Schooling." *New York Times,* July 22, 1962. Copyright by the *New York Times.* Reprinted by permission.

9. Daniel Schreiber, "School Dropouts." *NEA Journal,* 51: 51–52; May, 1962.

10. *Ibid.,* p. 52.

as "stay-ins," and nine of every ten dropouts have been retained in some grade at least one extra year.

3. The majority of dropouts are from lower socioeconomic families. They often come from families where the father is missing, where cultural background and horizons are limited, where education is viewed with indifference, distrust, or open resentment. Any redemptive or preventive effort of the school will have to take account of the student's total environment and will depend heavily on the school's staff of guidance counselors and school-community coordinators.

4. There is a high percentage of dropouts among minority groups. This fact was detailed as follows at the 1961 Conference on Unemployed, Out-of-School Youth in Urban Areas:

> Estimates of the number of Mexican-American youth who leave school before getting to high school range as high as 50 per cent in the major cities.

> Today, two thirds cf all Negroes live in urban areas, one third in urban areas outside the South.[11]

> In a slum section composed almost entirely of Negroes in one of our largest cities the following situation was found. A total of 59 per cent of the male youth between the ages of sixteen and twenty-one were out of school and unemployed. They were roaming the streets. Of the boys who graduated from high school, 48 per cent were unemployed in contrast to 63 per cent of the boys who had dropped out of school.

> An even worse state of affairs was found in another special study in a different city. In a slum area of 125,000 people, mostly Negro, a sampling of the youth population shows that roughly 70 per cent of the boys and girls ages sixteen to twenty-one are out-of-school and unemployed.[12]

> The problem of unemployed youth in the large cities is in no small part a Negro problem. We do not facilitate its solution by trying to find phrases to hide this fact.[13]

11. National Committee for Children and Youth. *Social Dynamite.* Report of the Conference on Unemployed, Out-of-School Youth in Urban Areas. Washington, D.C.: the Committee, 1961, p. 16.

12. *Ibid.,* p. 26.

13. *Ibid.,* p. 32.

5. Dropouts are not entirely from minority groups. Of the four special surveys made for the Conference on Unemployed, Out-of-School Youth in Urban Areas, two dealt with racially mixed urban school districts where the majority of the dropouts interviewed were white. Like the minority group dropouts, however, most of these white boys and girls belonged to lower income families who had recently arrived in the city. Theirs were families who had left subsistence farms, families said to be among the nation's least educated, with a lack of motivation no less deadening than that of darker-skinned families from depressed areas. But the problem of school dropouts is not confined to the big cities. It exists in small towns. It is particularly acute in rural areas, and the problems of the rural areas and the big cities are closely related.[14]

State-Wide Study of Dropouts

A state-wide study of dropouts by the Illinois Office of Public Instruction revealed the following:

Approximately 54 per cent of the students who took more than eight years to finish elementary school became high-school dropouts.

Only 2 per cent of the students who took college preparatory courses became dropouts, while 38 per cent of those who studied general curriculum left high school before graduating.

About 60 per cent of the students who were absent more than 25 days out of the normal 185-day school year became dropouts.

Over 30 per cent of the dropouts occurred before the end of the freshman year; another 30 per cent occurred during the sophomore year.

High-school graduates held more part-time jobs than dropouts held.

Dropouts had more frequent access to family cars and owned more cars than did those who graduated.

Students who finished high school engaged in more extracurricular activities than did dropouts.

A large percentage of dropouts came from broken homes.[15]

14. *Ibid.*, pp. 17–18.
15. "Late News." *Overview*, 3: 22; August, 1962. Copyright 1962, Buttenheim Publishing Corp.

WHAT HAPPENS TO SCHOOL DROPOUTS?

A number of studies have been made to discover what happens to young people who drop out of school. Among the more important findings are these:

1. A large percentage is unemployed. The U.S. Department of Labor in October 1960 surveyed the employment status of June, 1960 graduates and pregraduation dropouts. The survey found that

about three fourths of the male dropouts, but almost nine tenths of the high-school graduates (those not enrolled in college), were working. About two thirds of the unmarried female dropouts, but three fourths of the graduates, were working. Furthermore, the unemployed dropouts had been unemployed for longer periods than the unemployed graduates.[16]

Conant stated that

in the slums of the largest cities . . . the great need is for reduction of unemployment of male youth under twenty-one.[17]

The present (1960) unemployment rate nationwide is roughly 7 per cent for all age brackets, but unemployment among youth under twenty years of age is about 20 per cent, or nearly three times greater than the nationwide rate for all workers.[18]

A survey made in New York City in the summer of 1962 showed that 45,000 youths needed work but were unable to find it. Many of these were Puerto Ricans and Negroes, the groups which have the most difficulty in finding jobs. Many are school dropouts, and their lack of education and training further hampers them.

Ewan Clague, Director of the Bureau of Labor Statistics, stated at the Conference on Unemployed, Out-of-School Youth

16. Sophia Cooper, "Employment of June 1960 High-School Graduates." Special Labor Force Report No. 15. *Monthly Labor Review,* 84: 463–70; May, 1961.

17. Conant, *op. cit.,* p. 35.

18. James B. Conant, "Social Dynamite in Our Cities." *Social Dynamite,* p. 27.

in Urban Areas that 300,000 boys and 115,000 girls between the ages sixteen and twenty reported themselves out of school looking for work in October 1960.

2. Most school dropouts when employed work at unskilled jobs. Unskilled and immature, the dropout finds himself abandoned in a labor market where he has little to offer.

Casual jobs and work requiring little in the way of skills training typify the employment activity of most fourteen- to seventeen-year-olds. Job opportunities for youth in this age group are concentrated mainly in the trade and service industries and in agriculture.[19]

The jobs available to school dropouts are usually of the lowest order. Frequently they offer irregular employment and are the least open to advancement. Also, employers are loathe to employ and to provide on-the-job training to youths in the sixteen to twenty-one age group, since they may be subject to call for military service.

Two thirds of the nation's force of service workers and operatives and laborers are former dropouts. Two thirds of the unemployed men and women in the United States possess less than a high-school education.[20]

3. Dropouts face keen competition. Because of the rapid rise in births in the 1940's and 1950's, the population reaching age eighteen will shortly increase especially fast—from 2.6 million in 1960 to 3.8 million in 1965, up nearly 50 per cent in only five years. The 1965 rate will continue through 1970. Because of this increase, the number of new workers entering the labor force will mount steadily. Altogether 26 million young people will enter the labor force during the 1960's, almost 40 per cent more than during the 1950's.[21]

The estimated 7.5 million youths who, according to recent experience, will drop out of school during the 1960's may glut

19. White House Regional Conferences. *Young Workers Under 18.* Fact Sheet. Washington, D.C.: the Conferences, 1961.

20. Schreiber, *op. cit.*

21. U.S. Department of Labor, *op. cit.*

the labor market already overcrowded with unskilled workers at a time when the number of unskilled occupations is declining.

4. The life earnings of school dropouts are low. During his lifetime, the average boy who drops out of school before high-school graduation will earn much less than the average high-school graduate. "The typical male high school graduate can be expected to earn over his lifetime (from age twenty-five to death) $72,000 more than the typical male elementary-school graduate."[22]

School Dropouts and Delinquency

Exact numbers and percents of school dropouts who become delinquent are not known. It is claimed that they are relatively large. Out-of-school, unemployed youth are more apt to become delinquent. A youngster out of school and out of work is a potential source of trouble to himself and to the community. A youth who drops out of school and cannot find a job, which gives him a sense of belonging to the community and of purpose in life, is apt to feel at odds with society and is more likely to become delinquent.

Careful studies of juvenile delinquency show that this problem is not confined to communities and families of low socio-economic status. It occurs in favored communities and families, although at a lower rate of incidence. Nor is juvenile delinquency a peculiar problem of the United States. It is world-wide. These facts call for fundamental study of this disturbing problem and incisive action by responsible agencies, including the schools.

CONCLUSIONS

1. Today, for most youths under eighteen, work should be secondary to getting education and training appropriate to their abilities and needs.

2. Lack of basic education seriously complicates the retraining of the long-term unemployed.

22. Lambert, *op. cit.*, p. 171.

3. A substantial percentage on relief rolls are those who lose their jobs and lack the training for other employment.

4. Out-of-school, unemployed youths commit a disproportionately high percentage of juvenile crimes.

5. Full development of each youth's talents and abilities is the key to meeting future manpower needs. To assure such development, youths must have protection and guidance, jobs that provide productive experience, and, perhaps most important, the kind of education needed in our modern complex and technically oriented economy.

[These] conclusions raise many questions about the adequacy of today's public elementary and secondary schools. Is the guidance program adequate? Is the curriculum or program of studies broad enough to meet the present needs of America's children and youth? Are adequate provisions made for the children of "disadvantaged Americans"[23]—parents with low socioeconomic status, language handicaps, lack of vocational skills with resulting unemployment, and little interest in having their children continue in school? Are the quality of teachers and their training and teaching equal to the demands of a rapidly changing society?

The powerful impacts of our dynamic economy upon all Americans hold fundamental implications for public schools. The next section identifies some of the improvements required in these schools if they are to meet changing demands.

23. National Education Association and American Association of School Administrators, Educational Policies Commission. *Education and the Disadvantaged American*. Washington, D.C.: National Education Association, 1962. 39 pp.

". . . She cut me with the edge of the ruler there. So I got up and hit her."

DON'T BUG ME*
S. M. Miller

The abstracts of the dropout problem as presented by Norton do little to reveal the nature of the human relations that are often the cause of leaving school. In the course of a study of dropouts conducted at Syracuse University, S. M. Miller interviewed a group of boys to obtain their perceptions of the school situation from which they had withdrawn. In these excerpts from the interviews it is clear that, although the boys do not in general dislike school, they were bewildered by it, and objected to what they saw as the "bugging" they were forced to endure.

Miller offers several suggestions for revisions in work situations or training programs to meet the difficulties of dealing with the feelings of these boys. What practical steps might be taken by the schools to eliminate "bugging"?

* S. M. Miller, "Types of Dropouts: The Unemployables," presented at the Annual Meeting of the American Orthopsychiatric Association, Washington, D.C., March, 1963. Reprinted by permission of the author.

A FREQUENT explanation of difficulties, especially with police, employers, or school, is that someone was "bugging me." [Here are] two examples of bugging ("I" is the interviewer, WDO and NDO are "white dropout" and "Negro dropout"):

I	What did they (teachers) do when they picked on you?
NDO	Like sometimes, you know, I ain't doing nothing, they just start bugging me. They just started talking and all this trash.
I	What did they say?
NDO	Oh, like, what you doing, do your work and all that. Sometimes I can't quit talking cause I ain't been talking and it be somebody else that been talking.
I	Anything else you dislike about school?
NDO	No.
I	Why did you drop school?
NDO	I got expelled.
I	Can you tell me about that?
NDO	Well, you see, I was getting in a little bit of trouble, so one day, in the cafeteria; you know they have teachers that be in there, so this one teacher, he thought I snuck ahead in line but I didn't, so when I got up to get my milk, he told the boy not to give it to me, and then, so I said something, so then he grab me and then, you know, we sort of tussled a little bit and then I had to go down to the principal's office and he . . . ah . . . he . . . ah, Mr. ———, the principal, he expelled me. He kicked me out.
I	Why did you leave school?
WDO	Got sick and tired of school.
I	Got sick and tired of school? How did you get sick and tired of school? What happened?
WDO	Oh, the teachers keep on bugging me.
I	Bugging you?
WDO	Yes.
I	How do teachers bug students? I have heard this expression time and again. But I don't understand what it is. How do teachers bug a student?
WDO	They push me around, or something like that.

I	Push you around how?
WDO	Shove me or something.
I	Where do they shove you? Who shoves you?
WDO	The teachers.
I	Why do they shove you?
WDO	I talked in class or something like that. Fooled around a couple of times.
I	Why do you think they did that?
WDO	Oh, they got mad at me, and pushed me around, so I started pushing them around.

These boys frequently report the precipitating incident for their getting kicked out of school or being fired from a job was a situation in which they were not deliberately trying to do something wrong. (The earlier excerpt from the interview with the New York City boy in a rural school is a good example.) Someone was constantly nagging them, misinterpreting what they were doing; the adults' misperception led to the action which the adults feared.

WDO	Well, the teachers were okay up until the seventh grade. Then they started getting down my neck.
I	How they'd get down your neck?
WDO	Well, it started out when I moved into the seventh grade and there was a bunch of guys I knew that had failed. They were in my class. We started monkeying around and the teachers started to get mad.
I	Monkey around with you?
WDO	Yes.
WDO	Uh . . . oh boy . . . I can't right remember her name but it will come back to me. She was my home-room teacher in —— School and . . . well, she always jumped on all the boys' necks. It's like when we had study hall and when we had to go back to our room for a study hall seventh period and we did all our work during the class and she tell us to do anything we want. We go over and start talking to the girls; we start asking them questions and things like that, she started jumping on the boys' necks about that. Then she goes down to the principal and say

	we were molesting her. And I didn't like that a bit.
I	Is that the worst teacher you've had?
WDO	Oh boy, that's the worst teacher I've had yet—ever had.
I	Has she ever hit you or anything like that?
WDO	She's hit me. One time she wish she hadn't.
I	With what? Why did she hit you?
WDO	I was . . . well, she told us to do anything we wanted to cause I did my . . . we only had English homework one night and I did that all during English class. We have . . . I think it's fifteen minutes at the end of the class there to do our homework or anything like that or any homework we've got, so I did all my homework in that fifteen minutes so she told us that if we were tired, to lay our heads down on our desk or something like that, so I laid my head down on the desk and she come over with a ruler and hit me in the back of the neck just as hard as she could and that hurt too. She cut me with the edge of the ruler there. So I got up and hit her.

The boys in using this mode of explanation do not claim that they had always been good little conformists; no, they had been in trouble before, but the incident which led to their exile was not initiated by them.

They saw the adults' behavior in the situation as "unfair," falsely accusing them, and this seems to provide a basis for neutralizing the norms which restrain behavior in school or in the job world. Perhaps more importantly, they see many supervisory adults as bugging them, always "buzzing around," "riding" them, "going after them," looking for trouble even when it is not there. The boys frequently recognize that they are doing things which are difficult for teachers or bosses to accept but they do not do them to antagonize. These outcomes are the result of trying to have a good time, "kidding around," and the like. The constant nagging and riding, which is their interpretation of what is taking place, is thought of as "picking on" them and excessively irritating. Yet, they accept the idea of structure and discipline; it is the particular form of it which bugs them.

They see the adult mode of control as entrapment: "They're after me all the time until I finally get real angry and do something that is too much."

Yablonsky[1] reports the poignant feeling of being bugged:

> The essential meaning of the "permanent" clubroom to the gang was revealed by Jay. He would come regularly, pay his ten-cent dues, then go and lie down in a corner on the floor and stare quietly at the ceiling. One day I questioned him about what seemed to be a waste of money:
>
> L.Y.   Jay, how come you pay your dime and just lie around? Why don't you play checkers or talk to the guys or something?
>
> JAY   Look, man, this is the only place in the world they leave me be. *Don't bug me.* I hang on the corner or the park—the cops boot me. I go home—they throw me out. They don't let me in the [community] center no more. I hang in my hallway—the janitor yells. I go on the stoop—the neighbors bitch. I get a little peace here—so leave me be.

In the job world, the boys frequently mention that they have been fired because one boss wanted them to do one thing; another, a different thing and they got fed up and told off the boss.

> Makes me sick. I got so many bosses, I don't know who to mind. Even the bus boys had bus boys. "You bus that table." "No, I want you to bus that table: Come over here and bus this table." So I said, "Don't none of you say nothing to me. If you do, we're going to fight. I'm not taking any orders from anybody but the big boss. If I see something that needs to be done, I'll do it."

The precipitating incident is again that of a false accusation of aberrant behavior. Yet, here again as in the school situation, they accept the idea of authority and supervision. It is its concrete manifestation with which they have difficulty.

I   Is it ever really necessary for someone to give orders?

1. Louis Yablonsky. *The Violent Gang*, New York: Macmillan, 1962, p. 78.

NDO Yes, if nobody don't give no orders and everybody do what they want to do, somebody might not do the right thing.

Another boy:

I Well, is having someone give orders every time really necessary?

WDO Well, in ways it is and in ways it isn't. Because, let's say, one guy gives you orders and you go to do it and another guy gives you orders when you're just doing this one. When you're doing the other one, the other one come by and ask you why you aren't doing this one and then you get all mixed up and then you . . .

I That happen to you?

WDO It happened to me six times.

I Where was this?

WDO This company. Till the seventh time, I got sick and I slammed him. I gave him a black eye and a bloody nose. He said I was fired and I said, sorry, I quit two minutes ago and I want my check and he said he wasn't going to give it to me. So I took it to the labor board and I got $20 extra.

The frequency with which contradictory orders may be involved may be due to these boys' working in situations (like restaurants) where work rationality is limited and the organizational structure leaky. Their jobs are frequently in establishments where there is not a well-formalized work situation. (One action suggestion would involve setting up regularized grievance systems in places which employ many youths. Training programs might experiment with providing a neutralized mode of handling grievances.)

A central tension is that the boys seem to take criticism in a very personal way (not that all of us do not have difficulty in separating criticisms of our products from criticisms of ourselves). It is all right for a boss to exert authority—that's what being a boss is—but that is not the same thing as criticizing me, telling me what is wrong with what I do, especially if such comments are made in heat.

What does it mean to accept criticism? Is it considered a sign of weakness to let someone get away with it? Or is it taken as a sign of total rejection by the adult? Or as an effrontery and an invasion of privacy? We do not know; we suspect that the boys are asking for respect, a "rep," a status which we adults tell them has to be earned. But the boys frequently are not sure it is worthwhile to try to earn it, if it is not first accorded them.

". . . sins for which all Americans are in some measure guilty and for which all Americans owe some act of atonement."

THE CITY AND THE NEGRO *

Charles E. Silberman

In this Fortune article, Silberman raises and discusses just about every one of the important elements in the problem facing the urban school: the migratory movements of masses of Negroes, metropolitan growth patterns, the differences between the current problem and that of earlier waves of immigrants, the significance of the Negro revolution, the issues of the involvement of the poor in the solution of their problems, the alienation of the ghetto school, and the question of "positive discrimination." Because many big-city school teachers themselves have European immigrant backgrounds, an important part of the article for them to consider is Silberman's analysis of the

* Charles E. Silberman, "The City and the Negro," *Fortune Magazine* (March 1962). Reprinted from the March 1962 issue of *Fortune Magazine* by special permission. Copyright © 1962 Time, Inc.

Negro's singular position at the bottom of the economic and social ladder.

> *Silberman argues that it is specious to say that because earlier minority groups improved their social status by their own efforts alone, the Negro must be incompetent or lazy not to have done so. How valid are the arguments he advances against this view?*

"*THE APPROVED* way to talk about cities these days," Paul Ylvisaker of the Ford Foundation has observed, "is to speak solemnly, sadly, ominously, and fearfully about their problems. You don't rate as an expert on the city unless you foresee its doom." Doom is easy to foresee in the spreading slums, the increasing crime rates, the public disaffection of almost every large city. And yet the city can survive, as it has survived for a century and a half. Indeed, American cities today have a chance to achieve their greatest success and their greatest glory.

For this to happen, however, city planners and civic leaders will have to understand better than they now do what their cities' greatest problem is. It is not, as so many assume, to bring the wandering middle class back from the suburbs. The large city, as Jane Jacobs of *Architectural Forum* has put it, cannot import a middle class; it must manufacture its own. And, indeed, most of the huge middle class that dominates American life today was manufactured in the big-city slums of yesteryear. Cities always have had to create their own stable, cultivated citizenry out of whatever raw material lay at hand. For the American city during the past hundred and fifty years, the raw material was the stream of immigrants pouring in from Britain, Ireland, Germany, Norway, Russia, Italy, and a dozen other lands. The city needed these immigrants to build its streets and offices, to man its factories, service its homes and hotels and restaurants, and do all the dirty and menial jobs that older residents disdained. But the city did more than use its newcomers; it equipped them to take their place as fully participating members of U.S. society. Doing this—bringing people from society's backwaters into the mainstream of American life—has always been the principal business, and the principal glory, of the American city.

It isn't any longer; the city is in trouble today because it isn't dealing successfully with its newcomers. They are still pouring in—not from County Cork, or Bavaria, or Sicily, or Galicia, but from Jackson, Mississippi, and Memphis, Tennessee, and a host of towns and hamlets with names like Sunflower, Rolling Fork, and Dyersburg. The new immigrants are distinguished from the older residents not by religion or national origin, but by color. Between 1950 and 1960 the twelve largest U.S. cities lost over two million white residents; they gained nearly two million Negro residents.

It is the explosive growth of their Negro populations, in fact, that constitutes the large cities' principal problem and concern. When city officials talk about spreading slums, they are talking in the main about physical deterioration of the areas inhabited by Negroes. And when they talk about juvenile delinquency, or the burden of welfare payments, or any of a long list of city problems, officials are talking principally about the problems of Negro adjustment to city life. For the large city is not absorbing and "urbanizing" its new Negro residents rapidly enough; its slums are no longer acting as the incubator of a new middle class.

One reason for this failure is that city planners have been more interested in upgrading the value of the city's real estate than in upgrading the lives of the human beings who inhabit the real estate. They have tried to create middle-class neighborhoods by driving lower-class Negro residents out of the neighborhood being renewed, and bring white middle-class residents in; Negroes bitterly refer to urban renewal as "Negro removal." (An estimated 80 per cent of the families relocated by urban-renewal projects have been Negro.) The effort is doomed to failure. Driving the Negroes out of one area merely creates a new and frequently worse slum somewhere else in the city.

The city can be saved only if it faces up to the fact that "the urban problem" is in large measure a Negro problem. But the Negro problem is more than just an urban problem; it is also the problem of all the U.S., rural or urban, North or South—though it is in the large northern cities that the solution is most likely. Speeding the Negro's integration into American life—helping the big-city Negroes move up into the great American middle class—is the largest and most urgent piece of public business facing the U.S. today.

It is also the most difficult. There is a tendency among many well-intentioned Americans to underestimate this difficulty. Some people see the Negro problem as purely legal and social and assume that it will be solved automatically by desegregating schools, restaurants, bus terminals, and housing developments. Other people see it as purely economic, to be resolved by upgrading Negro jobs and incomes. And a good many Americans believe the problem would be solved if the Negroes would just decide to adopt white middle-class standards of behavior and white middle-class goals of economic success.

There are no cheap or easy answers to the Negro problem, however; it involves all these elements and a good many more besides. The problem's roots go back to slavery, whose impact is still being felt in the disorganization of the Negro family, and to the Negro's systematic exclusion from American society since slavery ended a century ago. These are sins for which all Americans are in some measure guilty and for which all Americans owe some act of atonement. Those who hesitate to act because of the magnitude of the problem should remember the stricture of Edmund Burke: "The only thing necessary for the triumph of evil is for good men to do nothing."

But the triumph of "good" in this instance (as in most others) requires a lot more than good will. To solve the Negro problem will demand difficult and occasionally heroic decisions on the part of civic and political leaders, and changes in the behavior of Americans in every walk of life: teachers and students; trade-union leaders and members; employers and employees. This article—the sixth in *Fortune's* series on "The Public Business"—will document what is being done across the country, and what needs to be done, to speed the Negro's advance and thereby save the large city.

FILLING THE VACUUM

The Negro has come to the big city because it needed his labor, especially after the cutting off of European immigration created a vacuum in northern labor markets. The Negro population outside the Deep South has increased fivefold since 1910; it has nearly tripled just since 1940. Part of this expansion, of course, has come from natural increase rather than migration;

but it is the migration of Negroes in the childbearing ages that enabled the natural increase to occur outside the South.

Most of the Negroes moving to the North have crowded into the slums of the twelve largest cities, which today hold 60 per cent of the Negroes living ouside the Deep South. Since 1940 the Negro population of New York City has increased nearly two and one-half times, to 1,100,000, or 14 per cent of the city's population. In Philadelphia, Negroes have doubled in number since 1940, to 529,000, or 26 per cent. The Negro population of Detroit has more than tripled, to nearly 500,000, or 29 per cent of the city's population. And the Negro population of Los Angeles Cunty has jumped a phenomenal sixfold since 1940, from 75,000 to 464,000.

The Negroes, to be sure, are not the only disadvantaged peoples coming into the large cities. In New York the Puerto Rican population swelled from perhaps 100,000 in 1940 to over 700,000 in 1960. And Cincinnati, Baltimore, St. Louis, Columbus, Detroit, and Chicago, among others, receive a steady stream of impoverished white hillbillies from the southern Appalachian Mountains. These Appalachian whites—of the oldest and purest U.S. stock—have at least as much initial difficulty adjusting to the city as do the Negroes and Puerto Ricans. But the Puerto Ricans and Appalachian whites affect only a limited number of cities, usually in only a limited way. There are a good many other city problems besides the Negro problem, in short. But the Negro problem is what city planners and officials are really talking about when they refer to The City Problem.

THE CRUCIAL DIFFERENCE

Migration to the large city has always involved a heavy cost in family dislocation, pauperism, crime, delinquency, and urban blight. Immigrants bring with them housekeeping and other habits that clash with city standards; and the impersonality of city life tends to erode the social relationships that regulated behavior in "the old country." Hence the U.S. middle class has always had the sense of being engulfed by uncultivated newcomers, and has always been on the move. As early as the 1840's, for example, New York City's Fourth Ward—the district in which George Washington had lived when he was inaugurated President—had become a slum so overrun by violence that even the police dared not enter except in parties of six or more. And by the 1870's New Yorkers were already lamenting the exodus of men of "moderate income to the suburban towns." With its "middle classes in large part self-exiled, its laboring population being brutalized in the tenements, and its citizens of the highest class indifferent to the common weal," a journalist commented at the time, "New York has drifted from bad to worse and become the prey of professional thieves, ruffians, and political jugglers." Measured against the backdrop of history, therefore, the gangs and crime and squalor of today seem almost benign, and some historians and sociologists have concluded that time and patience are almost all that's needed.

It will take more than that. The Negro is unlike the European immigrant in one crucial respect: he is colored. And that makes all the difference. The Irish, to be sure, faced job discrimination a century ago as severe as the Negro faces today. But the Irishman could lose his brogue; as soon as he was "Americanized," his problem was resolved. But the Negro cannot escape so easily. "All other slum dwellers, when the bank account permits it," James Baldwin has written, "can move out of the slum and vanish altogether from the eye of persecution." Not so the Negro.

There are other differences. The European peasant, no matter how depressed his position, had roots in a "whole society" with a stable culture and stable institutions and above all a stable family life. The Negro does not. Slavery made a stable life (and a stable culture) impossible. Husbands could be sold away from wives, children from parents. Such family life as did exist centered almost entirely around the mother.

What slavery began, prejudice and discrimination have helped perpetuate. Family disorganization is endemic. Negro women frequently find it easier to get jobs—e.g., as domestics—than Negro men, thus making them the financial center of the family. The inability of Negro men to find jobs that confer status and dignity, together with the servility required of them in the South, have led Negro men to sexual promiscuity, drinking, and violence as means of asserting their masculinity. Embittered by their experience with men, Negro mothers seem to take more interest in their daughters' than in their sons' upbringing. Twice as many Negro girls as boys go to college. (Among white college students, the reverse is true.) And family disorganization is compounded by the overcrowding and dilapidation of Negro housing.

Hence the Negro, all too often, is trapped in a vicious circle from which he cannot extricate himself. Little in the Negro boy's environment is likely to give him any sense of aspiration or any direction; he has no male model to follow and little reason to assume that education offers a way out of the slum. His lack of education and aspiration, in turn, makes it virtually impossible for the Negro youth to find a job with dignity and status, even where discrimination is absent. All too often, therefore, he decides that there is no point to trying, and he loses the capacity to take advantage of such opportunities as do arise. In the jargon of the social worker, he "develops a self-defeating mode of living" that keeps him trapped in the slum forever.

To make matters worse, the gap is widening between Negro education and training, on the one hand, and the requirements of the labor market, on the other. The Europeans immigrated during periods of rapidly expanding U.S. demand for unskilled labor; no great transfer of skill was needed to enable an Irish or Italian peasant to find a job on a construction gang. But in the U.S. today, the demand for unskilled labor is shrinking relative to the total labor force. Since 1947, employment of white-collar workers-executives, entrepreneurs, professional and scientific employees, clerks, and salesmen—has gone up 43 per cent, compared to only a 14 per cent gain in blue-collar and service-worker employment. By 1970 a substantial majority of workers will be in white-collar or highly skilled blue-collar jobs —in jobs that characteristically require real training and thought. Three out of four nonfarm Negro male workers, however, are in unskilled or semiskilled occupations, compared to only one in three among white workers.

In this new world of specialized skills, Negroes have more and more trouble finding and holding jobs. The unemployment rate among Negro men is more than twice that among white men. In some cities as many as one Negro male in three is out of work. The problem is particularly acute among Negro youths; in one northern Negro slum area surveyed by Dr. James B. Conant, 70 per cent of the young men who had left school were out of work; in another the ratio was over 50 per cent.

THE OTHER SIDE OF JORDAN

It would be a serious mistake to equate the Negro's apparent apathy and lack of motivation with a sense of contentment. It is a lot harder for today's Negro to bear his poverty and lack of status than it was for the European immigrant, who arrived at a time when the great majority of the population was poor. The Negro migration, by contrast, is occurring in an affluent society. Like the underdeveloped peoples everywhere, American Negroes have been fired by the revolution of rising expectations. In Harry Ashmore's phrase, Negroes have seen "the other side of Jordan"; they are in a hurry to cross. Among a good many Negroes, especially the college students involved in the sit-in movement, impatience with their rate of progress has conquered apathy and led to direct, disciplined, and frequently courageous action to improve the Negro position in American life. But among the great mass of working-class Negroes and a large part of the middle class, apathy exists side by side with a growing, festering resentment of their lot. These Negroes are more and more convinced that they should have a better life; they are less and less convinced that they themselves can do anything about it.

Impatience is greatest, perhaps, in the area of civil rights; the Supreme Court decision on school segregation raised expectations of a new era in race relations that has been painfully slow in coming. But Negroes are also impatient over their economic progress. During World War II and the early postwar boom, Negroes did make remarkable economic strides; the median income of urban Negro males shot up from less than 40 per cent of white income in 1939 to 60 per cent in 1952. Negroes have not been able to improve their relative position since 1952, however; the slowdown in the economy during the 1950's bore most heavily on the durable-goods industries, where many Negroes are employed. Thus the income of the average Negro male city dweller, which was 60 per cent of the average white income in 1952, had gone up only to 61 per cent by 1960. Outside the cities, average Negro income has actually declined since 1952.

As a result, impatience is turning into bitterness, anger, and hatred. The danger is not violence but something much deeper and harder to combat: a sense of permanent alienation from American society. Unless the Negro position improves very quickly, Negroes of whatever class may come to regard their separation from American society as permanent, and so consider themselves permanently outside the constraints and the allegiances of American society. The Negro district of every large city would come to constitute an American Casbah, with its own values and its own controls—and a deep hostility to the white community. In such a situation, communication between the races would become impossible. And life in the large city would become unbearable.

But the Negro advance depends on changes within the Negro community as well as within the white community. Understandably, Negroes have been reluctant to recognize this fact. They have assumed that an end to discriminatory practices will by itself solve the Negro problem. It will do nothing of the sort, although an end to discrimination certainly is a prerequisite to any solution. "If the color barrier could be eliminated overnight," Professor Eli Ginzberg of Columbia put the matter baldly in *The Negro Potential,* "that fact alone would not materially improve the position of the Negro."

The truth is that too many Negroes are unable—or unwilling—to compete in an integrated society. Because of the shortage of professional and technical personnel in industry and government, just about any qualified Negro can get a good job, but employers willing to hire Negroes have trouble finding Negroes to hire. Colleges and medical professional schools eager to admit Negroes (and give to them scholarships) cannot find as many qualified Negroes as they are willing to admit; the National Scholarship and Service Fund for Negro Students reports that there are five times as many places available in northern colleges as there are Negroes to fill them. Nor have Negroes been taking advantage of the professional and business opportunities that the growth of the big-city Negro population has offered. The number of Negro physicians in the U.S. has been static for fifty years. As the U.S. Commission on Civil Rights sadly concluded, a principal reason for continued Negro poverty is "the lack of motivation on the part of many Negroes to improve their educational and occupational status."

The Negro community also lacks the sort of self-help institutions through which the European immigrants climbed out of their slums. Negroes, as Professor James Q. Wilson of Harvard put it in *Negro Politics,* are "the objects rather than the subjects of civic action. Things are often done for, or about, or to, or because of Negroes, but they are less frequently done *by* Negroes." There is no tradition of Negro philanthropy. Because the Negro has no indigenous culture to protect, the Negro community has not seen the same need to organize itself that European ethnic groups felt. The paucity of Negro self-help organizations may also be due to the tremendous growth of public assistance during the past quarter-century. The fact that help now comes from the city or state or federal government, sociologist Nathan Glazer suggests, has tended to channel "social energies" into the formulation of demands for new governmental programs rather than into the establishment and financing of voluntary organizations among Negroes.

THE NEED FOR EXCELLENCE

This institutional vacuum must be filled. For one thing, charitable and social-welfare programs organized, staffed, and supported by Negroes are likely to have a much greater impact on Negro behavior than programs administered by government or by private white agencies, both of which tend to be viewed with suspicion and hostility. Then, too, as Professor Ginzberg has been reminding Negro audiences, freedom is only the precondition for equality, not its equivalent. The more Negroes get what they want in terms of formal rights —voting, education, desegregation, etc.—the more responsibility they will have to assume for their own well-being.

This fact is now beginning to get its due. Perhaps the most important single factor making for solution of the Negro problem is the emergence of pride of race among Negroes. This new pride is the product of many factors: the Negro gains during World War II, the independence of the African nations, the courage and dignity shown by the sit-ins and Freedom Riders. Pride, to be sure, is always a two-edged sword; among the Black Muslims it leads to hatred of everything white and to threats of anti-white violence. But overall, the new sense of pride is serving to raise the level of Negro aspirations and behavior; even the Black Muslims stress the importance of work, sobriety, chastity, and self-discipline.

A growing number of Negro leaders and spokesmen, moreover—particularly at the national level—are encouraging Negroes to assume more responsibility for their own fate. "All the intellectual arguments and sociological explanations in the world," the distinguished Negro journalist, Carl Rowan, now Deputy Assistant Secretary of State for Public Affairs, has written, "do not meet fully the need to do something about the fact that people are being killed and maimed, street gangs are spreading terror in big cities, young girls are bearing an increasing number of illegitimate children, and dope and gin mills are flourishing in our urban centers." Negro leaders must recognize, Rowan argues—and in fact, they are beginning to recognize—"that it is not enough to blame every Negro misdeed on segregation, or to pretend that integration will be a cure-all for every social problem in sight."

Significantly, Rowan's view is shared by the man who has given the most dramatic leadership in the fight against segregation and who, more than any other leader, has captured the imagination of the Negro rank and file, the Reverend

Martin Luther King Jr. "We have become so involved in trying to wipe out the institution of segregation, which certainly is a major cause of social problems among Negroes," Dr. King says, "that we have neglected to push programs to raise the moral and cultural climate in our Negro neighborhoods." Negroes, in Dr. King's view, must learn to strive for excellence in every field of endeavor—"not excellence as a Negro doctor or lawyer or a Negro craftsman, but excellence per se." He is urging his Southern Christian Leadership Conference to emphasize what he calls "the constructive program" of raising Negro standards as much as the program of "creative protest"—i.e., the sit-ins.

The National Urban League, moreover, is shifting its emphasis from opening up new job opportunities to preparing Negroes for the job opportunities that are opening up. "It's one thing to eliminate barriers," Dr. Whitney Young Jr., the league's dynamic new executive director, observes, "and quite another to get a previously depressed people to take advantage of the new opportunities." Dr. Young believes that Negro family life must be stabilized if Negroes are to be able to take advantage of these opportunities, and he's looking for funds to finance an ambitious new program in which the league would recruit a number of settled, well-adjusted middle-class Negro families to "adopt" a newly settled family and facilitate their adjustment to urban life.

"MORE POWERFUL THAN APATHY"

There is reason to think that Negroes, even those living in the worst sort of slum, can be mobilized to help themselves. In many ways the most impressive experiment affecting the Negro anywhere in the U.S. is going on now in Chicago's Woodlawn area, an oblong slum running south of the University of Chicago campus and containing about 100,000 people, almost all Negro. Woodlawn's physical decomposition is more than matched by its social disorganization. It is the principal port of entry for Negroes coming to Chicago from the South, and so has had a large transient population. It also contains a flourishing traffic in gambling, narcotics, and prostitution. Woodlawn, in short, is a social chaos of the sort that social workers have always assumed can never produce a large, active organization.

It's producing one now. The guiding genius is a highly controversial Chicago sociologist and criminologist, Dr. Saul D. Alinsky, executive director of the Industrial Areas Foundation. (No one else in the city of Chicago, as two Woodlawn ministers have written, "is as detested or as loved, as cursed or blessed, as feared or respected.") Alinsky was one of the principal architects of Chicago's much-admired Back of the Yards Neighborhood Council, which has turned a white slum area that had been the locale for Upton Sinclair's *The Jungle* into one of the most desirable working-class neighborhoods in Chicago. Alinsky was asked by three Protestant ministers and a Catholic priest to organize Woodlawn; the project is being financed by grants from the Catholic Archdiocese of Chicago, the Presbyterian Church, and a private philanthropy, the Schwartzhaupt Foundation.

If Alinsky succeeds, it will be the first time a large, broadly representative organization will have come into existence in any Negro district in any large American city. Alinsky is trying to create an organization that, as one local leader puts it, "will be the most powerful thing in Woodlawn—more powerful than the political party . . . more powerful than the apathy that holds the community in its grasp." He eschews the usual appeals to homeowners' interests in conserving property values or to a general neighborhood spirit or civic pride—appeals, in his view, that apply only to middle-class neighborhoods. Alinsky, instead, uses the classical approach of trade-union organization. He appeals to the self-interest of the local residents and to their resentment and distrust of the outside world, and he develops a local, indigenous leadership.

"THEY'RE PAYING ATTENTION"

The issue that is principally animating Woodlawn now is the University of Chicago's proposal to annex a strip a block wide and a mile long adjacent to the campus. The Negro residents have no particular attachment to the strip in question, but they suspect that its annexation will be the prelude to bulldozing a large part of the area for middle and upper-income apartment houses. There is ample basis for their fears; urban-renewal projects have been going on for some time under university sponsorship in the Hyde Park-Kenwood district north of the university, designed in good measure to clear Negroes out. To force the university and city-planning officials to bargain with the Woodlawn residents, Alinsky is mobilizing the residents into a group called the Temporary Woodlawn Organization; he had 8,000 Woodlawn people enrolled in the T.W.O. within six months of the project's inception. The T.W.O. organized an impressive campaign to get the usually apathetic Woodlawn residents registered and voting; during the registration period last August, a caravan of forty-six buses took some 2,300 members down to City Hall to register.

What makes the Woodlawn experiment significant, however, is not what it is doing *for* its members but what it is doing *to* them. "The most important thing to me about the forty-six busloads of people who went to City Hall to register," Alinsky says, "was their own reaction. Many were weeping; others were saying, 'They're paying attention to us.' 'They're recognizing that we're people.' " What is crucial, in short, is not what the Woodlawn residents win, but the fact that *they* are winning it. This fact seems to make the Woodlawn members see themselves in a new light, as people of substance and worth. While Alinsky's methods create a sense of militancy that could be misused, they create a sense of responsibility as well, and this is their most important product so far.

THE TWENTY-POINT DROP

The Negro problem is not just the responsibility of the Negro community, of course; its resolution requires drastically changed policies by a variety of governmental agencies. The social institution that touches the Negro problem most directly is the public school, which since the 1890's has been the

principal means by which newcomers to the city, or their
offspring, have been able to move out of the slums. The public
school offers the greatest opportunity to dissolve the cultural
barrier that blocks the Negro's advance into the mainstream
of American life.

The opportunity is being muffed. Admittedly the problems
encountered in the Negro (or for that matter, the white) slum
school are enough to discourage the best-intentioned. Children
entering school are ill-prepared, poorly motivated, and badly
behaved; teachers must spend inordinate amounts of time main-
taining order, and they are occasionally in danger of physical
harm. Because families move from tenement to tenement with
great frequency, pupil turnover is incredibly high—more than
100 per cent in some New York slum schools; the standard
quip has it that if a teacher is absent a week, she won't recognize
her class when she returns. Under these conditions one might
reasonably expect that cities would spend more per Negro
pupil than they do per white pupil. The reverse is generally
true; the schools in Negro slum areas are the most overcrowded,
are manned with the least experienced teachers, and have the
highest ratio of students to teachers.

The results are predictably poor. Coming from semiliterate
or illiterate backgrounds, which not only offer no incentive
to learn but rather frequently regard the school as a hostile
force, many children never learn to read properly. Their inability to read at grade level in turn makes them fall behind
in every other subject, even vocational courses; for example,
shop students can't learn carpentry if they can't read blueprints
or calculate fractions of an inch. The result is that their learning ability itself becomes atrophied; I.Q. typically drops twenty
points as the Negro child progresses through school. By junior
or senior high, it is almost impossible to reach him or teach
him; three out of five Negro youngsters drop out of school
before completion—uneducated, seemingly uneducable, and
virtually unemployable. And yet these children can be educated; New York City and St. Louis, in particular, as we shall
see, have demonstrated the fact beyond doubt.

The question first is, what kind of education can they—

and should they—be given? Unfortunately, the current discussion is being shaped by Dr. James B. Conant's recent *Slums and Suburbs,* which has been accepted blandly and uncritically by almost everyone concerned with the problem, Negro or white. Dr. Conant has performed a great public service in calling attention to the dimensions of the problem and to the need for immediate action. But he has prescribed the worst possible remedy: a great expansion of vocational education for Negro youth.

If Conant's advice were followed, it would doom the Negro permanently to the bottom rung on the economic ladder. "A generation or two ago," as Professor Eli Ginzberg put it in *The Negro Potential,* "a man with negligible formal education could become a skilled worker. Today, participation in the industrial process requires of the worker not only basic literacy but a fairly high level of ability to deal with words and figures." The worker must be able to follow written instructions, to read the bulletin board, to keep various kinds of records, to master considerable technical knowledge. And he must be able to learn new skills, for nobody knows what job skills will be needed ten years from now.

What the Negro child needs, in short, is the same kind of education the white child needs and is beginning to get: an education that teaches him how to learn, that gives him the intellectual discipline and depth of understanding that will enable him to meet new conditions as they arise. But it will take more than a return to the three R's to give Negro children this kind of education. To penetrate the environmental and cultural curtain that keeps the Negro child from learning, the school must take on a whole range of functions that lie outside its normal sphere.

A SUCCESS STORY

The most spectacular demonstration of what can be done to raise the aspirations and performance of Negro slum children is occurring in St. Louis, in the "Banneker group"— twenty-three elementary schools enrolling 16,000 children, 95

per cent of them Negroes living in the city's worst slum. Dr.
Samuel Shepard Jr., the assistant superintendent in charge of
the Banneker district, decided to take action four years ago,
when the city's high schools instituted a three-track system
of ability grouping. Only 7 per cent of the Banneker graduates
were able to make the top ability track; nearly half were put
in the bottom track. In three years Dr. Shepard has been able
to triple the proportion of Banneker graduates admitted to the
first track, from 7 per cent to 21 per cent. Last June, in fact,
Shepard's eighth-graders actually exceeded the national norm
in reading; three years before the Banneker eighth-graders had
been a full year behind.

The results largely reflect the impact of Shepard's powerful
personality and dedicated leadership. He has changed teachers'
and principals' attitudes toward their students from one of
condescension to one of sympathy and challenge. More important, he has changed the Negro community's attitude toward
the school. He keeps up a steady fire of meetings and of assemblies, field trips, pep talks, contests, and posters, designed
to inculcate a respect for learning. For the children, he sets
up a very competitive athletic-like atmosphere, in which the
kudos goes to "the achievers." For the parents, Shepard uses
an extremely blunt approach. He shows them by slides, charts,
and film strips exactly how poorly their children are doing and
warns them that unless the children do better in school they'll
be no better off than their parents. He explains that things *can*
be different for children, he shows in great detail the relation
between education and employment, pointing to specific jobs
now open to Negros in St. Louis for which no qualified Negroes
can be found. He also explains at length how the school operates at each grade, what the parents should demand of their
children, and how they can help. And through all of this he
emphasizes reading as the key to academic—and vocational—
success.

Shepard has achieved these results without the use of extra
resources; the greatest strength of his program is the fact that
it depends on the ordinary classroom teacher. But remedial-
reading teachers, guidance counselors, psychologists, and social

workers can also be used to good effect, as New York City has shown with its Demonstration Guidance Project and its Higher Horizons program. In the first year of the Higher Horizons program the city was able to cut third-graders' retardation in reading from six months to only one month. Under grants from the Ford Foundation's Great Cities School Improvement Project, other cities are experimenting with a variety of techniques. Detroit and Philadelphia, for example, are employing "school-community agents" in slum schools to try to break down parental suspicion and hostility and persuade parents of the importance of education.

The programs now in operation, however, affect only a minute fraction of the children needing special help. What must be done is to put these programs into effect on a mass scale. To do so will cost money, of course. But the cities will get the money back—and a lot more besides—in lower relief costs, decreased juvenile delinquency and crime, and increased income for its residents—not to mention a radical improvement in the whole quality of city life. "A community which made its schools rather than its central business district the tender object and physical center of its urban-renewal operations," Paul Ylvisaker recently suggested, "would be taking one of the noblest and shrewest steps forward in the civic progress of this century."

THE UNDERDEVELOPED COUNTRY

The city, in short, must exercise "positive discrimination" in favor of the Negro if it is to enable the mass of Negroes to compete with whites on equal terms. The U.S. must learn to look upon the Negro community as if it were an underdeveloped country.

One thing that must be done—by industry and labor, as well as by government—is to develop long-range programs to educate workers who are already out of school, and whose lack of education makes them particularly vulnerable to technological unemployment. Armour's experience in trying to retrain workers made idle by automation has shown clearly that crash programs can provide only limited help. Of the 170 employees who applied for retraining when the company closed its Oklahoma City meat-packing plant, for example, 110 could not be given any training because they lacked the minimum skills in reading and mathematics. (See Labor, *Fortune,* July, 1961.)

There must also be a broadening of job opportunities for Negroes. There has been a significant reduction in job discrimination against Negroes in recent years, largely because of government prodding, but Negroes still find it very difficult to obtain jobs in the skilled trades, where union prejudice is a big stumbling block, and in clerical and sales jobs. It isn't enough for employers to make jobs formally available to Negroes; as a result of generations of discrimination, Negroes tend to assume that prejudice exists even where it has ended. A special effort must be made, therefore, to publicize the new job openings; Negroes must be brought within the web of job gossip through active recruitment.

Meanwhile, cities must try to alleviate some of the disorganization of Negro family and community life. The city has a vast panoply of services designed to prevent, relieve, and cure problems of individual and family behavior and circumstance. But each service deals separately with the individuals involved, sometimes in bureaucratic competition with the others. As often as not, the Negro—or the white slum dweller, for that matter— sees the bewildering array of police, school, and welfare agencies as enemies to be played off one against another.

It is possible to close the distance between the individual and government, and to coordinate the activities of the agencies affecting him. Wayne Thompson, the young city manager of Oakland, California, has pulled together seven public agencies representing four levels of government into something called the Associated Agencies. Fortnightly meetings of the A.A. workers in each section of the city are held to coordinate their work. In dealing with one school marked by frequent violence, for example, the school superintendent allowed the police to seal off the school area and then clean out the guns and knives in the school lockers. The school, police, recreation, probation, and welfare workers then culled a list of trouble-makers, letting each agency take responsibility for the children it already knew, or upon whom it had some particular claim. Out of 2,800 pupils, only fifty-four turned out to be real trouble-makers; when the whole job had been finished, only two had to be moved out of school and into detention. Since the Associated Agencies program started in late 1957, Oakland has been relatively free of trouble. The city recently received a $2-million grant from the Ford Foundation to extend the program.

New York City is trying to accomplish somewhat the same thing through its Neighborhood Conservation Projects. The coordination is not as complete, and the emphasis is fairly heavy on conservation of real estate rather than of human beings. But several projects have gone beyond physical rehabilitation —e.g., in the Bloomingdale district on Manhattan's West Side. The projects, in a sense, are designed to create a modern-day (but honest) counterpart to the old Tammany district leader, who served a very important function for the European immigrant, in effect locating him in the city and providing a channel to its government.

THE HOUSING DILEMMA

More must also be done about Negro housing. Despite a remarkable improvement in the condition of Negro housing since the end of World War II, nearly half of all the houses and apartments occupied by Negroes are still classified as "dilapidated" or "deteriorating" in the census rolls, compared to only 15 per cent of white homes. And Negroes live under far more crowded conditions. While good housing doesn't guarantee good behavior, bad housing does contribute to family disorganization and hence to delinquency.

The deterioration and overcrowding of Negro housing are due in good measure to the poverty of Negroes as a group. A study of the Philadelphia housing market by Chester Rapkin and William Grigsby of the University of Pennsylvania, for example, disclosed that only about 5 per cent of all Negro households had incomes sufficient to buy houses costing $12,000 or more—about the minimum price at which private builders were able to erect houses in that city. But discrimination as well as income robs the Negro of freedom of choice. Housing, as the U.S. Civil Rights Commission puts it, with only slight exaggeration, is "the one commodity in the American market which is not freely available on equal terms to everyone that can afford to pay."

Because economic and social factors bar Negroes from the market for new construction—and because Negro population is growing at an explosive rate in most large cities—Negroes are constantly looking for homes in the older, less expensive areas of the city. This pressure is as unsettling for the white community as it is for the Negro, for it leads to unstable and rapidly changing neighborhoods. To most white persons, as Eunice Grier of the Washington Center for Metropolitan Studies puts it, "there is no such thing . . . as a stable and permanent integrated neighborhood." Hence, when Negro demand appears in a neighborhood, the community either resists Negro entry—sometimes with violence—or it abandons the neighborhood completely. The latter usually occurs in any case. As Negroes start moving in, the whites start moving out—some because of prejudice, others because they fear that if they remain they will rapidly become a minority. Integration, as Saul Alinsky sardonically observes, "is usually a term to describe the period of time that elapses between the appearance of the first Negro and the exit of the last white."

There is considerable evidence to suggest that whites *will* live in integrated neighborhoods if they have some assurance that they will not be swamped. For that reason a number of housing experts now advocate the use of "benign quotas" as the best—or only—means of solving the Negro housing problem. New York City's Housing Authority, for example, is using a quota system to try to integrate its low and middle-income housing projects, with fair success.

But the benign quota is no panacea and will work only where there is some authority able to decide how many Negroes will be admitted, and to determine which Negroes will be admitted. The authority must be powerful enough to enforce compliance after the quota has been filled. Enforcing a quota, moreover, frequently involves a painful conflict between two laudable objectives—housing integration and an increased supply of housing for Negroes. In order to maintain the desired racial balance, a housing authority frequently has to turn down qualified Negroes in desperate need of housing in favor of whites whose need is far less acute.

It's doubtful, in short, whether any simple, dramatic approach can solve the Negro housing problem. So long as the great majority of Negroes have slum incomes, they are going to live in slums. In the long run, therefore, the only way to solve the problem of Negro housing is to solve the problem of Negro people—to raise the economic and social level of the Negro community.

THE COST OF DELAY

A new pride in self that is developing among Negroes is a powerful lever to raise Negro aspirations and achievements. The Negro's growing political activity is a powerful lever to force cities to face up to the problem; the Negro vote was decisive in last fall's mayoralty elections in Atlanta, Detroit, and New York.

And the U.S. economy itself should facilitate the Negro's advance during the 1960's. In a rapidly expanding economy employers will have to end job discrimination and upgrade unskilled and semiskilled Negro workers if they are to produce all their markets will demand. The training programs developed during World War II show what industry can do when the stakes are high enough. And with a shortage of skilled labor likely, unions will have far less incentive to restrict entry into the skilled occupations.

These trends will make solution of the Negro problem less difficult; but they will not solve it. If the Negroes are to take their proper place in U.S. society, millions of hard decisions will have to be taken by people of both races. And the longer the U.S. delays those decisions, the more painful this most urgent piece of public business will become.

". . . [they] add to a rather tough and knowing cast of New York characters a new type—softer and milder, gayer and more light-spirited."

THE PUERTO RICANS *

Nathan Glazer

This article on the Puerto Rican adjustment to the big city takes, on the whole, a more cheerful and optimistic view of it than do many other commentaries on the problem, although it does not overlook the dark side of the picture. As a companion piece to Silberman's article on the city and Negro, it raises a number of interesting questions for educators:

Teachers often feel more positive toward their Puerto Rican pupils than they do toward Negro pupils. What is there in Glazer's piece that might explain this difference? In the picture he presents of the Puerto Rican's relation to the city, what are the most crucial problems for the schools? A major distinction between Negro and Puerto Rican children, from the school's point of view, is the language diffi-

* Nathan Glazer, "The Puerto Ricans," *Commentary* (July, 1963). Reprinted by permission of *Commentary* and of the author.

culty of the newly arrived Spanish-speaking child. Although policy has varied nationally, the schools in New York City, for one, have until recently taken the view that in order for the child to learn English as rapidly as possible the use of Spanish-speaking teachers should be discouraged. Should this view have been modified?

IF SOMEONE twenty-five years ago had looked around at the potential sources of new immigration to New York City, his eye might well have fallen on Puerto Rico, but he would probably also have concluded that the Puerto Ricans, if they came to New York, would have a very hard time adapting. Puerto Rico in the middle 30's—after thirty-five years of American administration—was a scene of almost unrelieved misery. It was overcrowded and disease ridden, almost without industry, suffering from the collapse of its major cash crop (sugar), its population undereducated and underemployed. Puerto Rico was also unsure in its cultural traditions and without a powerful faith. Nor was there much strength in the Puerto Rican family. In some ways, it was a family similar to the type we find in peasant Europe—patriarchal and authoritarian, the man reigning as absolute despot, demanding obedience and respect from wife and children. However, this was not the family of the Polish or South Italian peasant. The major difference was the wide extent of unstable consensual or common-law marriage; more than one-quarter of the marriages were of this kind, and as a result about one third of the births were formally illegitimate. In both legal and consensual marriage, moreover, concubinage and sexual adventurism on the part of the men were widely accepted, which meant that children often grew up in confused family settings and that great strain existed between husbands and wives. Children were loved in Puerto Rico—this was fortunate since there were so many. And yet it has frequently been said that their mothers perhaps loved them as much as they did in order to make up for neglect by their husbands.

Marriage in Puerto Rico was typically a matter of the young daughter—as young, even, as thirteen or fourteen—making an escape from home with a man whom her parents had not chosen and whom she herself scarcely knew. A random sample of the island's population in 1947-48 showed that 6 per cent of the married women had been married at fourteen or younger, a fifth had been married at fifteen or sixteen, a quarter at seventeen and eighteen, and another fifth at nineteen or twenty

—seven out of ten, in other words, were married before the age of twenty-one! This, combined with the feeling that a man and woman living together should have children as soon as possible, resulted for women in a very early induction into child-bearing and for men in a very early induction into the burdens of adulthood.

Still, the family, despite these weaknesses, was perhaps one of the stronger elements in the Puerto Rican situation. Men might have children with a number of different women, but they took responsibility for all of them; there was (for a peasant culture) a relatively high degree of marital breakup, but there was always a place for the children. The institution of the godparents, the *compadre* and *comadre,* provided a second set of parents who stood ready to take over if the first was over-burdened with too many children and too many woes, or was broken up by death or desertion. Children in Puerto Rico were neither resented nor neglected; if anything, they suffered from being overprotected.

Nevertheless, this was not, by the standards of other peasant cultures, a tightly knit and well-integrated family system, and when Puerto Ricans first began coming to New York, it did not hold up too well. Indeed, as early as 1930 a social worker at a meeting of the National Conference of Catholic Charities stated that the Puerto Rican family was the biggest social-work problem in New York at the time.

Given all this, who could have expected that the postwar Puerto Rican migration to New York City would turn out to be so successful? It was as little to be expected as the transformation of the island itself—a transformation so startling, and so little heralded by anything in Puerto Rico's earlier history that by 1960 it was reasonable for two new books on Puerto Rico to bear the titles: *Puerto Rico: Land of Wonders* and *Puerto Rico: Success Story.* The great advances in education, health, self-respect, work capacity, and training that have taken place under Luis Muñoz Marin's regime have benefited New York no less than Puerto Rico itself.

New York City had 500 persons of Puerto Rican birth in 1910; 7,000 in 1920; 45,000 in 1930. This group already included some professional people and some small storekeepers, but the overwhelming majority were employed—when they were employed at all—in unskilled work, as laborers, porters, factory operatives, and domestic help. In Manhattan, where three quarters of the Puerto Ricans lived (in an area bounded by 97th Street on the south, 125th Street on the north, Fifth Avenue on the west, and Third Avenue on the east), they met the old East Harlem Italian community and the growing community of Negroes to the north and west. There was also a large Jewish group in East Harlem, which was then beginning to withdraw to other parts of the city, principally to the Bronx.

There is no record of any conflict between the Puerto Ricans and the Jewish group. With the local Italians, relations were cool. The tight Italian community did not find it easy to open up to strangers: the youth, of course, simply followed in the pattern of adolescent ethnic hostility, and the mild Puerto Ricans, whose history had had plenty of misery but remarkably little violence, were taken aback.

As for relations between the Puerto Ricans and the Negroes, they were more complex, even in those early days. The Puerto Ricans are a mixed people, and though a man's color meant something very different to them from what it meant to white Americans, they knew very well its meaning for Americans. About one fifth of the Puerto Rican group in New York in the 1930's was listed in census returns as Negro (a slightly smaller proportion than was then listed as colored in the census taken in Puerto Rico itself). Lawrence R. Chenault, who made the first book-length study of the New York Puerto Ricans in the mid-30's, believed that the American Negro was "inclined to resent all of the people from the West Indies [he included the Puerto Ricans in this group] because of their competition in the labor market," while on his part "the Puerto Rican, if white or slightly colored, deeply resents any classification which places him with the Negro. . . . Finding the American-born Negro confronted with serious disadvantages in this country, the Puerto Ricans want to maintain their own group and to distinguish themselves from him. . . . People who have studied the relations of the West Indian groups in Harlem report that

. . . the darker the person from the West Indies is, the more intense his desire to speak only Spanish, and to do so in a louder voice."

But whatever the complications introduced in Puerto Rican attitudes toward Negroes by this factor of color, relations actually seem to have been pleasanter than with the Italians. In later years, the young people coming into this first section of Puerto Rican settlement, *"El Barrio,"* would find their adjustment made more difficult by the hostility of Italian youth; Negro youth were on the whole more willing to accept them.

During the war, Puerto Rico, four days from New York by boat, was cut off to normal passenger movement, and there was almost no addition to the Puerto Rican population until 1944. Then there was a heavy migration of 11,000. The next year, with the end of the war, air service between San Juan and New York was introduced, which immediately transformed the situation of the potential migrant. In 1945, 13,500 entered the city; in 1946, almost 40,000: New York was in the middle of a mass migration rivaling the great population movements of the first two decades of the century. By 1961, there were 613,000 people of Puerto Rican birth or parentage in the city (representing about 60 per cent of the total number of Puerto Ricans in the continental United States). Since 1961, the number of new arrivals has fallen off sharply and will probably remain low, but the high birth rate of the Puerto Rican group guarantees that it will make up an increasing proportion of the city's population.[1]

By 1961 also, Puerto Ricans were no longer living almost exclusively in El Barrio in East Harlem. The desperate housing shortage made it impossible for El Barrio to expand into the areas to the north, east, and west, and the vast program of slum clearance and public housing not only broke up the Puerto Rican concentrations (in the oldest and most decrepit buildings, of course) as soon as they were formed, but prevented new

1. In 1961 the crude birth rate of the Puerto Rican population of New York was 40 per thousand, as compared with 30 for nonwhites and 20 for non-Puerto Rican whites.

concentrations from forming. And so Puerto Ricans spread rapidly throughout the city in the late 1940's and 1950's—to the West Side, to Washington Heights, to Chelsea, to the Lower East Side; and outside of Manhattan, to the downtown Brooklyn and nearby Bedford-Stuyvesant areas; to the Bronx, through Morrisania, Melrose, and other districts; and to various sections of Queens. Thus, unlike the older immigrant groups, they rubbed shoulders with almost everybody in the city.

The Puerto Rican migrants of the 1950's were much better equipped for life in New York than those who came in the 1920's and 1930's. Thanks to Muñoz Marin's programs of economic development, island incomes steadily rose during the 1940's and 1950's, as did the urban population and the number of workers with schooling and experience in manufacturing. And all this naturally reflected itself in the character of the new migrants, who, if anything, represented a better-than-average sample of the island population.

The links between the New York Puerto Ricans and the island Puerto Ricans are, indeed, close and complex, and quite different from the relationship of earlier migrant groups to their homelands. Puerto Rico is a part of the United States, and there is no control over movement between the island and the mainland; air passage is not too expensive; and the island government takes a strong interest in its people. Many, in fact, would be hard put to say whether they belonged to the city or the island. A great part of the movement between New York and San Juan consists of people going back and forth for visits, to take care of sick relatives or to be taken care of, of children being sent to stay with one family or another. In other words, going back is usually not, as it was in earlier migrations, either the return of someone who is defeated and incapable of adjustment, or of someone who has made a small competence that will look big in the homeland. Something new, then, has perhaps been added to the New York scene—an ethnic group that will not assimilate to the same degree as others have, but will resemble the strangers who lived in ancient Greek cities, or the ancient Greeks who set up colonies in cities around the Mediterranean.

There are interesting consequences for the community in this. Relatively few Puerto Ricans—as compared with Negroes or with the non-Puerto Rican white groups—register and vote. One reason may be that the state constitution requires all voters to be literate in English. After Mayor Wagner's election to his third term in 1961, it was estimated that no fewer than 200,000 Puerto Ricans were in effect disfranchised by this provision, and in December, 1961, the city filed a proposal for a constitutional amendment that would permit residents to take literacy tests in any language in which a daily or weekly newspaper was published in the state. Clearly, people active in politics and the leaders of the Puerto Rican community expect that Spanish will be the major language in use in the community for as long ahead as anyone can see. As against the situation in some earlier immigrant groups, where dominant opinion both in the city and in the group insisted on the need to learn English and to relegate the immigrant tongue to a lesser status, many Puerto Rican leaders—and they are young people—expect and hope that Spanish will maintain an important foothold in their community. The city government, on its side, encourages city employees to learn Spanish, and issues many announcements to the general public in both languages. Conceivably this will change, but Spanish already has a much stronger official position in New York than either Italian or Yiddish ever had. This is one mark of the closeness of the island—physically, politically, and culturally.

Closeness to the island is unquestionably a factor in another interesting characteristic of the Puerto Ricans in New York— the relative weakness of community organization and community leadership among them. The early migrants were so completely working-class and below that the few Puerto Rican professionals and businessmen in the city tended to blend into the non-Puerto Rican Spanish-language group, consisting of immigrants from Spain, Cuba, and other parts of Latin America. But as the number of Puerto Ricans in the city grew, something happened to the general Spanish-speaking group similar to what had happened to the high-status German Jews when the poor East-European Jews arrived—the effort to maintain a separate image for themselves in the public mind failed. When the Puerto Ricans became the overwhelming majority of the city's Spanish-speaking population, the status of all Spanish-speaking people became involved in that of the new immigrants.

These circumstances have led to a recapture by the Puerto Rican group of some of the leadership elements from the longer settled, and perhaps better educated, non-Puerto Ricans. Thus, Emilio Nuñez, the first Spanish-speaking city magistrate (he was appointed in 1951) was born in Spain. Thus, also, the five Spanish-speaking members of the executive board of the Shirtmakers' Union, Local 23 of the ILGWU, include one South American, one Mexican, one Cuban, and only two Puerto Ricans, though Puerto Ricans make up by far the largest part of the Spanish-speaking rank-and-file. And thus, finally, *La Prensa*, an old and established Spanish daily, which never had much Puerto Rican emphasis, was a few years ago completely revamped as a tabloid to appeal directly to the Puerto Rican population.

The fact that a newspaper originally designed for another group—and owned, to boot, by an Italian, Fortune Pope—could so easily be turned into a Puerto Rican organ, is a sign of the relative weakness of what may be called indigenous organization among the Puerto Ricans. The other and much larger newspaper read by Puerto Ricans, *Il Diario*, was originally owned by a Dominican, and edited by a New York newspaperman who had formerly edited a newspaper in the (then) Ciudad Trujillo. Both *La Prensa* and *Il Diario* were bought by the transit operator O. Roy Chalk, who is also not a Puerto Rican, and have recently been merged. This newspaper performs many of the services other immigrant-group newspapers have performed, but it is not the *creation* of the community itself. And this is the kind of situation one finds in many other areas of Puerto Rican life as well. But just recently a new Spanish newspaper was started in the city; the change to a larger degree of self-sufficiency has already begun.

So far as religion is concerned, most of the Puerto Ricans in the city are Catholic, but their participation in Catholic life is small. It is interesting, for example, that only 15,000 Puerto

Rican children are in parochial schools in the New York Archdiocese, against almost ten times as many in the public schools
—a much smaller percentage than for any other Catholic group
in the city. There are only 250 Spanish-speaking priests in the
Archdiocese of New York, and most of these—like many priests
in Puerto Rico itself—have expressly learned Spanish in order
to minister to Puerto Rican Catholics.

As the problems of the first generation are overcome, as
families become stabler, incomes higher, and the attachment
to American middle-class culture stronger, Catholicism will
probably also become stronger among the Puerto Ricans. But
it does not seem likely that the Church will play as large a role
in their life as it plays for Catholics of European origin. Indeed,
there is already a well-established rival to Catholicism in the
Puerto Rican community, and if we were to reckon religious
strength not by mild affiliation but by real commitment, we
might find almost as many Puerto Rican Protestants as Catholics. All told, about 14,000 Spanish-speaking people belong to
the major Protestant denominations in the city, about 10,000
of them in their own all-Spanish churches. Attendance in these
churches is high, evangelical zeal puts most Anglo-Saxon Pro-
estantism to shame, and the willingness to spend money on the
church is also great.

But the most vigorous and intense religious movements
among the Puerto Ricans are the Pentecostal and independent
Pentecostal-type churches. The 1960 study of the Protestant
Council of New York located 240 such churches with an estimated total membership of 25,000—but the Council's estimates
are certainly too conservative. These tiny churches generally
run services every day of the week. They demand that their
people give up smoking and alcohol and fornication. They are
completely supported by the membership, and often a church
of 100 members will keep a full-time minister. Here, where the
preachers and ministers are all Puerto Ricans, if a stranger
comes in, he is warmly greeted, and if a member falls sick, he
is visited. The tight Pentecostal congregation is one of the most
important expressions of community that exists among Puerto
Ricans in New York.

Aside from these churches, however, the Puerto Ricans do not have a strong organizational life. To be sure, there are many social organizations, based on place of origin on the island, but they do not have the importance that the early immigrant societies in New York used to have. That they should not is understandable: movies and television and other forms of commercialized recreation have usurped one major function of such societies in the past, while public and private welfare agencies have usurped the other. Moreover, the rise of organization has been inhibited by the same factors (urban renewal, public housing, etc.) that have dispersed the Puerto Rican population throughout the city and prevented the development of a great residential center for the group.

The ways in which the relation to the island affects the organizational life of Puerto Ricans in New York are probably many and subtle, but one clear impact is seen in the role of the Office of the Commonwealth of Puerto Rico in New York City. This office (maintained by the Department of Labor of the Commonwealth of Puerto Rico) is for the Puerto Rican community of New York what the NAACP and the National Urban League are for the Negroes. It serves as an employment agency and an orientation center for new migrants; it represents Puerto Ricans and Puerto Rican interests on committees; it helps organize the Puerto Rican community where such organization seems necessary (as for example, in the 1960 campaign to increase registration, in which it took a leading and active role); it is concerned with the public relations of the Puerto Ricans, supplying information and correcting misconceptions.

But it is again a special twist for New York's Puerto Ricans that their equivalent of NAACP and NUL, or of the Jewish community organizational complex, should be a *government office,* supported by *government* funds. That we no longer leave newcomers to New York to sink or swim is undoubtedly a good thing; yet because the Puerto Ricans have been so well supplied with paternalistic guidance by the island government, and with social services by city and private agencies, the group has not been forced to develop powerful grass-roots organizations of its own. Despite (or perhaps because of) this, however, the Puerto

Ricans have achieved a sizable degree of success in adjusting to life in New York. Much of this success has been obscured, for adjustment means inconspicuousness and the well-adjusted Puerto Rican is often not seen as a Puerto Rican; he tends to be only someone with a Spanish name. The successful and adjusted withdraw to Washington Heights and two- or one-family houses in the Bronx or Queens. The newcomers, crowding the rooming houses of the West Side and Chelsea, are in some of the busiest sections of the city, with a large and active, previously settled population that is made all too aware of their problems and difficulties.

One important index of success is business, and according to a recent estimate by the Puerto Rican migration division, there are, all told, 4,000 Puerto Rican-run businesses in New York. This is an amazing figure. It is considerably higher, for example, than the much bigger and longer-settled Negro population has achieved, and it suggests that one of the widely accepted reasons for the low participation of Negroes in small business—discrimination in loans—is probably not of primary importance. (The Puerto Rican, after all, with his characteristically accented and poor English, would not be likely to impress the banker or supplier any more than a Negro does.) Other factors, like the demand for special items by the group and the bond of language, seem to explain the difference better.

As for Puerto Rican workers, the 1950 census already indicated a remarkable shift upward in the occupational profile of the second generation. In 1950, 37 per cent of Puerto Rican men were semiskilled operatives (in toy factories, plastics, and the like) and 28 per cent were service workers (porters, elevator operators, kitchen helpers, etc.). For those Puerto Ricans born in this country who were under twenty-four and at work—still a small group, but suggesting the shape of the future—there was a radical decline in these categories and a sharp increase in the sales and clerical category (from 9 per cent for the Puerto Rican-born to 24 per cent for the native born). And the changes among women are even more striking. In 1950, more than four fifths of young Puerto Rican women migrants were working in factories (mostly clothing factories) and only 7 per cent were in clerical and sales. Among the young native-born, on the other hand, the proportion working as operatives dropped by half, and the number employed in clerical and sales rose to 43 per cent!

For all this, however, it takes no special discernment of eye to see that a great many of the newcomers live in a veritable sea of misery.

As to its extent: Puerto Rican median family income was considerably lower than even non-white median family income —$3,811 as against $4,437—in 1960, and unemployment among Puerto Ricans also seems to be consistently higher than among nonwhites. The census of 1950 showed, for men, 7 per cent of the non-Puerto Rican whites, 12 per cent of the Negroes, and 17 per cent of the Puerto Ricans unemployed; for women, 5 per cent of the non-Puerto Rican whites, 8.5 per cent of the Negroes, and 11 per cent of the Puerto Ricans. In 1960, 5 per cent of all New York males, 6.9 per cent of non-white males and 9.9 per cent of all Puerto Rican males were unemployed.

In explaining misery among the Puerto Ricans, their high birth rate must be taken into account. Puerto Ricans begin bearing children younger, and bear more of them. A 1950 analysis showed that for women between the ages of fifteen and nineteen the Puerto Rican birth rate was about five times the continental white rate (the Negro rate for this age group was almost as high); for women twenty to twenty-four it was almost twice the white rate, and a third higher than the Negro rate.

We see the strain in a number of ways. For example, it is interesting to note how many of the adjusted Puerto Rican families have only one or two children. The job at $50 a week, which manages to support a small family in an apartment in the Bronx and which, compared with the $12-a-week income that was left behind on the island, represents real advancement, is completely inadequate to support five children or more. All problems tend to pile up. The bigger family may not get into a good apartment or a housing project. The crowding in a small apartment may mean more illness and poor management of children. And the difficulty of feeding so many mouths on $50 a week means that welfare has to be called in to help. One

half of all families in New York receiving supplementary assistance from the Department of Welfare are Puerto Ricans; one
quarter of all Puerto Rican children in the city are on some
form of assistance; and about one seventh of all Puerto Ricans
are on public assistance. The Puerto Rican (especially the
Puerto Rican male) is not happy about going on relief; no
one is, but it is perhaps even worse for Puerto Ricans since their
culture places so high a value on the maintenance of dignity
and self-respect.

Everything can contribute to breaking this circle of dependency—more education, more training, fewer children, fewer
illnesses, better housing, dedicated social workers, etc., etc.
Sometimes, however, at the bottom of the scale, things are too
far gone for the circle to be broken. Here are the "multi-prob-
lem" families, afflicted simultaneously by a variety of miseries
—a child who is a drug-addict, another who is delinquent, a
father who is psychologically or physically unable to work, or
perhaps is not there at all.

One of the greatest misfortunes of this bottom layer of unfortunates who cannot help themselves is the enormous difficulty of managing one of the most complex and ingrown
bureaucracies in the world—harried city employees, probation
officers, welfare workers, rent administrators, etc., etc., etc. An
equal misfortune is the housing situation, which consigns those
without sufficient resources and without energy to the frightful
one-room furnished dwellings carved out of brownstones and
apartment houses principally on the West Side of Manhattan.
Better living quarters are available, and at cheaper rents, in the
Bronx and Brooklyn, but when one is overwhelmed by so many
troubles, the energy to take the subway to look for an un-
furnished apartment, to get together the few sticks of furniture
and the minimal kitchen equipment (the Welfare Department
will pay), is often literally beyond the capacity of many families.
And so they migrate dully from one of these awful dwellings to
another, scarcely better, a few blocks away. Meanwhile, one generation on relief gives rise to another. The culture of public
welfare, which Julius Horowitz has so vividly described in his

novel, *The Inhabitants,* is as relevant for the future of Puerto Ricans in the city as the culture of Puerto Rico itself.

And yet despite all this, there was not an exceptionally high rate of delinquency among Puerto Rican children during the 1950's. Today, a good deal of Puerto Rican violence consists of crimes of passion involving members of the community only (though it is not unreasonable to expect that in the future, as the community becomes more and more "Americanized," more and more of this violence will be turned outward). As for that other index of social strain—illness—Puerto Ricans seem to enjoy poorer health than other groups in the population, and their rate of admission to mental hospitals is higher than on the island, or for New Yorkers in general. The migration, it seems, has hit them very hard.

A typical pattern of migration for families with children is for the father to go alone, stay with relatives or friends, find a job and living quarters, and then gradually bring over the rest of the family. Many families are consequently divided between Puerto Rico and New York, and when they are united, if ever, they show wide differences in degree of knowledge of English, assimilation, and the like. A second pattern of migration involves a woman with children—her husband has deserted her, or she has decided to leave home and go to New York, where jobs are abundant, where the government is reputed to be "for the women and the children," and where relief is plentiful.

The Puerto Rican mother works here much more often than she does in Puerto Rico, but women still tend, if at all possible, to stay home to take care of the children. Fewer of them work than do Negro mothers. The question, then, is what kind of care the children get from these mothers, many of whom have been married since what could be considered childhood. In Puerto Rico, it is perfectly clear how one raises children. The boys are praised for their manliness and aside from being required to act respectfully toward their fathers (whether or not their fathers still live with their mothers), they are left to raise themselves. In radically different fashion, the girls are carefully watched, warned to keep their virginity—without which a proper marriage is inconceivable—and then relatively early they flee from this restrictive and stifling atmosphere into marriage and motherhood.

In New York, however, both traditional patterns raise serious problems. If the boys are left to themselves, they find bad friends, may take to drugs, will learn to be disrespectful and disobedient. And even if a boy survives the streets morally, how is he to survive them physically, with cars and trucks whizzing by, and tough Negro and Italian boys ready to beat him up at the slightest provocation? If the girls are guarded and confined to the home (i.e. a tiny, overcrowded apartment) as proper girls should be, they become resentful at a treatment that their classmates and friends are not subjected to.

Thus the radical boy–girl disjunction does not work in New York City. To the social workers or young ministers in the slums, the dances and other coeducational activities they run are means of teaching young boys and girls how to relate to each other in ways that are not purely sexual and exploitative, and perhaps in a measure they do accomplish this. But to the Puerto Rican (and often Negro) parents, what goes on in the settlement houses and the church socials simply looks like a shocking invitation to premature pregnancy.

In this confusing situation there are two possibilities. One is to give up altogether and simply let the children run wild. But a more typical reaction is a tightening of the screws, not only on the girls but on the boys, too. Many cases of disturbed Puerto Rican boys that come to the attention of social agencies are cases of overprotection, anxiety stemming from an exaggerated fear of the dangers of the streets. With the girls, a tightening of discipline makes life seem even more stifling, and there is less chance of escaping into an early marriage here than there is in Puerto Rico. When a social worker suggested to a Puerto Rican girl who had a job and was expected to scurry home from the factory as fast as she had from school, that she ought to get away from the traditionally strict supervision of her father by moving into a residence, the girl was shocked. "She seems to think that in Puerto Rico they would consider any girl who moves away from her family into a residence as someone who goes into a house of prostitution."

The changing city no longer provides the neighborhood that is exclusive to one ethnic group, and so the models for new conduct in rearing one's children vary. There are Negro, Jewish, and Italian models, as well as the "American" models of the welfare workers and the settlement houses. What degree of discipline is proper, what kind of punishment and rewards ought to be enforced, what expectations should one have of one's children? The Puerto Rican mother is at a loss in deciding on the right course.

And then there is the role of the school in the lives of the children. Even the least schooled migrant knows the value of education; Puerto Ricans universally would like to see their children well educated, and hope they will grow up to be professionals. But school is often a frustrating experience. The shift to a new language has been peculiarly difficult for the Puerto Ricans. We can only speculate as to why Jews and Italians, coming into the city at roughly the same ages as the Puerto Ricans have, and with less formal knowledge of English to begin with, should have made a less problematic linguistic adjustment. Certainly the schools did much less to ease their path. (Of course in the years of the heaviest Jewish and Italian migration, the school-leaving age was considerably lower, so that the children who could not learn English got out before their problems became too noticeable.)

Probably no public school system has spent as much money and devoted as much effort to a group of minority children as the New York public school system has devoted to the Puerto Ricans. There are now hundreds of special personnel to deal with parents, to help teachers, to handle the special difficulties of students. The magnitude of the problem is barely communicated by figures. "On October 31, 1958," reports the Board of Education, "of the 558,741 children in our elementary schools, there were 56,296 children of Puerto Rican ancestry whose lack of ability to speak or understand English represented a considerable handicap to learning."

The numbers alone are enormous, and there is the additional problem of the rapid movement of the newcomers. On the West Side of Manhattan—one of the major sections of entry for Puerto Rican migrants—the turnover in an area containing sixteen schools has been 92 per cent, which means that each year the school confronts what is in effect a completely new student body.

It is probably particularly hard for adolescent boys to adjust to this situation, for the Puerto Rican emphasis on masculine dignity makes it embarrassing to speak English with an accent. Meanwhile, there is a good deal of school-leaving at the earliest possible age and relatively small proportions today go into the academic high schools. The register for New York City schools in October 1960 showed that 18 per cent of the elementary-school students, 17 per cent of the junior high-school students, and only 8 per cent of the high-school students were Puerto Rican. The proportion in the academic high schools was 5 per cent.

The other side of the coin is an impressive amount of activity by young, educated Puerto Ricans to raise the level of concern for education in the group. For example, Puerto Rican social workers, professionals, and teachers have set up an organization called *Aspira*, which is devoted to helping students and their parents to take all possible advantage of educational opportunities. The young Puerto Rican leaders clearly see Puerto Ricans as following in the path of the earlier ethnic groups; and these leaders speak of the earlier ethnic groups as models for emulation, not as targets for attack. They identify, that is, with the Jews and Italians of forty years ago, rather than with the Negroes of today, and they have a rather hopeful outlook, which stresses the group's potential for achivement rather than the prejudice and discrimination it meets.

New York's folk culture is already deeply affected by the Puerto Rican migration—and in time, one feels sure, its commercial culture will be similarly affected. In every area of Puerto Rican settlement little record stores carry a remarkable variety of Latin American music; the same records, and live music, pour from hundreds of rooms and apartment houses, and from small and large (and even internationally known) dance halls. As the group becomes larger and more self-conscious, the special Puerto Rican passion for music and dancing will cut more and more into the coldness and sharpness of the city. Indeed, the Puerto Ricans in general add to a rather tough and knowing cast of New York characters a new type—softer and milder, gayer and more light-spirited.

But the most significant Puerto Rican contribution to the city of New York, one suspects, will be in the area of attitudes toward color. The Puerto Ricans introduce into the city a group that is intermediate in color, neither all white nor all dark, and they also carry with them a new attitude toward color. There is no strong sense among Puerto Ricans of difference based on color; intermarriage is common, and people are aware of color and hair and facial features as they are aware of any other personal and defining characteristics of an individual. In Puerto Rico, in fact, there seems to be much less concern over color than there is in Jamaica, where subtle distinctions are made in shade, and persons try to marry someone lighter than themselves.

In the 40's, it was widely believed that the Puerto Rican group would eventually split, with the darker members being absorbed into the over-all American Negro community, just as West Indians and other colored immigrants had been. But Father Joseph Fitzpatrick's study of marriage among New York Puerto Ricans reveals that the newcomers still maintain the pattern of a single Puerto Rican community in which people mingle freely in disregard of the color marks that so affect American social behavior. Even more interesting: Father Fitzpatrick's study shows a sizable proportion of marriages between persons of different color; at least a sixth of Puerto Rican marriages in New York are of this type.

The break between colored and white Puerto Ricans, then, has not yet occurred. And if the cancer of color consciousness fails to develop among them, the Puerto Ricans may yet bring a greater gift to New York than any special cultural contribution could ever be.

PART II

The Alienated Learner

The process that finds its terminal point in the low skill levels, unemployment, and poverty described in the first section begins years earlier, when the child comes to school. In fact, it begins considerably before that, but school represents the first direct confrontation for the slum child with a social institution that demands more of him than mere behavioral conformity and that sets out to shape him into the kind of person the culture approves. In this institution, so comfortable and familiar to the middle-class child, the slum child finds himself a stranger.

It is particularly useful to look at the slum child's difficulties in adapting to this new environment as a form of alienation, one of many that some social observers suggest began with the breaking up of feudal institutions and accelerated with the economic revolution that created modern industrial life. In a general social order in which most persons confront the danger of alienation, the American lower-class and particularly the Negro lower-class person faces his own peculiar and magnified estrangement, a counterpoint to that of the society's of which he is a part and yet not a part.

The concept of alienation includes a loss of identity, a loss of self, a sense of helplessness, detachment, and isolation. At its best, the human condition is an anxious state; we are never sure when our own small flicker of existence will be wiped out, and in the pursuit of our own human needs we can be sure only of some measure of frustration at least and never certain of fulfilment. For such existential anxiety the human animal finds two solutions: a clear enough sense of his unique self to work toward what he really wants, and a sharing of purpose and meaning with others in the same situation. "In this staggering disproportion between man and no-man," says Kenneth Burke, "there is no place for purely human boasts of grandeur, or for forgetting that men build their cultures by huddling together, nervously loquacious, on the edge of an abyss."[1]

The conditions of modern life, the argument runs, have eroded the possibility of both of these underpinnings of life. The individual no longer grows up in a network of stable, accepted relationships, to take his place in an expected and established status. In a traditional society, the child finds a world that is all of one piece; the values familiar to him in the family are those he finds in the church, and they suffuse the community as a whole. He has a very good idea of what he will become as an adult and thus is assured of some recognizable status among his fellows, whether that status is important or not. And *what* he does is likely to have some clear relationship to the web of community life; he will provide food, clothes, shoes, she will take care of the children and the home.

In such a life, one does not ask *"Who am I?"* because the answer is clear. A sense of identity develops as we interact with others, as they tell us who we are by their behavior towards us. We accept our self if others consistently accept it, and if what we do and what we are to do and be makes sense to us. But the

1. Kenneth Burke, *Permanence and Change,* quoted in R. S. Lynd, *Knowledge for What?,* Princeton: Princeton University Press, 1948, p. v.

modern world, as Fromm has argued, frees us to become one of a great variety of selves, and in so doing, removes the security of knowing in advance who we are. We are not restricted by birth to a narrow band of possibilities. We no longer live in a world of certain values, moreover, but are free to choose our own, to move from one group membership to another in pursuit of them, if we are strong enough to relinquish the human ties with which they are identified. The work we grow up to do is likely to have lost its functional relation to life and its recognizability as "something *I* have made." To take pride in something one has produced is to say "there is something of me in it, and if it is worthy then I am worthy," but where can a man see himself in the complicated product of an assembly line?

If the over-all result for urban, industrial man is an anxiety about his own identity and a sense of detachment from both work and society, it has far more serious consequences for those at the bottom of society, those facing the most severe status deprivation and the most crucial identity loss. The papers in this section document from a number of different perspectives the form of that alienation with which the slum school must deal.

Perhaps the most important source is in the value conflicts between the school as a solidly middle-class institution and the culture of the lower class. The excerpt from Gans' *Urban Villagers* includes a detailed account of the differences among the values of the various social classes, a summary of the findings of a great number of researchers over the past several decades. Gans' book is particularly valuable for the thoroughness with which it makes an important distinction between two quite different cultures in lower-class life, the working class and the lower-lower. The "urban villagers" he studied, a group of Boston Italian-Americans, are working class, and their social values are predominantly influenced by what he calls the "peer group culture," an emphasis on the close personal ties among small groups of friendly couples, which persist as centers of social interaction and as a kind of defense against the outside middle-class world.

A considerably more stable life economically and socially

than that of the lower-lower class world, it is oriented toward routines rather than action-seeking. Thus it presents rather different requirements for social strategy for what Gans calls the "caretakers"—the social workers, teachers, and other personnel whose job it is to help people in trouble. But both cultures share a feeling of suspicion, distrust, and rejection of what they perceive as a vast middle-class bureaucracy, manned by people who do not appreciate the importance of personal ties and loyalty, who instead appear to be motivated by distant and impersonal goals and for whom abstractions seem to be more important than people.

It is difficult to overemphasize either the extent to which the lower-class child sees the school through the screen of these values or the effect of this perception on his adjustment to school demands for achievement. What is the sense of exerting great effort for dim, future goals which do not have anything to do with present realities? What is the use of all the nonsense about honesty and neatness and individual integrity, when often enough they mean being different from those whom you admire and identify with, or even worse, require a violation of loyalty to friends? The total inability of most of the middle-class public to understand how a labor leader can be stigmatized as crooked in the press, and indicted for "improper practices" in the courts, yet retain his position in his organization, parallels the exasperation of school administrators and teachers over the inability of their slum children to grasp the importance and truth of such values as ambition, honesty, integrity, and other virtues high in the middle-class lexicon of eternal verities.

For not only are the schools committed by tradition to communicate and enforce these values, but also they are staffed, as Spindler points out, by teachers who themselves originate in that "traditionalist" value system. The complex quesion of whether the school *should* attempt to transmit that value system is related to many of the professional issues raised in the companion volume, *Policy Issues in the Inner City School*. Is it a viable structure for those children who will be spending the rest of their lives in a different subculture? Indeed, as Coles argues in the article reprinted in this section, providing illustrations for Gans' earlier generalizations, many of the poor do not want to be middle class precisely because they distrust and dislike the attitudes and life style they naturally associate with that class. On the other hand, are not middle-class values demonstrably better ones, leading more surely to the good life, and do we not then have a responsibility to transmit them? Still a third position suggests that some middle-class values are required for the achievement in schools of the basic skills necessary to any kind of decent survival in this society, and that we should stress these and forget about attitudes relevant only to a particular life style and a limited subcultural world. The assumptions lying below the surface of each of these positions deserve thoughtful exploration.

A second source of alienation is revealed by the materials describing the physical and social environment of the children, and especially the interview accounts which permit us to look at it through their eyes. In presenting the interviews, Fine raises one issue particularly relevant to the question of alienation. The boys do not take the disorder and sordidness of the life surrounding them as something natural, as something to be accepted because it is all they know. They are aware, sharply and wistfully, of a life in which there are flowers on the sill, no empty wine bottles littering the alleys, no quarrelsome couples waking one up.

One often hears teachers in the slum schools say that the discipline and order imposed within the school represent for these children a unique island of organization and cleanliness in otherwise chaotic lives. Administrators use the same line of argument to justify such rules as that requiring pupils to wear white shirts and ties to school on assembly day. These assertions have the ring of solid sense to them, at least on the surface. Yet one wonders why, in these interviews and in the book from which they were excerpted, school occupies such a minimal part of the psychological life space. Some of the explanation may lie in the kind of bitterness expressed by James Baldwin when, recalling his own childhood, he thinks of the white-shirt rule as simply another example of the dominant whites' prejudice against color. Perhaps, too, the order and beauty children want in their own lives are unacceptable in school because there it is merely a part of an alien world, and often offered with a considerable amount of unconscious condescension. Hiram, whose "Report From a Spanish Harlem 'Fortress' " finds school routines meaningless and demeaning, responded only to the one teacher who took the trouble to engage his interest with such works as *The Threepenny Opera*. The savage world reflected in Brecht's play is the antithesis of the antiseptic and orderly world of the school, but Mack the Knife is at least a recognizable figure for boys like Hiram.

The readings also suggest not only a sharp sense of difference in environment but also the ways in which the children are made to feel actively excluded by those who live in the world outside their islands of poverty. This sense of restriction and exclusion is an inevitable consequence of the social-class patterning noted in the first section. But for the Negro lower class in particular, of course, it is made much more severe by their realistic sense that even an improvement in economic circumstances may not increase their chances of getting out of the ghetto.

Given this situation, one is impressed by the similarities between the school in the slum and the classic colonial image of the foreign enclave within the native settlement. The school is a middle-class island in an alien sea of despair and disorder, run by a staff of brisk authorities who live off in their own sections and who set up the rules and the rewards and punishments according to their own standards. It is hardly surprising that both teachers and pupils think and talk in terms of "We" and "They," or that more often than one would think conceivable visitors to these classrooms are treated to explanations delivered with piercing audibility to the effect that " 'They' really are pretty stupid, so that's why I have to give them these special materials."

Although common enough, teachers with this degree of insensitivity to the feelings of the "natives" are in the minority. One is probably likelier to find the unconscious cruelty of the teacher Dick Gregory describes in "You Don't Have a Daddy." Most teachers in the slum schools feel some sense of nurturance for their children and sufficient professional commitment to try very hard to help them learn. But if their attempts to induce pupils to adopt middle-class mores and habits are frustrated by an alien system of class values, their efforts to teach simply the straightforward intellectual skills which are the major domain of the school must overcome another set of handicaps which one might think of as a sort of cognitive alienation.

"Cognition" is the generic term that stands for all of the human processes involved in knowing, the intricate business of categorizing and differentiating the world of stimuli into patterns of meaning. One cannot learn to read unless one has grasped the difference between a "C" and an "O," for example, and has developed the ability to recognize the similarity between one "C" and all other "C's"—that is, until he has conceptualized the letter. One cannot do simple arithmetic until one is able to understand the abstract conception of "oneness," apart from a variety of single, concrete objects. Schools have always operated on the assumption that by the time children come to them they will have already developed to a fairly high degree the basic cognitive skills necessary for formal education, and for the middle-class child the assumption is quite correct.

Children from stable, fairly well-to-do families get, first of all, an extraordinary amount of attention from adults, who patiently point out differences and similarities to the child, and who pressure him toward the development of basic language skills. They fill his environment with arrays of richly colored and often well-designed toys which instruct him in textures, sizes, colors, and relationships. The contrasting poverty of the cognitive world of the lower-class child is described in Martin Deutsch's article, as he notes the links between the environmental characteristics of lower-class life and the cognitive requirements of schooling.

Deutsch himself, on the basis of these facts, has set up a large-scale experiment to determine whether one can overcome these early cognitive deficiencies by bringing the child very early into a richly patterned nursery-school environment, staffed with skilled and understanding teachers. If he succeeds, there will still remain the question of whether we can duplicate the results of his experimental situations routinely and on a large scale, as Project Head Start has attempted to do. Recent studies in developmental psychology suggest, too, that there might well be a limit to what one can do even at the age of three to overcome a thoroughly impoverished background during the early years, that if some basic cognitive processes are not stimulated very early, they may be permanently impaired.

One can view all of these forms of alienation as inextricably linked to both school failure and decreased life chance if one sees them in relation to the need for status, a relationship Cohen makes explicit in his piece "The Bottom of the Heap." Our need to have a recognized position in the eyes of our fellows is a compelling one; in our society, where status is not fixed, where everyone is assumed to have a chance to achieve it, boys in particular recognize that they are in competition with others. The whole atmosphere of school as an institution emphasizes that competition, if not with individual others, then with an abstract standard of excellence.

But we compete with a sense of confidence only when we feel comfortable, when we are on familiar ground. The lower-class boy is in strange surroundings when he is in school, and he is made sharply aware that his own familiar values and the behavior based on them are not acceptable, hence unworthy. Furthermore, it soon becomes clear to him that he is not equipped to compete on equal terms because of the cognitive handicaps he begins with, which sharply increase the probability of early failure in school work. Thus, striving for status that depends upon academic success appears totally unrealistic to him.

But the hunger for position, for status, is no less strong in the healthy child, although the sick ones withdraw from the situation through drugs or other denials of reality. It is far easier to carry on the search, however, in familiar territory, in the neighborhood, in the gang. And once he has rejected the school as a meaningful context for status strivings, he can easily reject everything that goes along with it—the middle-class values, the abstract goals, and the effort required to succeed at the really very difficult intellectual tasks the school sets for him. In the first chapter of *The Cool World*, one finds the perfect expression of the utter lack of meaning of school activities for Duke and his friends. It is not that they dislike Mr. Shapiro, or object to the field trip, it simply has no *connection* with them, they are not engaged. The rest of the novel exposes the other side of the coin as it describes Duke's rise to leadership in his gang. The satisfaction he gets from that achievement is precisely the feeling of any young, successful executive rising to the top; that Duke failed to get anything like it in school is the essential problem we face, for one of the solutions to alienation is to help people gain position and status.

How a set of relatively weak social institutions, including the school, can succeed in bringing the poor into the mainstream of the culture, without necessarily imposing an alien set of values on them, is the current dilemma. As the study by Suzanne Keller indicates, it is by no means a Negro dilemma only. The early life of the poor white child handicaps him in many ways for existence in a predominantly middle-class, industrial society; Keller's report confirms what everyone knows, however, that the handicaps are very much greater for the child in the Negro family. Indeed, Moynihan's summary excerpted here of the pathological elements in Negro family life leads him to suggest that only by restructuring that family can the child's alienation be mitigated. Even if he is correct, if educators generally adopt his view as a comfortable escape from the necessary and difficult task of restructuring the school, they are surely evading a moral as well as a professional responsibility.

A CLASS VALUE SCALE

Before you read the selections on the values of the American social class system, you may be interested in taking a brief assessment of your own values. The following statements were taken from an instrument used in a study of the values of high-school students, and the scores successfully differentiated middle-class students from lower-class ones.* The key that follows the items identifies the middle-class ends of the scale for each statement.

Circle: 1 if you strongly agree
2 if you agree somewhat
3 if you disagree somewhat
4 if you strongly disagree

1. Even though parents often seem too strict, when a person gets older he will realize it was beneficial.   1 2 3 4
2. Nowadays, with world conditions the way they are, a wise person lives for today and lets tomorrow take care of itself.   1 2 3 4
3. All a person should want out of life in the way of a career is a secure, not too difficult job with enough pay to afford a nice car and eventually a home of his own.   1 2 3 4
4. Parents should be greatly upset if their child ended up doing factory work.   1 2 3 4
5. Planning only makes a person unhappy, since plans hardly ever work out anyway.   1 2 3 4
6. The best kind of job is one where you are part of an organization all working together, even if you don't get individual credit.   1 2 3 4
7. When the time comes for a person to take a job, he should stay near his parents, even if it means giving up a good job.   1 2 3 4
8. Even when teenagers get married, their main loyalty still belongs to their mother and father.   1 2 3 4
9. Parents ought to take teenagers seriously.   1 2 3 4

* B. C. Rosen, "The Achievement Syndromes," *American Sociological Review*, XXI, April 1956, 203–11.

10. When a person is born, the success he is going to have is already in the cards, so he might just as well accept and not fight against it.   1 2 3 4

11. It is silly for a teenager to put money in a car when the money could be used for his educacation or to get started in business.   1 2 3 4

12. If parents tell a teenager to stop seeing a friend of his own sex, he has a right to see that friend anyway.   1 2 3 4

13. Nothing in life is worth the sacrifice of moving away from your parents.   1 2 3 4

A person with middle-class values would check the items as follows:

1. disagree	8. disagree
2. disagree	9. agree
3. disagree	10. disagree
4. agree	11. agree
5. disagree	12. agree
6. disagree	13. disagree
7. disagree	

"... what West Enders disliked most about the outside world and the middle-class culture is their stress on object-goals that interfere with person-oriented relationships."

THE SUBCULTURES OF THE WORKING CLASS, LOWER CLASS AND MIDDLE CLASS*

Herbert J. Gans

Gans is a sociologist whose training and interests are in urban planning. The study from which this chapter is excerpted, *The Urban Villagers,* was undertaken to answer the question of why people who live in areas undergoing urban renewal accept the disruption of their lives so passively. To find the answer Gans lived among a group of working-class Italian people living in a section of Boston's West End, from which they were soon going to be forced to move. In this chapter he compares the value system he found among this group with the findings of other studies of

* From Herbert J. Gans, *The Urban Villagers,* New York: The Free Press, 1962, pp. 230–41, 244–62, 264–65. Copyright © 1955, reprinted by permission of the publisher.

working-class cultures, and contrasts it with what we know of lower-class and middle-class cultures. (His extensive footnotes are omitted here; several pages of them may be found in the original text.) In so doing, he provides a remarkably condensed view of the spectrum of values one finds among the subcultures that make up the American society which, if applied cautiously, can vastly increase our understanding of the problems of urban education. Educators may find it useful to read the material with questions like the following in mind:

Gans distinguishes between two types of lower-class value systems; what is the heart of that distinction? What differences would teachers be likely to perceive in a classroom between children from each of these subcultures?

The chapter raises the crucial issue of whether the school should try to make the child middle class in value orientation; Gans himself struggles with the question and decides that for the lower-lower class it should. Are his reasons valid? What are the social consequences if we should decide that it is an unreasonable aim for the working class?

It is very difficult to persuade a person to adopt a value system different from the one he has been raised with, and which is supported by group memberships which are important to him. In another part of the book Gans criticizes social workers and teachers who work with the people he studied for the way in which they approached these value conflicts; what would the school and the teacher have to do to maintain their own system of values and at the same time be sympathetic enough to the child's values to reach him?

A WEALTH of evidence from other studies indicates that the peer group society is a class, rather than an ethnic, phenomenon. My survey of these studies will be cursory. It will consider various social structural and cultural characteristics in the order in which I have described them among the West Enders.

Although the existence of a peer group society has not been reported in other working-class populations, Walter Miller's study of an Irish and Negro neighborhood did conclude that: "Lower class society may be pictured as comprising a set of age-graded one-sex peer groups which constitute the psychic focus and reference group for those over twelve and thirteen." The distinction between the peer group society and the outside world is much like Hoggart's dichotomy of "us" and "them" in the British working-class. He writes:

> . . . the world outside is strange and often unhelpful . . . it has most of the counters stacked on its side . . . to meet it on its own terms is difficult. One may call this, making use of a word commonly used by the working classes, the world of "Them.". . . The world of "Them" is the world of the bosses, whether those bosses are private individuals or . . . public officials. . . . "Them" includes the policemen and those civil servants . . . whom the working classes meet. . . . To the very poor, especially, they compose a shadowy but numerous and powerful group affecting their lives at almost every point. . . . "They" are "the people at the top" . . . who . . . "get yer in the end," "aren't really to be trusted," "are all in a clique together," "treat y'like muck."

Similarly, a study of American working-class women notes their separation from "the outer world," and their fear of its " 'chaotic and catastrophic' qualities." In some ways Redfield's conception of the relationship between the peasant and the elite is like that between the West Ender and the outside world. Moreover, Lewis's description of the Mexican "culture of poverty" bears a number of resemblances to the way of life of the poorest West Enders.

My description of routine- and action-seekers is paralleled in many ways by S. M. Miller and Frank Riessman's distinction between the "unskilled, irregular worker . . . [who] . . . lacks the disciplined, structured and traditional approach of the stable worker and stresses the excitement theme." Their analysis, based on a review of American working-class studies, reflects the general sociological distinction between working and lower class. Walter Miller's study of lower-class culture describes in more systematic detail what I have called action-seeking. He notes its "focal concerns" with such qualities as toughness, daring, adroitness in repartee, excitement, and rejection of superordinate authority. His discussion of excitement observes that:

> For many lower-class individuals the rhythm of life fluctuates between periods of relatively routine or repetitive activity and sought situations of great emotional stimulation. Many of the most characteristic features of lower-class life are related to the search for excitement or "thrill."

The largest amount of data is available on family life. The segregation of family roles and the separate lives of husbands and wives have been reported in studies of the English working class, among Puerto Ricans, both in Puerto Rico and in New York, in a Mexican family, and in a national American working-class sample. A study of Polish-Americans describes this segregation as follows:

> . . . the pairs are not "one" . . . the marriage relation is not intensive. There is not a ceaseless seeking out of the other's motivations, no rigid set of expectations to which the other must conform.

The same study also notes the men's need to display and defend their masculinity. Similar findings have been reported in most working-class populations regardless of ethnic origin. The subordinate role of children in what I have called the adult-centered family has been observed among New York Puerto Ricans and in a general survey of working-class culture. Two American studies point out the lack of interest in children as individuals. The pattern of permitting freedom to boys, and of keeping girls at home has also been found among Puerto Ricans.

The central role of the peer group has been suggested, as previously noted, by Walter Miller's study of Irish and Negro lower-class adolescents. Another American study found that:

> Husband and wife tend to have few, if any friends in common. Relationships with friends tend to be on a single-sex basis. . . . Often relatives are the only friends. If husband or wife do have friends who are not relatives, they have them as individuals and not as couples.

Many studies have shown the existence of the family circle, notably in England, and among New York Puerto Ricans. The prevalence of spending one's social life with relatives more than with friends has been reported in England and in a variety of American working-class groups.

A number of findings on group life and personality have suggested that many of the elements I have summarized as person-orientation are found among working-class people generally, and one survey of American studies describes them as person-centered. This article also notes the practice of personalizing bureaucracy and other outside world situations, as does an account of English working-class life. A study of American working-class women describes their problems in regard to self-control, and shows how lack of self-control encourages their children in turn to express anger through violence. It also suggests that working-class adolescents express themselves motorically, or physically, while middle-class adolescents use conceptual and symbolic modes. Another study of American working-class women stresses the importance of group life, the fear of loneliness, and their concern with what others think of them. An analysis of lower-class interview respondents has described in considerable detail their tendency to be concrete and particularistic, to think anecdotally, to personalize events, and to see phenomena only from their own perspective: they do not "assume the role of another toward still others." The limited repertoire of roles also has been described in a study of an English group, and the inability or unwillingness of people to adopt other roles has been reported as lack of empathy in a previously mentioned study of Middle Eastern peasants.

A number of American studies have shown the scarcity of working-class participation in what I have described as community life. For example, the West Enders' pattern of being religious but not being identified with the church has been found among other American groups, both Protestant and Catholic, and in England as well.

Both American and English studies have reported the working-class detachment from work, the concern with job security, and the negative evaluation of white-collar workers and bosses. The West Enders' ambivalence about education is also widely shared. The conception that school should teach children to keep out of trouble has been described by an English study; that education must contribute to the occupational success of the individual, by many studies, including an American and a Puerto Rican one. Two studies have indicated that working-class mothers want more education for their children than do the fathers.

I have already reported the prevalence of the general conception that the outside world is not to be trusted. This extends also to a skepticism about caretakers, a reluctance to visit settlement houses, and a fear of doctors and hospitals that seems to be found in all countries. Similarly, working-class people everywhere believe—or know—the police to be crooked, and politicians, corrupt. In America, England, and Mexico, researchers have described the working- and lower-class antagonism toward law, government, and politics.

Conversely, the mass media are accepted, often more enthusiastically than by other classes. A recently published study of American television viewers has made this finding, and noted the working-class audience's interest in and identification with performers. Several studies have also suggested the preference for action dramas over other forms of media content, not only in America, but all over the world. In Green's study of a Polish group, the rejection of romantic films by young working-class adults was described as follows: "At the local movie house, when the hero pauses in pursuit of the villain to proffer the heroine a tender sentiment, whistling and footstamping greet his fall from grace."

As I have not attempted to make a complete survey of the literature, I have mentioned here only some of the many similarities between the West Enders and other groups. Even so, it should be evident that, by and large, the peer group society is associated with working- and lower-class life. Moreover, the data show that many of its features are found among other ethnic groups who have come to America from Europe—notably the Irish and Polish—as well as among racially differentiated groups, such as the Negroes and the Puerto Ricans. Incidentally, the peer group society also cuts across religious lines, for many of its characteristics appear not only among Protestants in England and America, but among European and Latin Catholics as well.

Some differences—including a few ethnic ones—do exist between the West Enders and other working-class people. Yet many of these differences can be traced to class factors operating in past and present generations. Italian-Americans, for example, differ from the Irish-Americans in a number of ways. The Irish are more respectful of paternal authority, of the older generation, of the church, and of authority in general. Irish men are also much closer to their mothers than are Italian men, a fact that has a number of implications for family structure, family dynamics, and even for the ways in which mental illness is expressed.

Many of these differences can be related to the fact that the Irish immigrants came from landowning, peasant families. In Ireland, the father was the sole owner of the family farm, and thus was free to choose as to which of his sons would inherit it. As a result, sons were in a subordinate position. One study of the Irish peasantry notes, in fact, that sons were called boys until the day the father surrendered the farm to one of them, even if they themselves were middle-aged adults. The conditions which the Irish immigrants found in America evidently did not encourage any major change in family structure. Certainly, one could argue that those Irish-Americans who turned to politics and the priesthood found that the relationship between the political boss and his underlings and between the Bishop and his priests was much the same as that between the farm owner and his sons. Needless to say, not all Irish-Italian differences can be explained purely by class factors, or by cultural differences which developed from economic conditions in Europe. They do seem, however, to be of primary importance.

West Enders also differ from other working-class, and especially lower-class, groups in the role that the mother plays in family life. Studies of the English working class, for example, have stressed the importance of the "Mum" and the dominance of the mother-daughter relationship over all others, even when the daughter is married and has children of her own. Similarly, studies of the Negro, Puerto Rican, and Carribean lower classes have shown the family to be what anthropologists call matrifocal. The mother is the head of the household, and the basic family unit includes her, her children, and one or more of her female relatives, such as her mother or aunt. Often the man is a marginal and only intermittent participant in this female-based household. American studies of the lower class have reported what Walter Miller calls "serial monogamy"—a pattern in which a woman lives and has children with a series of men who desert her or whom she asks to leave.

The reason for this pattern among Negroes can be found in the fact that in past and present, they have lived under conditions in which the male's position in the society has been marginal and insecure. Under slavery, for example, the formation of a normal family was discouraged, although the female slave was allowed to raise her own children. Since the days of slavery, the Negro's economic position has been such as to maintain much of this pattern. The man who has difficulty in finding a steady job and is laid off frequently finds it difficult to perform the functions of a male breadwinner and household head. Moreover, when the woman is able to find steady employment or can subsist on welfare payments, she tends to treat the man with disdain and often with open hostility, especially if he complicates her life by making her pregnant. Under these conditions, there is no incentive for the man to remain in the family, and in times of stress he deserts. Moreover, when the male children grow up in a predominantly female household—in which the man is a .powerless and scorned figure—their upbringing en-

courages ambivalence as to male functions and masculinity.
Thus, the pattern is perpetuated into the next generation.

The hypothesis that the female-based family can be traced
to class and, more specifically, to occupational factors is supported by studies describing this family type among peoples
who have not been slaves. It has been found, for example,
among Puerto Ricans, both on the island and in New York. It
seems, however, to be more prevalent among Puerto Ricans
from sugar cane areas, which have a plantation economy much
like that under which the Negro endured slavery. The hypothesis is supported in another way by the fact that a somewhat
similar family constellation prevails when the man's occupation separates him from his family for long periods. Thus, a
study of sailors' families in Norway indicates that the woman
takes over the dominant role in the family, and overprotects
her children. Although the girls show no negative consequences,
the boys seem to develop what Tiller calls a defensive feminine
identification, and compensatory masculine traits. When such
boys become adults, they thus favor occupations that stress
masculinity and minimize female contact and the family role.

The female-based family, however, is not found among West
Enders, and the reasons perhaps can also be traced to occupational factors. Although the West Enders' ancestors suffered
from unemployment, the totally agrarian economy of Southern
Italian society and the extremely strenuous character of farm
labor created no employment opportunities for women. Indeed,
the family could best survive if the woman stayed home and
bore a large number of children who could eventually add to
the family's income. As a result, the woman did not take on
an economic function, and the man maintained his position
in the family even though he could not always support it
adequately. This family constellation seems to have been strong
enough to endure in America during those periods when the
man was unemployed and the woman could find a job. Needless to say, some family instability and male marginality or
desertion has occurred among the immigrants and the second
generation, but such cases have been considerably fewer than
among newcomers with female-based families.

Finally, the West Enders may be contrasted to the Jews, an ethnic group which came to America at about the same time as the Italians, but with a different occupational history. The Jews who emigrated from Poland and Russia around the turn of the century were neither farm laborers nor peasants, but peddlers, shopkeepers, and artisans with a more middle-class occupational tradition. They also differed from their fellow immigrants in their belief in education, partly for reasons related to this tradition. Although they worked initially as unskilled and semiskilled laborers in America, they reacted differently to their environment than did the ethnic groups from peasant and farm labor origins. Superficially, the Jewish family structure resembled the Italian one, with a nuclear household surrounded by a large family circle. Because of the high value placed on education, however, the immigrants did not restrain their children from contact with the outside world. As already noted, they encouraged the children to use the schools and settlement houses to prepare themselves for white-collar and professional occupations. Thus, the Jewish young people pursued careers that drew them apart from the parental generation at the same time that their Italian neighbors rejected such careers as "lonely ventures" that could only break up the cohesion of the family circle. Although the Jewish immigrants did bemoan the children's acculturation into styles of life congruent with their higher occupational level, they also took pride in the successful mobility of their offspring.

The voluminous literature of class studies in America and elsewhere and the considerable similarity of the classes all over the industrialized world have made it possible to begin a delineation of the principal class subcultures. While I shall not attempt this task here, I do want to suggest what seem to me to be some of the major "focal concerns" of four of the subcultures: working class, lower class, middle class, and professional upper-middle class. These brief outlines are based on observations made in the West End and elsewhere, and on the research literature. For the most part, they describe the subcultures in America and in one period of the life cycle: that of the family which is rearing children.

Perhaps the most important—or at least the most visible—difference between the classes is one of family structure. *The working-class subculture* is distinguished by the dominant role of the family circle. Its way of life is based on social relationships amidst relatives. The working class views the world from the family circle, and considers everything outside it as either a means to its maintenance or to its destruction. But while the outside world is to be used for the benefit of this circle, it is faced with detachment and even hostility in most other respects. Whenever feasible, then, work is sought within establishments connected to the family circle. When this is not possible—and it rarely is—work is primarily a means of obtaining income to maintain life amidst a considerable degree of poverty, and thereafter, a means of maximizing the pleasures of life within the family circle. The work itself may be skilled or unskilled; it can take place in the factory or in the office—the type of collar is not important. What does matter is that identification with work, work success, and job advancement—while not absolutely rejected—are of secondary priority to the life that goes on within the family circle. The purpose of education is to learn techniques necessary to obtain the most lucrative type of work. Thus the central theme of American, and all Western, education—that the student is an individual who should use his schooling to detach himself from ascribed relationships like the family circle in order to maximize his personal development and achievement in work, play, and other spheres of life—is ignored or openly rejected.

The specific characteristics of the family circle may differ widely—from the collateral peer group form of the West Enders, to the hierarchical type of the Irish, or to the classic three-generation extended family. Friends may also be included in the circle, as in the West Enders' peer group society. What matters most—and distinguishes this subculture from others—is that there be a family circle which is wider than the nuclear family, and that all of the opportunities, temptations, and pressures of the larger society be evaluated in terms of how they affect the ongoing way of life that has been built around this circle.

The *lower-class subculture* is distinguished by the female-based family and the marginal male. Although a family circle may also exist, it includes only female relatives. The male, whether husband or lover, is physically present only part of the time, and is recognized neither as a stable nor dominant member of the household. He is a sexual partner, and he is asked to provide economic support. But he participates only minimally in the exchange of affection and emotional support, and has little to do with the rearing of children. Should he serve as a model for the male children, he does so largely in a negative sense. That is, the women use him as an example of what a man should not be.

The female-based family must be distinguished, however, from one in which the woman is dominant, for example, the English working-class family. Although this family may indeed revolve around the "Mum," she does not reject the husband. Not only is he a member of the family, but he is also a participant—and a positive model—in child-rearing.

In the lower class, the segregation of the sexes—only partial in the working class—is complete. The woman tries to develop a stable routine in the midst of poverty and deprivation; the action-seeking man upsets it. In order to have any male relationships, however, the woman must participate to some extent in his episodic life style. On rare occasions, she may even pursue it herself. Even then, however, she will try to encourage her children to seek a routine way of life. Thus the woman is much closer to working-class culture, at least in her aspirations, although she is not often successful in achieving them.

For lower-class men, life is almost totally unpredictable. If they have sought stability at all, it has slipped from their grasp so quickly, often, and consistently that they no longer pursue it. From childhood on, their only real gratifications come from action-seeking, but even these are few and short-lived. Relationships with women are of brief duration, and some men remain single all their lives. Work, like all other relationships with the outside world, is transitory. Indeed, there can be no identification with work at all. Usually, the lower-class individual gravitates from one job to another, with little hope or interest of keeping a job for any length of time. His hostility to the outside world therefore is quite intense, and its attempts to interfere with the episodic quality of his life are fought. Education is rejected by the male, for all of its aims are diametrically opposed to action-seeking.

The *middle-class subculture* is built around the nuclear family and its desire to make its way in the larger society. Although the family circle may exist, it plays only a secondary role in middle-class life. Contact with close relatives is maintained, but even they participate in a subordinate role. Individuals derive most of their social and emotional gratifications from the nuclear family itself. One of the most important of these is child-rearing. Consequently, the middle-class family is much more child-centered than the working-class one and spends more of its spare time together. Outside social life takes place with friends who share similar interests. The nuclear family depends on its friends—as well as on some caretaking institutions—for help and support. Relatives may also help, especially in emergencies.

The middle class does not make the distinction between the family and the outside world. In fact, it does not even see an outside world, but only a larger society, which it believes to support its aims, and in which the family participates. The nuclear family makes its way in the larger society mainly through the career of its breadwinner. Thus work is not merely a job that maximizes income, but a series of related jobs or job advances which provide the breadwinner with higher income, greater responsibility, and, if possible, greater job satisfaction. In turn his career enhances the way of life of the rest of the family, through increases in status and in the standard of living.

Education is viewed, and used, as an important method for achieving these goals. The purpose of education is to provide the skills needed for the man's career and for the woman's role as a mother. In and out of school, it is also used to develop the skills necessary to the maintenance and increase of status, the proper use of leisure time, and the occasional participation in community activities. Thus, much of the central theme of education is accepted. But the idea that education is an end in itself, and should be used to maximize individual development of the person, receives only lip service.

The subculture I have described here is a basic middle-class one; a more detailed analysis would distinguish between what is currently called the middle-middle class and the lower-middle class. The upper-middle-class subculture is also a variant of the basic middle-class culture. There are at least two such subcultures, the managerial and the professional, [the latter of which] is of primary interest here.

The *professional upper-middle-class culture* is also organized around the nuclear family, but places greater emphasis on the independent functioning of its individual members. Whereas the middle-class family is a companionship unit in which individuals exist most intensely in their relationships with each other, the upper-middle-class family is a companionship unit in which individuals seeking to maximize their own development as persons come together on the basis of common interests. For this subculture, life is, to a considerable extent, a striving for individual development and self-expression, and these strivings pervade many of its relationships with the larger society.

Therefore, work is not simply a means for achieving the well-being of the nuclear family, but also an opportunity for individual achievement and social service. Although the career, income, status, and job responsibility are important, job satisfaction is even more important, although it is not always found. Indeed, professional work satisfaction is a focal concern not only for the breadwinner, but often for the woman as well. If she is not interested in a profession, she develops an alternative but equally intense interest in motherhood, or in community activity. Child-rearing, moreover, gives the woman an opportunity not only to maximize her own individual achievements as a mother, but to develop in her children the same striving for self-development. As a result, the professional upper-middle-class family is not child-centered, but adult-directed. As education is the primary tool for a life of individual achievement, the professional upper-middle-class person not only goes to school longer than anyone else in society, but he also accepts its central theme more fully than do the rest of the middle class.

This concern with individual achievement and education further enables and encourages the members of this subculture to be deliberate and self-conscious about their choices. They are a little more understanding of the actions of others than the members of less educated strata. Their ability to participate in the larger society, plus their high social and economic status, also gives them somewhat greater control over their fate than other people, and make the environment more predictable. This in turn facilitates the practice of self-consciousness, empathy, and abstraction or generalization.

The possession of these skills distinguishes the upper-middle class from the rest of the middle class, and even more so from the working and lower class. For the latter not only live in a less predictable environment, but they are also detached from the outside world, which increases their feeling that it, and, indeed, all of life, is unpredictable. In turn this feeling encourages a pervasive fatalism that pre-empts the optimism or pessimism of which the other classes are capable. The fatalism of the working and lower classes, as well as their lack of education and interest in personal development and object goals, minimizes introspection, self-consciousness, and empathy for the behavior of others.

CLASS: OPPORTUNITY AND RESPONSE

The subcultures which I have described are *responses* that people make to the *opportunities* and the *deprivations* that they encounter. More specifically, each subculture is an organized set of related responses that has developed out of people's efforts to cope with the opportunities, incentives, and rewards, as well as the deprivations, prohibitions, and pressures which the natural environment and society—that complex of coexisting and competing subcultures—offer to them. The responses which make up a subculture are compounded out of what people have retained of parental, that is, traditional responses, the skills and attitudes they have learned as children, and the innovations they have developed for themselves in their own encounters with opportunity and deprivation.

These responses cannot develop in a vacuum. Over the long range, they can be seen as functions of the resources which a society has available, and of the opportunities which it can offer. In each of the subcultures life is thus geared to the availability of specific qualitative types and quantities of income, education, and occupational opportunities. Although I have used occupational labels to distinguish between the major subcultures, a man's job does not necessarily determine in which of these he shall be placed. In the long run, however, the existence of a specific subculture is closely related to the availability of occupational opportunities. For example, the functioning of the family circle and the routine-seeking way of life in the working class depend on the availability of stable employment for the man. The lower-class female-based family is a response to, or a method of coping with, the lack of stable male employment. The goals of middle- and upper-middle-class culture depend on the availability of sufficient income to finance the education that is necessary for a career and on the availability of job opportunities that will allow middle-class individuals to find the type of job satisfaction for which they are striving.

When these opportunity factors are lacking, the cultural responses made by people are frustrated. Should opportunities be deficient over a long enough period, downward mobility results. Should they disappear entirely, the subculture will be apt to disintegrate eventually. For example, working-class culture can function for a time in a period of unemployment, but if no substitute sources of stability are made available, people initially resort to protest. Eventually, the family circle begins to break up under the strain, and its members adopt many if not all of the responses identified with the lower-class subculture.

Similar reactions take place in the other subcultures, although the ways in which they are expressed may differ. If job opportunities are lacking so as to frustrate the career desires of the middle class, or the professional desires of the upper-middle class, one reaction is to transfer aspirations elsewhere, for example, into nonwork pursuits. Since upper-middle-class people are able and willing to act in the larger society, they may also develop social and political protest movements in order to create these opportunities, or to change society. Bourgeois socialist movements in America, taking their lead from the Marxist aim to "humanize" work so that it will provide quasi-professional job satisfaction to all people, are examples of such a reaction. Although downward mobility in the working class results in the adoption of lower-class responses, middle-class downward mobility does not bring about a working-class response. People may depend more on relatives as adversity strikes, but other differences between middle- and working-class subcultures remain in effect.

Downward mobility is also possible in the lower-class subculture. Since this culture is initially a response to instability, further instability can result only in family disintegration, total despair, and an increase in already high rates of mental illness, antisocial and self-destructive behavior, or group violence.

Conversely, when opportunity factors are increasingly available, people respond by more fully implementing their subcultural aspirations, and by improving their styles of life accordingly. For example, working-class people responded to the post-World War II prosperity by selecting from the available opportunities those elements useful for increasing the comfort and convenience of their way of life. They did not strive for middle-class styles. Nor did they reshape the family, adopt careers, or surrender their detachment from the outside world.

Periods of increased opportunity also encourage marginal members of each subculture to move into others to which they are aspiring. For example, lower-class women with working-class goals have been able to send their boys to school with the hope that they will be able to move into working-class culture. Whereas some of them have been able to make the move as adults, others have found that they could not summon the emotional and other skills necessary to succeed in school or job. In many cases, opportunities simply were not as freely available as expected, and sudden illness or other setbacks propelled them back into the lower-class culture.

Upward mobility that involves movement into another class subculture is relatively rare because of the considerable changes which people must make in their own lives, often against great odds. Thus the majority are content to improve the style of life within their own subcultures. They may, however, encourage their children to make the move in the next generation.

Although opportunities can increase or decrease rapidly and drastically over time, the subcultures I have described are relatively slow in changing their basic structure and content. In many ways contemporary working-class culture is a continuation of European peasant cultures, and some features of the middle- and upper-middle-class subcultures can be traced back to the post-Renaissance and to the beginnings of the urban-industrial revolution. Improvements and changes in the level of living take place all the time, as modern ideas, habits, and artifacts replace traditional ones. But the focal concerns of each subculture change more slowly.

Changes in the distribution and quality of opportunity factors do, of course, have significant effects. They influence the extent to which subcultural aspirations can be realized, and they help to determine the position of each subculture within the over-all class hierarchy. This in turn affects the political influence that each of them can exert on many matters in the national society, including the distribution of opportunities itself.

Moreover, new opportunities and the need for new skills can increase the number of people found in any one subculture, just as the demise of opportunities can reduce it. For example, whereas the reduction of temporary, unskilled labor is likely to shrink the lower-class subculture, the increased need for professionals has led to the enlargement of the middle and upper-middle class. In short, new opportunities bring higher incentives, which in turn encourage people to move into other subcultures, although a generation or two may pass before they adopt all of the primary focal concerns of their new way of life.

At any one point in time, then, many people could be said to be living between subcultures. Radical changes in the society can even bring entirely new subcultures into being, although this has happened only infrequently in the course of history.

CLASS AND MOBILITY
AMONG THE WEST ENDERS

I have tried to show that the movement from one class to another is a cultural change that requires not only access to the prerequisite opportunities, but the willingness and ability to accept them. This is especially true of the move from working class to middle class, and may be illustrated by a description of the mobility process among the West Enders. This analysis will require some prior comments about class and ethnicity that will apply the definition of class proposed in the previous section to the West Enders and that will summarize the relationship between class and ethnic origin in the life of the peer group society.

So far, West Enders have had relatively few of the opportunities necessary for entry into the middle-class subculture, and even those few are of recent vintage. On the other hand they have not demanded access to these opportunities. For example, a number of college scholarships offered by one of the area settlement houses had frequently gone begging ever since the Jewish exodus from the West End. In short, it should be clear from the picture of the peer group society I have drawn in the preceding chapters that the West Enders are not yet eager to move into the middle class. While they now have many of the comforts and artifacts that once only the middle class could buy, they have not thereby become middle class. Their culture is still that of the working class.

This applies not only to the routine-seekers, but even to some of the action-seekers as well. Aside from the never married, only the married action-seekers who have effectively detached themselves from their families, and made them female-based, can be considered lower class. The remaining action-seekers have at least one foot in the working-class culture, and participate sufficiently in the family to maintain a viable role. Thus their children are likely to grow up without the characteristics found in children from female-based families.

One of the distinguishing marks of a working-class group is its detachment from the larger society. This is found also among some ethnic groups, but it is not an ethnic phenomenon per se. While it is true, for example, that the West Enders' detachment from the larger society has been supported by ethnic differences between themselves and the outside world, it is also true that the detachment has not been caused by these differences. Indeed, the review of other working-class studies has indicated that this detachment from the outside world can be found among all working-class populations even when they are not ethnic minorities. Conversely, the high degree of Jewish mobility would suggest that ethnic status is no significant hindrance in entering either the larger society or the middle class.

Because working-class culture is different from middle-class culture, the move from one to the other is a difficult one, requiring behavior and attitude changes of considerable social and emotional magnitude. The most important changes are cutting the attachment to the family circle and the peer group society, and a concurrent shift from person- to object-orientation.

Thus, in order for a West Ender to begin the move into the middle class, he must first break—or have broken for him—his dependence on family and peers. His striving must shift moreover from peer group goals toward object-goals, such as a career, prestige, wealth, or individual development. And these goals must be pursued alone, or with people of like mind.

Since these goals conflict with family and peer group relationships, the peer group society naturally discourages such striving. The opposition to mobility which I described in the previous chapter is specifically directed against object-orientation. Indeed, what West Enders dislike most about the outside world and the middle-class culture is their stress on object-goals that interfere with person-oriented relationships. This is clearly illustrated by the West Enders' belief that suburbanites are lonely people and that the middle-class career requires inhuman exploitation of others. It is also exemplified by their complaints that adults today are striving for individual goals, and children for things, rather than for the emotional satisfactions of a cohesive family circle, as in the past. . . . the peer group society's opposition to mobility is such that movement into the middle class must therefore be an individual venture.

This venture, a process which seems to begin in childhood or adolescence, requires that the young person be isolated from his family and peer group by a combination of pressures which push him out of these groups, and incentives which pull him into the outside world. Many events can produce the requisite isolation, but among the most frequent are the possession of special talents, personal crises, and late arrival into the peer group.

Every population—even a low-income one—produces a number of young people with special gifts or talents, be these intellectual or artistic. Among the West Enders, however, young people with such talents are generally ostracized by their peers. And, unless their gifts are athletic or forensic and are useful to the group, these young people are often forced to choose between their talents and their peers. Parents are more tolerant of their talents, but since they are detached from the children's activities, they can offer little overt support. In fact, they may even discourage the child should his talent be identified with the opposite sex. On the other hand, representatives from the outside world, such as teachers and settlement house workers, do offer incentives. They encourage the young person to develop his talent, and provide opportunities for proper training. At the same time, these caretakers also make special efforts to draw gifted West Enders out of the peer group society. This in turn helps to isolate the youngster even further from his peers.

When the individual's talents are moderate, and his motivation to develop them weak, he is likely to suppress them in order to stay with the group. Should he be especially talented and strongly motivated, however, the peer group ostracism and the incentives from outside world representatives can combine and take him out of the peer group society, and into the training grounds of the middle class. Even so, he is likely to be ambivalent about this break. One West End youngster, for example, who wanted to be a singer of semiclassical music practiced on the sly, because his friends made fun of him. Another West Ender, an extremely creative adult, has never reconciled the conflict between his desire to use his talents and his wish to be a part of a peer group that shows little interest in and even some hostility toward them. Still ambivalent as to these gifts, he envies creative people who are encouraged by their families and friends. Needless to say, in a low-income group, hurdles are also placed in the way of the talented person by economic considerations and the immense social distance between the low-income person and the upper-middle- and upper-class world of the arts.

A second impetus to mobility seems to come from crises or traumatic experiences that are accompanied by unexpected isolation from the peer group society. This hypothesis is based on the experiences of two West Enders. One, a young man who had contracted tuberculosis in adolescence, developed a new set of goals while spending a year in a hospital bed. After recovery, he went to college and, later, into a profession. Another young man, who comes from a respected West End family, had been failing in school and participating in delinquent acts. Finally, when his life had reached an absolute nadir, he spent an entire night sitting up with his father, reviewing his past and his prospects for the future. He explained that as a result of these experiences, he developed a new set of goals. Subsequently, he too entered the professions. Such instances as these suggest that, for some, the move into middle-class culture requires a personal crisis, which is followed by a transformation that bears some resemblance to a religious conversion.

A third factor that encourages mobility is delayed entrance into the peer group society, which thus isolates the individual from the group during his formative years. This possibility was suggested by the fact that two of the most mobile individuals whom I encountered in the West End had both been born in Italy and had come to America just before their teens. Only marginally attached to peer groups as adolescents, both have departed considerably, although not entirely, from the ways of the peer group society in adulthood.

Another factor that acts on the individual is parental or familial encouragement to become upwardly mobile, but . . . this is largely absent among the West Enders, although it seems to be important among Jews.

These factors function as pressures on the individual. In addition, almost all young West Enders are exposed to some pulls from the outside world—albeit in varying degrees of intensity—which offer them incentives for leaving the group. These come from the mass media, as well as from the schools and the other caretakers. But as only a few individuals respond to them, it must be assumed that the incentives themselves are not sufficient. Isolating pressures which push the individual out of the group are also necessary, and seemingly even more important.

This difficulty of breaking from the group and becoming mobile has also been observed by other researchers. Ellis' study of unmarried career women, for example, concluded that:

> The evidence is consistent with the theory that upward social mobility is likely to be an outgrowth of basically neurotic drives resulting from unsatisfactory early primary group relations, and that mobility leads to a continuation of superficial, impermanent primary group relationships and other overt manifestations of emotional maladjustment.

Another study found vertical mobility "to be a factor in both schizophrenia and psychoneurosis. . . . This does not necessarily mean that mobility is the only or even the principal causative factor." At present, it is not known to what extent mobility is a result of difficulties experienced early in life, and to what extent it stems from parental desires for their children or from other incentives, and is a cause of these difficulties.

In associating mobility with object-orientation, I have considered only what might be called *total* mobility, that is, instances of people who make the move from working class to middle class in one jump of relatively short duration. There are other people whose mobility is more *segmental*. They enter occupations associated with the middle class—including the pro-fessions—but rather than seeking object-goals, they only want to be among people of higher status. Lacking any strong identifica-tion with their profession or with other middle-class values, they may not shift from person- to object-orientation at all. Instead, they merely apply person-oriented ways amid middle-class colleagues and friends, meanwhile retaining many of their other old behavior patterns and attitudes. Since such people are culturally between two classes, they are often described as "social climbers."

Finally, my discussion here has been limited to cases of suc-cessful mobility. Other individuals may break with the peer group society, but then fail to find a niche in the larger society. In this case, such people are likely to suffer considerable pain and even mental illness, especially if their unsuccessful break results eventually in downward mobility. I did not encounter such individuals during my stay in the West End, but, then, one would not expect them to come back to the area once they had broken with the group.

I have suggested that one of the steps in becoming middle class is the development of object-goals. But while it might follow that the middle class is a subculture of the object-oriented, I do not believe this to be the case. Indeed most middle-class people are not noticeably more object-oriented than working-class ones. The striving for object-goals, therefore, seems to be a temporary phase that is associated with the in-dividual type of mobility. If and when the sought object is achieved, many people "settle down" and become more person-oriented again, only this time with a new group of friends who share their characteristics and interests. Examples of this settling-down process may be found among the ambitious young corporate executives who later become "organization men," or among intellectuals who give up creative work for faculty poli-tics and sociability once they have achieved their academic career goals. The pleasures of group life then become more important than the socially isolating pursuit of object-goals.

Some people, of course, never stop striving for object-goals, and are likely to be socially marginal all their lives. The more

successful become leaders. The less successful may become the
isolates on the block who ceaselessly compete for status, and try
to keep up with real or imagined Joneses.

Whereas such people may be quite visible to the superficial
observer, they are numerically a minority in the total population. Most middle-class people—whether they have come from
the working class or not—are quite person-oriented. Their career
moves and their choices of residential areas, organizational affili-
ations, cultural interests, and leisure-time activities usually depend more on the wishes of family and friends than on specific
object-goals which they are pursuing. In this respect, they differ
little from the West Enders. The major difference—and it is an
important one—is that among the West Enders, person-orientation is based on a close association with the family circle and
the peer group which the individual maintains all his life, and
which is built into his personality structure. Middle-class people,
on the other hand, choose from a wider range of people the
individuals and groups with whom they spend their lives, remain somewhat more detached from them, and can even leave
them for others without serious feelings of loss.

This kind of middle-class person-orientation is perhaps similar to that which David Riesman and his associates have described as "other-direction," and which they have contrasted to
a striving for object-goals that they call "inner-direction." If
my hypothesis is correct, however—that object-orientation is
only a temporary phase for most people—the historical shift
from inner- to other-direction which they describe could be
interpreted differently.

Insofar as inner-direction is similar to what I have called
object-orientation, it would appear to be an infrequent, but
ever present, phenomenon, which accompanies individual mobility. Consequently, one might argue that it was neither as
prevalent in nineteenth-century America, nor as likely to disappear in the twentieth century, as the authors of *The Lonely
Crowd* have suggested. The historical evidence on this subject
is scattered and poor, and, indeed, most of what we know about
the past has come from people who made their mark in the
world. They were highly visible to contemporary observers and

historians precisely because they were pursuing some object-goal with fanatic determination. Such people continue to appear in American society today, although the inreased size and complexity of the society make it more difficult for them to operate as individual entrepreneurs. Today, moreover, they are likely to be heading a corporate board or executive committee, where they are somewhat less visible. The people who carried out the day-to-day operations that enabled the nineteenth-century entrepreneurs to succeed—and the pioneers who were in the center of the convoys of covered wagons that opened up the frontier—were surely less inner-directed or object-oriented than those at the head. Indeed, they probably functioned as part of a family circle or other group much as do the majority of twentieth-century Americans.

Object orientation is thus a minority pattern in any era, past or present. The professional upper-middle-class subculture, however, is particularly object-oriented, and does have a larger than average contingent of intensely mobile people. Moreover, it encompasses the intellectuals, who have a virtual monopoly on the public analysis and evaluation of society. Like all other subcultures, it tends to see the world from its own perspective. Therefore, it is particularly sensitive to the differences between itself and the rest of society, and much of the subculture's social analysis is concerned with examining these differences. For example, such distinctions as other-direction and inner-direction, local and cosmopolitan, person-orientation and object-orientation are in many ways dichotomies between "them" and "us." If they are not intended as such by their formulators, they are often interpreted in this way by the upper-middle-class subculture itself.

Moreover, much of its critique of the "mass society" proceeds from a value judgment that all people should live by the standards of this subculture. This critique bears some similarity to the peer group society's rejection of the outside world. In both cases, "they" are criticized for lacking "our" attributes. Yet there are also many differences between the two critiques. For example, while the peer group society rejects those who differ, upper-middle-class professionals encourage them to give up their differences and to adopt the principal behavior patterns and values of the upper-middle-class subculture.

The programs that professionals have developed to achieve this aim are intended to make people object-oriented. . . . the missionary caretakers' stress on self-development, on cultural achievement, and on activity as an end in itself is based on the identification of object-orientation with middle-class culture. This object-orientation can be found not only in the goals of the settlement house and public library, which I described earlier, but also in those of public recreation, the community center movement, public education, adult education, the mental health movement, the good government movement, and a host of other public, semipublic, and philanthropic endeavors.

It now becomes possible to understand why so many of these movements have had relatively little success in converting clients, not only among the West Enders, and in other working- and lower-class neighborhoods, but in middle-class ones as well. They have attempted to make people object-oriented simply by attracting them to their facilities, and hoping that their participation in agency programs and contact with agency staff might result in conversion through a kind of osmosis. They have failed, however, to provide the social and economic opportunities that encourage the object-oriented response, and they have vastly underestimated the difficulty of the change from person- to object-orientation. Most of the successful conversions have taken place among young people who have left home and family emotionally, and who have developed surrogate relations with caretakers, be these settlement house workers, librarians, or youth group leaders. But if the number of people who are ready to leave their families is small, so is the number of trained workers who can function effectively as surrogate parents or siblings. The caretakers' success with the mobile Jewish youngsters earlier in the century must probably be attributed to qualities within the Jewish subculture which predisposed the children to object-orientation at home before they arrived at the caretaking institution. These predispositions, however, are not to be found among most of the children from other European ethnic groups or from Negro and Puerto Rican populations who have subsequently come into the schools and settlement houses.

THE EVALUATION OF WORKING- AND LOWER-CLASS SUBCULTURES

. . . I believe the working-class subculture to be a generally satisfactory way of adapting to the opportunities which society has made available. Even so, it does have a number of negative features that constitute disadvantages both to working-class people and to the larger society.

One of these is the inability to participate in formal organizations and in general community activity. Although the lack of interest in voluntary associations is relatively unimportant, the inability to organize per se deprives working-class people of a method of political representation that is very important in a pluralistic society. Generally less well represented in the political arena than the economically more powerful, and socially more skillful groups, they are thus hampered in expressing their point of view, and in defending their interests. Consequently, they delegate the political representation function to others, yet only at some cost. Urban political machines and labor unions defend their interests, but the leadership of these organizations is not always fully representative. Moreover, when these agencies are not responsive, working-class people may turn to authoritarian and occasionally violent forms of protest—more out of desperation than choice. But such solutions are not always desirable or effective.

A related drawback is the general inability to understand bureaucratic behavior and object-orientation. This encourages the development of a conspiracy theory to explain the outside world, and breeds suspicions that are frequently inaccurate. As a result, the already existing gap between the working class and the larger society is widened.

Much of the time, the working class can protect itself from real or imagined injury by minimizing its dependence on the larger society. But this solution, which may work in prosperous times and in periods of social stability, is not always effective.

In depressions, emergencies, and periods of rapid social change, however, the many indirect relationships to the larger society become apparent, mainly as they are being interrupted or altered. It is at these times that normal methods of class conflict over the distribution of opportunities go awry, and the gap between the working class and the larger society—notably the government—threatens to become harmful to both. The former is hurt by its inability to understand and deal with the changes that are taking place; the latter, by its inability to develop methods to solve the resulting problems even when it wants to do so. This state of affairs was illustrated only too well by the redevelopment of the West End. . . . the West Enders could not defend their interests, and the redevelopment agency was unable to understand their needs. Similarly, as automation and other technological changes alter the labor market, and reduce the need for semiskilled and unskilled workers, the working-class subculture's detachment from the larger society hampers the adjustment to changing conditions. Fortunately, the belief in education as a means to occupational success has allowed many working-class people to train themselves for the new job types that are now needed, and the problem is not as severe as it is in the lower class.

Another disadvantage of the working-class subculture is its rejection of certain types of caretakers, especially those whose services cannot be provided by the family circle. I am thinking here especially of the unwillingness to use medical specialists and psychotherapists. Although such caretakers may treat their clients as if they were middle class—which explains why they are so often rejected even when cost is no problem—the health goals which they further are sought by the working class as much as by any other. The family circle does provide a considerable amount of advice and emotional support to its members, but not always of the right kind. Indeed, some forms of care cannot be given by laymen, especially if the latter share the patient's mistaken beliefs. In dealing with mental illness, for example, the aid given by the family circle can even be harmful.

Finally, the emphasis on group life, the low value placed

on privacy, and the general conservatism of the working-class culture all penalize those who deviate. For most people, this is no problem. Those who deviate by being mobile, for instance, are able to leave. But for people who are not mobile and who are different without wanting to be—such as those with neuroses that detach them from the group—the sanctions against deviance are harsh.

More intensive research of the dominant cultural patterns would undoubtedly indicate other patterns with deleterious consequences. For example, the impulsive child-rearing methods may have undesirable effects for some children who, for one reason or another, do not learn to cope with them. Only a highly detailed and longitudinal study of the subculture, however, will be able to unearth such patterns.

My limited observations suggest that, on the whole, the advantages of working-class subculture do outweigh the disadvantages. The latter are real, and ought to be removed, but they are not overwhelming. Thus, given our present knowledge, there is no justification for planning and caretaking programs which try to do away with the working-class subculture. John Seeley has suggested why it should not be done away with in his description of a Polish working-class group with whom he once lived:

> . . . no society I have lived in before or since seemed to me to present so many of its members . . . so many possibilities and actualities of fulfillment of a number at least of basic human demands: for an outlet for aggressiveness, for adventure, for a sense of effectiveness, for deep feelings of belonging without undue sacrifice of uniqueness or identity, for sex satisfaction, for strong if not fierce loyalties, for a sense of independence from the pervasive omnicompetent, omniscient authority-in-general which at that time still overwhelmed to a greater degree the middle-class child. . . . These things had their prices, of course—not all values can be simultaneously maximized. But few of the inhabitants whom I reciprocally took "slumming" into middle-class life understood it or, where they did, were at all envious of it. And, be it asserted, this was not a matter of "ignorance" or incapacity to "appreciate finer things," but an inability to see one moderately coherent and sense-making

satisfaction-system which they didn't know as preferable to the quite coherent and sense-making satisfaction-system they did know.

Although his evaluation puts the case a little more enthusiastically than I might, it says very well that working-class culture is a positive response to the opportunities and deprivations which it encounters.

This is not true, however, of the lower-class subculture. Like all other cultures, it too tries to cope with the existing opportunities and deprivations, and to make life as bearable as possible. That it fails to succeed is largely the result of the intense deprivations with which it is saddled. Moreover, the response to these deprivations has consequences which make it difficult for lower-class people to accept opportunities for improvement if and when they are available.

Although lower-class culture has innumerable problems, perhaps the basic one is occupational. It seems to produce people who can work only in unskilled jobs. These jobs, however, are becoming more and more scarce, and they may virtually disappear in the not so distant future—surely to no one's sorrow. But while lower-class women have developed working-class or quasi-working-class aspirations, the female-based family seems to raise men who find it difficult to develop the skills and the motivations that are necessary for obtaining and holding the jobs that will be available. In addition, these men are ambivalent about themselves and their role in society, and thus have considerable problems in achieving some sort of personal stability even when they want it, and even when they have gained some measure of economic stability. At present, then, lower-class culture breeds men who find it increasingly difficult to survive in modern society, and who, in a more automated future, will be unable to do so.

Lower-class women seem to be able to achieve some measure of stability—however problem-laden it may be—within and through the family. Even so, they are content neither with the subculture, nor with the female-based family, and try to see that their children escape it. This in itself suggests a major difference between the lower class and the other subcultures. The people within other subcultures are by and large satisfied with them and pass them on much more willingly to their children, at least to the extent that culture is ever transmitted deliberately. Lower-class women may not often succeed in raising their children to reject the culture they live in, but the mere fact that they try illustrates the absolute qualitative difference between the lower-class subculture and all the others.

There are more persuasive illustrations of this difference. Many lower-class children grow up in homes ravaged by alcoholism, drug addiction, and mental illness, and the subculture that they inherit is overlaid with pathology, for besides the comparatively more functional elements of lower-class subculture, there are many that are the results of pathological conditions, such as being raised by mentally ill parents. For example, many of the focal concerns of lower-class culture described by Walter Miller are useful methods of coping with the environment, but there are some forms of action-seeking that reflect desperation more than adaptation. The episodes of riotous pleasure do not make up for the depression and self-destruction that accompany them. Significantly, the lower class not only has higher rates of mental illness than the others, but these rates are considerably higher than those of the working class. Indeed, the difference in rates between these two classes is so great as to suggest that many elements of lower-class life are not merely culturally different from other ways of life, but that they are in fact pathological.

"Our culture is patterned in conflicts that in part mirror
the struggle between the puritan ethic and the demands
of an industrializing society of abundance."

George Spindler

THE TRANSMISSION OF
AMERICAN CULTURE*

George Spindler

Spindler is one of a growing number of anthropologists who are turning their attention to the culture of
the school. In this thoughtful report, he traces the
value conflict one often finds in the slum school to
what happens during teacher training to the values
the future teacher brings with him into the college.
The same caution necessary to one's application of
Gans' generalization obviously applies here as well;
not all teachers share what Spindler describes as a
traditionalist value system, and not all of those who
train them accept emergent values. It is valuable to
compare Spindler's emergent type with the values
Gans assigns to the upper-middle professionals, and

* From George D. Spindler, "Education in a Transforming American
Culture," *Harvard Educational Review*, 25, Summer 1955, 145–56. Re-
printed by permission of Harvard University Press. Copyright © 1959 by
President and Fellows of Harvard College.

the traditionalist with those he describes as generally middle class. It is useful, too, to examine one's own values in relation to his typology and consider whether one has ever adopted any of the kinds of adjustment he describes. Educators might consider the question:

> *Which of the two types of values Spindler describes would be most useful for working with disadvantaged children? Why?*

THE AMERICAN CULTURE is notable for the conflicts woven into the very fabric of its value system, which is the core of any culture. For example, we appear to believe in the value of thrift, but believe even more strongly in the value of keeping up good appearances that depend upon mortgages and installment payments that strain our budgets. We believe in deferring satisfactions to the future but want the benefits of deferment now. We believe that success is to be won by hard work, but emphasize personality and social contacts as alternative techniques. We laud honesty as a virtue but acknowledge the need for pragmatic expediency in real life. We are egalitarian in ideal and in much of our practice but indulge in wide-ranging expressions of invidious prejudices. We deny sexuality but are titillated by sex in our mass media, dress, and imagery.

There are many more such internal contradictions in our valuing system, but these suffice as examples. Our culture is patterned in conflicts that in part mirror the struggle between the puritan ethic and the demands of an industrializing society of abundance.

Convinced that educators-in-training needed to know more about these kinds of conflicts in our culture so that they could come to some resolution of them in their teaching, I began in 1952 to administer some simple value-projective techniques to my education classes. The two basic techniques were open-ended sentences, such as "The individual is _____ _____," "All men are born _____ _____," "Intellectuals should _____ _____," and a request that the students write a brief paragraph describing their concept of the "Ideal American Boy."

Each year since then I have analyzed the responses to these techniques from the hundred or more students in the new classes, using a form of content analysis, and have integrated the data into a treatment of education in American culture for my course lectures. What started as a pedagogical technique has become also a research project of modest dimensions. Some of the results are reported in an article published in the *Har-*

vard Educational Review.[1] I want to summarize the salient features of these results, both to underline the concept of patterned conflict in values in our culture and to establish the framework for a step in analysis that I will need to take later.

Brief examples of the content of the responses to these techniques are necessary. In response to the item, "Intellectuals should _____ _____," 40 per cent of the respondents wrote "be more sociable, more practical, more down to earth"; 20 per cent wrote, "keep it under cover, drop dead, shut up"; 30 per cent said, "apply their intellect, study, create, think." Approximately the same results issued from a similar item on college professors, though a new category emerged—that they should "not be boring." In response to the item, "The individual is _____ _____," 60 per cent of the respondents wrote "all-important, sacred, supreme"; 20 per cent wrote, "unique, independent"; 10 per cent wrote "a part of the group or the community."

Analysis of the content of the Ideal American Boy paragraphs produced a definite pattern of character values. The rank order of these values from most to least frequently mentioned is as follows: He should be sociable, well-rounded, athletic (but not an athlete), healthy, popular, clean-cut, ambitious to succeed, and considerate of others. Leadership, independence, high intelligence, high academic ability rank low in comparison to these first items. The keynote of the valued character type is balance and an outward orientation. The *social* attributes are most highly valued. Individuality, creativity are not stressed. Deviation is tolerated only within narrow limits of sociability and activistic orientation. It is clear that even with respect to trends in the sample as a whole, and without regard to patterns in individual protocols, there are certain contradictions between responses to the open-ended sentences and the content of the projective paragraphs.

Through an analysis of individual protocols, including both responses to the open-ended items and the paragraphic pro-

1. George D. Spindler, "Education in a Transforming American Culture," *Harvard Educational Review*, Vol. 25, pp. 146–156, Summer 1955.

jection, it became clear that there were essentially two basic types of value systems represented in my sample of nearly six hundred students. One of them I have labeled "traditional," the other, "emergent." The traditional pattern includes values placed upon thrift, self-denial, delay of satisfactions to the future (and a belief that there will be one), strong emphasis on success and a belief that the means to it is hard work, a belief in absolute morals and elevation of the *individual* as an end rather than the group. The emergent pattern includes values placed upon sociability, sensitivity to the feelings and needs of others, a relativistic attitude toward moral norms, a present-time orientation that reflects uncertainty about the future and includes a certain kind of hedonism, and an elevation of the harmony of the group as an end (rather than the individual) that subsumes at least resignation to group conformity.

It is apparent that these two patterns of values are internally consistent and that they are diametrically opposed. The probability of their widespread existence helps to account for many of the public and private arguments between individuals and groups in our society and is reflected in many of the current attacks on our educational system by the public. There is evidence that educational philosophy and, to a lesser extent, practice, particularly in the elementary schools, approach the emergent typology in value orientation more closely than do the statements of the attackers, who sound, in general, like traditionalists.

For my last example of direct transmission of obvious but culturally patterned contradictions, I would like to cite briefly from one of my own case studies of teachers and their classrooms. Later on I will describe a more complex situation.

The cultural transmitter in this case was a highly respected teacher in a large elementary school, who had certain duties as a counselor. He originated from a respectable immigrant family and had improved his social status during his lifetime by becoming a schoolteacher. The particular situation from which I have extracted certain verbatim records to follow was one of the "rites of passage" that occur now and then throughout the educational life cycle of children. The students in the eighth grade were being prepared for the choice of programs in high school and were making out proposed study lists under his guidance. The class group consisted of thirty-five children, twenty-four of whom were Mexican-Americans. The range of scores on the California Mental Maturity test was 80 to 120, with a median of 102. There was a broadly corresponding variety of reading and academic achievement represented in the group. I will present a few items from the verbal interaction of the teacher-counselor and the students.

T: You must be a good citizen, or they won't accept you. Now, what do you need to get into Orthodox State College? (*Children raise hands, repeat answers previously learned.*) What do you need to get into Junior College? (*Students respond likewise.*)

T: In arranging your programs for next year, there are certain things that everyone must take, so we'll just put them down. You will all take P.E., English, and Social Studies. (*Teacher writes these down on the board opposite numbers 1, 2, and 3.*) Now you have to decide whether you want to take Algebra or not. You have to take math all the way through high school if you want to be an engineer. Now, if you've gotten B's and C's all the way through eighth grade, what are your chances of doing well in ninth-grade Algebra? (*Students murmur various things.*) That's right! Not so good! So what can you do?

S: Try to raise your grade.

T: Yes.

S: Work harder.

T: That's one thing. But what else? . . . Do like I did when I wanted to be a singer but found I couldn't sing. What did I do? Yes . . . that's right; I changed my plans. . . . With respect to language, how many here speak Spanish? (*Six of the Mexican-Americans raised their hands, but all speak some Spanish.*) It will help you if you do. But you have to realize that there is some work to do—homework! It is good to take Spanish if you want to go on to college and need a language. But you can't take Spanish and General Business. They come at the same period.

Now, one of the things you have to do is to be neat and orderly. If you aren't good at that it might be hard for you until you learn to do it better.

T: Now here we have Mechanical Drawing. This is exclusively a boy's class. I don't know why some girls couldn't take it if they wanted to. But only boys take it. Now Home-making is for girls, so you can take that.

T: Now when you come to see me, if I tell you to take General Business instead of Spanish, it should be understood that you don't have to take it. You can do as you wish. But it means that I think you will do better in General Business. (*Several more subject choices are covered.*)

T: And here is typing. It looks interesting when you pass the typing room, doesn't it? But do you know there aren't any letters on those keyboards? You have to watch a chart at the front of the room, and if you look at the keyboard, you fail!

Of course a great deal more went on during this hour of counseling. I have purposefully selected those verbal items that constitute the most clear indications of bias in cultural transmission. And this is always unfair to the cultural transmitter. But I believe the extracted items accurately reveal persistent trends in his counseling of the mixed Mexican-American and Anglo groups in the eighth grade.

After this particular class session, the teacher-counselor said, "This is a passive group. There is no spark in there. The better groups get quite excited about this. Of course, most of the better groups are college-preparatory and perhaps only three or four of these students will go to college." Previous to the session, in his statement of educational philosophy, he had commented, "I believe that our job is to make the most of the potential of each child. Of course there is a wide range of ability among our students. A good many of them will never go on to college. And we have to do the best we can to help them on to a satisfactory adjustment."

I propose that he was defeating his own aims in the way he handled this crucial rite of passage, this point of compression in the relation of the child and his culture where choices made affect future development decisively. He opened the gates to valued channels of development and then shut them in the children's faces. And he did not open the gates to any alternative channels. What he transmitted, it seems to me, was that the only worthwhile goal was to go to college so that one could become an engineer or something equivalent, that if the child did not have the necessary qualifications there was no other dignified and worthy choice, and that most of the members of this class group did not have the necessary qualifications.

I would be less concerned if I thought this person were a small, mean individual with explicit prejudices, and if I thought he were not concerned with making the most of the potential of each child. But he is not small and mean. He is a generous, well-intended person, and believes in democratic opportunity. In his counseling he projects his own struggle to improve his status, mirrors the discrepancy in our culture between ideal and real in the definition of opportunity, and inadvertently defeats his own professed aims.

THE ACCULTURATION OF
THE SCHOOL TEACHER

What I hope has been established so far is that our culture is one in which conflicts in values, and between goals and the means to them, are present and patterned. And that teachers, as cultural transmitters, convey these patterned conflicts to children in their classrooms, with the consequence that many professed goals are defeated, or at least obscured. I hope that it is also clear that I have not been castigating teachers. They are the agents of their culture.

A further step must be taken if we are to see the full meaning and scope of the problem. Teachers are a special group. They are not selected at random as official culture transmitters; they are trained and accredited to that status and role. They must take courses in educational psychology, the social foundations of education, curriculum design, philosophy and history of education, the methods of education, and must do supervised practice teaching. In short, they must attend teacher-training institutions and graduate with the stamp of approval from the established professional cadre. But professional educational instruction and training consist not alone of courses and training in techniques. Every institution with a history and internal organization, and a specialized personnel, has a culture—or, more properly, a subculture. Certain values, symbols, beliefs and certain basic premises are patterned into the structure and process of the institution. The institutions of professional education—the teacher-training schools and the literature of education—are no exception.

What I am going to try to say now may be misunderstood. I am going to state some generalizations about the subculture of education. Some of my educational colleagues will disagree, but objectively. Others will disagree and be offended. Some will agree and approve. Others will agree but be unhappy about doing so.

I must refer back to the traditional and emergent value patterns revealed in the responses of education students to the values projection techniques. You will remember that the traditional pattern included emphasis on thrift, self-denial, faith in the future, a strong emphasis on success and a belief that hard work was the means to it, absolute moral norms, and a strong value placed upon the individual as an end. The emergent pattern included value placed upon sociability, sensitivity to the feelings of others, a relativistic attitude, a present-time orientation, and high value placed upon the group. The modal type of person with respect to these dichotomous value patterns is a mixed type that embraces values from both in varying degrees of coherence.

I believe that many of the conflicts between school boards and educational personnel, between parents and teachers, and between teachers and pupils can be seen as projections of differences in value commitments that represent various approximations to the traditional and emergent positions. But the dynamic process of greatest relevance to us at the moment is the relationship between the culture that the elementary-school teacher brings to the professional teacher-training institution subculture and the patterning of that subculture, the adaptation that the teacher-in-training makes to this patterning, and the consequences in selective culture transmission in the class-room.

This is a complex relationship with many subtle ramifications. I must dissect it with bold and clumsy slashes rather than precise incisions. It is well established that school teachers originate from a middle and lower-middle social class culture. I believe that it can also be demonstrated that the value pattern that I have termed "traditional" is found in this cultural context in its most purely puritanic form. To the extent this is so, it means that whatever selective processes are operating tend to bring many people of traditionalistic value orientation into teacher-training.

The question that the anthropologist raises is "What are the characteristics of the subculture of the teacher-training institution to which these students bring their traditionalist orientations?" Analysis of a sample of some of the influential literature of curriculum design for elementary education reveals that there is present a strong values bias that fits in general terms the "emergent" pattern. The literature of child development and educational psychology reveals some of the same trends. Interpretations of the social behavior of boys and girls, intended for educational consumption, provide both implicit and explicit value judgments in the same pattern. The popularity of sociometric techniques is diagnostic of this orientation. The topical content of many of our teacher-training courses suggests it as well.

The basic premise underlying the superstructure of specific emergent values is that what is most important is the social adjustment of the child. His place in the group, the responses of his peers to him, his ability to get along well, to work and play with others are penultimate concerns. I personally do not regard this as all bad. The emphasis on social adjustment is the educator's attempt to meet the demands of a new kind of society, where this kind of adjustment is of vital importance. When balanced by a concern for individual differences, support for the deviating child, for intellectual development and the acquiring of cognitive skills, and when it does not become a form of "groupism," this emphasis on social adjustment is a necessary compensation for what I regard as many of the harshly competitive, egocentric patterns of our culture.

But the point is that however understandable and useful the emphasis may be, this pattern of values incorporated in the ethos of professional education may be at variance with what the new teacher in training brings into the situation. The neophyte in training must reorient his value system wherever the conflict in values is encountered.

This places many new teachers in training in a situation similar to that of acculturating populations all over the world. These populations are attempting to rechannel their emotional and intellectual commitments as they adapt to conflicts between their indigenous culture and the new culture diffused to them or appropriated by them. Anthropological studies of such populations provide the models for characterizations of adaptive consequences for teachers that I wish to make now, but these models are rebuilt in terms of empirical case studies of teachers in classrooms.

When acculturating teachers in training or people in any other acculturating group adapt to sharply disjunctive value systems, essentially four adaptive responses may occur. The individual meets the new value system and feels threatened because it challenges his established, familiar, and comfortable values. He does not, of course, necessarily interpret the experience in these terms. He is more likely to see it as a personal conflict, which heightens the threat. After some exploration in the new dimensions of feeling and belief offered to him by the opposing system, his feeling of threat overcomes him and he seeks refuge in the comforting shelter of his established values. But something has changed. He has been driven back to his "native state" by threat. Therefore he overcompensates, and rigidifies the original system in what may be psychologically termed a reaction formation, or culturally termed a "nativistic reaffirmation." I would call him a "reaffirmative traditionalist" in the framework of this analysis. The teacher of this type will tend to be rigid in his uncompromising projection of traditional values in his classroom behavior.

An alternative adaptive response is represented by the person who encounters the new value system which is sharply disjunctive with his own, likewise feels threatened by the conflict in personal terms, but adapts by overcompensating in the direction of the new system. Perhaps he is more threatened by the possibility of being left behind or out of step than he is by the requirement to change. He uncritically appropriates the new values in their entirety and frequently becomes a strident proselytizer for them. This kind of teacher I term a "compensatory emergentist." His channels of communication with children, and his criteria for their behavior, become narrowed to individual-in-harmony-with-the-group. "Groupism" reigns in his classroom. Individualistic differences and deviations become smothered by group conformity.

The third alternative adaptive response is exhibited by the person who encounters the conflict of value systems and superficially internalizes segments of both but does not rework them into any coherent synthesis. He is a mixed type but quite different from a type that I shall describe shortly. He is usually not particularly thoughtful about the conflicts he encounters and leaves them unresolved, but still a part of his acquired culture. This person as a teacher is likely to vacillate between different modes of group leadership and different modes of interaction with individual children. Obvious discontinuities in his classroom management cause trouble for both him and his students. I term his type, the "vacillator."

The fourth alternative is a happier one than the others. This person comes into the acculturative situation with a capacity for adjustment to differences in values and conflicts between them. Usually he is thoughtful and has the ability to combine useful features from more than one system of belief on a rational basis. He does not need to overcompensate as a defense against conflict because he is not threatened by it. He is a mixed type but does not internalize the mixture segmentally. He recombines the aspects from both systems into a creatively coherent synthesis. I have labeled this an "adjusted" type.

As a matter of fact I believe increasing numbers of students in our senior and graduate education classes are of this latter type. They exhibit workable combinations of what seem to be the best of both the emergent and traditional values. For instance, they accept the need of the individual to be a member of the group but believe that the individual must be self-possessed and self-actualized in order to be a useful participant in any group. They believe that hard work is necessary for success but that there is no point in being unpleasant about it. Whether they represent a shift in the kind of training they receive in the school of education, or whether they represent a change in the culture of generations, or both, I do not know. In any event, I am happy to see them and hope their numbers increase, for I am convinced that large numbers of teachers, at least new ones, are reaffirmative traditionalists, compensatory emergentists, or vacillators.

I make a value judgment here because it seems clear to me that teachers falling into the first two adaptive categories tend to exhibit highly selective biases as culture transmitters. They transmit in narrow channels with few alternatives, due to their reactive rigidity. Without intending to do so, they open some doors to self-cultivating developments for some children but lock them for many others. And the vacillator, though he is not rigid and transmits along many channels, issues only weak signals and produces little but static as a result.

"... an down on the floor these men was running aroun
with little bits of paper an yellin like they was a
rumble on."

THE FIELD TRIP *
Warren Miller

In his novel *The Cool World* Warren Miller tells the
story of an adolescent boy in Harlem and his rise to
the leadership of his gang. Duke is engaged throughout most of the novel in proving himself by getting
a gun for the gang to use in its fights, the "piece"
referred to in this excerpt. The story of the class field
trip not only serves to illustrate the theoretical value
materials in the preceding articles, but also is a caustic expression of the total alienation of the slum child
from the school and its values. The boys' attitude
toward the teacher and trip is not hostile; Duke

* From Warren Miller, *The Cool World*, New York: Crest Books, 1964,
pp. 9, 15–17. Copyright © 1959 by Warren Miller, reprinted by permission
of Little, Brown and Co., Publishers.

seems to like Mr. Shapiro. They simply are indifferent to his purposes and involved in this own affairs.

Miller seems to be saying in this chapter, and in the novel as a whole, that what is valuable about the world of the gang is that the boys find status and recognition in it. If he is correct, what can the school do to substitute for it?

THREE BIG BUSES lined up waitin. Mister Shapiro say "Custis. Summer. You almost missed the outing. Line up now boys."

We go to the bus with a card stuck to the door sayin

8TH GRADE

MR. SHAPIRO

an we got on. Handy savin me a seat up front. "You get it?" He say. And then the others stick they faces over the back of my seat. "You get it Duke?" They all asking.

Mr. Shapiro get on the bus. He say. "All right boys. Now I know we are going to enjoy this trip."

So we go down to Wall Street that day Mister Shapiro he took us. Shapiro is okay he aint always yellen at us like the rest of them. Some of the teachers tell you. "Stay out. Dont come to school an we wont report you. You co operate with me an I will co operate with you." They dont want to be bothered. Mister Shapiro he aint like that. A little man. He look worried all the time. Got lines in his forhead like they been cut in.

First we went to the George Washington Museum. It has this big statue of him out front. The place where we went was the cellar of this building where they got cases full of things from histry. Mister Shapiro he lead us around explainin this an that. Histry make Mister Shapiro get all hopped up you know. He say. "Think of it boys where you standen right now maybe the Father of our Country once stood." Evrybody look down at they feet.

Handy and Summer an me was in the back an all they talken about was the piece. Handy say. "Shitman you get yourself a piece you gonna be President of the Crocadiles. Aint no doubt about that."

"Where you hear that?" I ask him.

He just shrug. He just shrug. "Hear it around." He say. "Blood is getten old. He gonna be 20 soon. He cant swing with the gang for ever. Time he moved up."

Summer say to me. "Whut kind of piece you say it was Duke man?" Summer talk like a big shot because his father a big man in the numbers.

I tell him it was a Colt.

"Birettas is better." Summer say.

Handy say. "Dint Priest spread the word whut he had was a Biretta?"

"That whut he say. But whut he got is a Colt." I tell them.

"I like the Biretta my self." Summer say.

"Biretta the best Duke." Handy tell me. "That is one sweet piece the Biretta."

"I like the Biretta." Summer say.

"Biretta is for women." I tell them.

"Now hold on Man." Summer say. "Now jus a minute. Lemme tell you something Man. Colt dont have the improvements Man. Why shitman them Colts is the same motheren piece they was usen at Cussers Last Stan."

Then Handy get into it. Like he knew whut he talken about you know. He say. "The man is right."

"Improvements." I say. "Shitman you can take those improvements. I want a piece I can be sure of. Colt is sure. Lemme ask you somethin Man lemme ask you somethin. Why you think the headbreakers usen a Colt if it no good? Let me ask you that Summer? Man you got Biretta on the brain. You dont have the bread to buy a cap pistol an all you talken is Biretta."

"The Man is right." Handy say. Meanin me. That I am right.

Summer say. "Shitman the reason headbreakers usen the Colt is because they dont know no better. Thats all."

Mister Shapiro he call us over. He tell us not to get lost an stay with the class. Then he say. "Just think boys. This is the place where George Washington tooken the Oath of Office an become our first president."

"Now whut do you think of that." Someone say.

Mister Shapiro dont pay no attention to him. He say. "Do you never think boys that they was a time this nation of ours was just *one day old?*"

"Jus a goddamn baby." Same person say. George Cadmus. Mister Shapiro know but he dont pay any atention. He talken about how rough things was in the old days. Man it was rough at Valley Forge an places like that he tellin us.

Then we walk aroun an look at the sords an things like that from histry an then Mister Shapiro tooken us across the street to the stock exchange. They got these little streets down in that part of town. On one corner they was a man a white man wearin a derby hat tellin a crowd of people about the Bible an they was hecklin him. He was standin on a box with the American Flag painted on it. Some of the guys lit up butts while we was crossin the street an Mister Shapiro made out like he dint notice.

We went into this big bilding then an befor we got on the elevator Mister Shapiro made evrybody throw away his butts. He knew we was smoken. Then we went up to the stock exchange an looked at the exibits about the City of the Future. These rocket ships kept flyin back an forth over it. They were on wires you could see the wires. An the City of the Future it was jus a big housing projeck. If you wanted to know whut it all about they had these phones an you could listen in.

When you picked up the phone you could hear this TV announcer tellin you how much steel they gonna need to bild the City of the Future. George Cadmus was breaken evrybody up. He standen there with the phone saying things like. "Uh huh. You dont say Man. Well uh listen Man how things in Pittsberg?" Like this TV announcer was talken to him.

Then we looked at other exibits about tires an aluminum and then we went inta this big room. We was up on a little balcony an down on the floor these men was running aroun with little bits of paper an yellin like they was a rumble on. Hangin on the wall was the biggest American Flag I ever see any where.

Then it was time for the movie and we all went in to this little movie and saw a movie about America. It show rivers an factories & farms & mountains & a workinman in a blue shirt buyin stocks. Flash Gordon he was sittin in front of me slash the back of a seat with his blade and all the stuffin started fallin out. An Lonesome Pine unscrewed the arm of his chair with a dime. When the lights went on we made a lot of noise and Mister Shapiro hussled us out an never noticed the damage.

On the way out they give us these little books about how

we could own a Share of America an about how to orginize a club an buy these stocks.

When we got out to the street the bus driver threw his butt away and he say. "All right. This bus was hire for 2 hours and the time is up." An he got in an drive off. Mister Shapiro took us back up town on the subway.

So that was the last day of school an summer started.

". . . he necessarily looks with . . . disapproval and vexation on the lusty, irrepressible, boisterous young-sters who are destructive of order, routine and predict-ability in the classroom."

THE BOTTOM OF THE HEAP: PROBLEMS OF THE WORKING-CLASS BOY*

Albert Cohen

In this excerpt from his book *Delinquent Boys,* Cohen generalizes about the school problem that lies be-neath the surface of Duke's field trip. The book it-self is a classic exposition of what one might call the "group theory" of delinquency, which holds that any group confronting status deprivation develops shared norms for coping with it. The values of the delin-quent subculture is such a set of norms, and because membership, and therefore one's status, depends on

* From Albert Cohen, *Delinquent Boys,* New York: The Free Press, 1960, pp. 109–19. Copyright © 1955, reprinted by permission of The Free Press.

whether one shares the norms, they are far more potent and attractive than the conflicting values which the school sets out to transmit.

Cohen here views the school as one setting in which lower-class children must compete with middle-class children, almost inevitably committed to failure in such a competition by their backgrounds. If he is correct, what implications can one draw from the fact for the school's attempts to develop middle-class attitudes in all children? Does it necessarily mean that schools would be better off if they were restricted to a narrow range of social class?

FIRST and most obviously, the working-class child shares the social class status of his parents. In the status game, then, the working-class child starts out with a handicap and, to the extent that he cares what the middle-class persons think of him or has internalized the dominant middle-class attitudes toward social class position, he may be expected to feel some "shame." Margaret Mead has put the point with characteristic trenchancy if somewhat dubious melodrama:

> Shame is felt perhaps most strongly over the failures of other people, especially one's parents, who have not been successful, who have not worked hard enough to have an inside bathroom or an automobile or to send one to a private school, to live on the right street, or go to the right church. As class is an expression of economic success, then it follows that to belong as a child or an adolescent to a class below others is a statement that one's parents have failed, they did not make good. This is bad enough when they have not risen, unbearable if they have started to fall even lower. Deeper than our disapproval of any breaking of the Ten Commandments lies our conviction that a failure to keep moving is an unforgiveable sin.[1]

Furthermore, people of status tend to be people of power and property. They have the means to make more certain that their children will obtain respect and other rewards which have status significance even where title in terms of deserving middle-class conduct is dubious. Hollingshead, in his *Elmtown's Youth*, stresses throughout the importance of parental status in obtaining special consideration in school activities and on the job through "connections" and other means of exerting pressure. Finally, parents of good standing in the class system can usually provide their children with money, clothes, cars, homes and other material amenities which not only function as external trappings and insignia of status, but which serve also as means and avenues to activities and relationships which

1. Margaret Mead, *And Keep Your Powder Dry*, New York: Murrow, 1942, p. 197.

confer status. Like his parents, a child is unlikely to be invited to participate in activities which require a material apparatus he cannot afford; if invited, he is less likely to accept for fear of embarrassment; and if he accepts, he is less likely to be in a position to reciprocate and therefore to sustain a relationship premised on a certain amount of reciprocity. It seems reasonable to assume that out of all this there arise feelings of inferiority and perhaps resentment and hostility. It is remarkable, however, that there is relatively little research explicitly designed to test this assumption.

However, invidious status distinctions among young people are, after all, a result of individual differences in conformity to a set of conduct norms as well as simple functions of their parents' social status. Havighurst and Taba in their *Adolescent Character and Personality* have shown that variations in "character reputation" scores cannot be explained simply as a result of social class membership. The existence of "achieved" as well as "ascribed" criteria of status for children makes it possible for some working-class children to "rise above" the status to which the social class position of their parents would otherwise consign them. However, this does not make the situation psychologically any easier for those of their brethren who remain behind, or rather, below. Low achieved status is no pleasanter than low ascribed status, and very likely a good deal more unpleasant for reasons we have indicated earlier; it reflects more directly on the *personal* inadequacy of the child and leaves him with fewer convenient rationalizations.

One of the situations in which children of all social levels come together and compete for status in terms of the same set of middle-class criteria and in which working-class children are most likely to be found wanting is in the school. American educators are enamored of the idea of "democracy" as a goal of the schools. An examination of their writings reveals that "democracy" signifies "the fullest realization of the individual's potentialities," "the development of skills to an optimal level," "the development of character and abilities which can be admired by others," "preparation for effective participation in the adult vocational world."[2] Despite reservations such as "with due regard to individual differences," this conception of "democratic" education implies that a major function of the schools is to "promote," "encourage," "motivate," "stimulate," in brief, *reward* middle-class ambition and conformity to middle-class expectations. However sincerely one may desire to avoid odious comparisons and to avoid, thereby, injury to the self-esteem of those who do not conform to one's expectations, it is extremely difficult to reward, however subtly, successful conformity without at the same time, by implication, condemning and punishing the non-conformist. That same teacher who prides himself on his recognition and encouragement of deserving working-class children dramatizes, by that very show of pride, the superior merit of the "college-boy" working-class child to his less gifted or "corner-boy" working-class classmates.[3]

There are three good reasons why status in the school, insofar as it depends upon recognition by the teacher, should be measured by middle-class standards.

First, the teacher is *hired* to foster the development of middle-class personalities. The middle-class board of education, the middle-class parents whom they represent and, it is to be presumed, many of the working-class parents as well expect the teacher to define his job as the indoctrination of middle-class aspirations, character, skills and manners.[4]

2. See, for example, the following statements by educators: Elizabeth M. Fuller, Helen Christianson, Nelth Heedly *et al.*, "Practices and Resources in Early Childhood Education," in *The Forty-Sixth Yearbook of the National Society for the Study of Education*, Part II, Chicago: University of Chicago Press, 1947, pp. 103–105, and Samuel Smith, George R. Cressman and Robert K. Speer, *Education and Society: An Introduction to Education for a Democracy*, New York: Dryden, 1942, pp. 154–5.

3. On the mental hygiene implications of failure in conforming to teacher expectations, see Fritz Redl and William W. Wattenberg, *Mental Hygiene in Teaching*, New York: Appleton, 1940, pp. 245–7; and an excellent short article by Roger G. Barker, "Success and Failure in the Classroom," in Wayne Dennis (ed.), *Readings in Child Psychology*, New York: Prentice-Hall, 1951, pp. 577–82, reprinted from an article in *Progressive Education*, XIX, 1942, pp. 221–4.

4. W. Lloyd Warner, Robert J. Havighurst, and Martin B. Loeb, *Who

Second, the teacher himself is almost certain to be a middle-class person, who personally values ambition and achievement and spontaneously recognizes and rewards these virtues in others.[5]

The third relates to the school itself as a social system with certain "structural imperatives" of its own. The teacher's textbooks in education and his own supervisors may stress "individualization" and "consideration for the needs, limitations and special problems of each student." Nonetheless, the teacher actually handles 20, 30 or 40 students at a time. Regardless of what he conceives his proper function to be, he necessarily looks with favor on the quiet, cooperative, "well-behaved" pupils who make his job easier and with disapproval and vexation on the lusty, irrepressible, boisterous youngsters who are destructive of order, routine and predictability in the classroom. Furthermore, the teacher himself is likely to be upwardly mobile or at least anxious about the security of his tenure in his present job. He is motivated, therefore, to conform to the criteria in terms of which *his* superiors evaluate *him*. Those

---

Shall Be Educated? New York: Harper, 1944, is an excellent discussion of the way in which school policy is shaped by middle-class values. The functions of teachers, they say, are two: "They train or seek to train children in middle-class manners and skills. And they select those children from the middle and lower classes who appear to be the best candidates for promotion in the social hierarchy" (p. 107). A public-school superintendent, critical of current guidance philosophy, states: "Boards of Education and Parent-Teacher Associations are invariably Calvinists. . . . They believe that a Director of Guidance in the high school will be able to elevate every student, that is, to lead him into some pleasant and dignified occupation, to guide him so that his will not be a life of toil or manual work or degrading forms of labor. A school with a real guidance program should raise all pupils to a high social and economic position." Ernest W. Butterfield, "Our White-Collar Guidance Psychology," *The Clearing House,* XIII, May 1939, p. 516.

5. Percival M. Symonds, "Personality Adjustment of Women Teachers," *American Journal of Orthopsychiatry,* XI, January 1941, p. 15, comments, on the basis of a study of 50 biographies of women teachers: "It is because the need for achievement is so strong among teachers that competition is used as a motivating force so widely in schools. The teacher with strong drive for achievement is likely to overestimate the bright, and show unjust discrimination against the dull and failing."

superiors may themselves be "progressive" and in teacher meetings preach "democracy in the classroom" and "individualization" and indeed genuinely believe in those goals. However, the degree to which a teacher tries to achieve these goals or succeeds in doing so is not highly visible and readily determined. On the other hand, grades, performance on standardized examinations, the cleanliness and orderliness of the classroom and the frequency with which children are sent to the "front office" are among the most easily determined and "objective" bases for the evaluation of teacher performance. A good "rating," then, by his supervisors is possible only if the teacher sacrifices to some degree the very "individualization" and "tolerance" which those same supervisors may urge upon him.

Research on the kinds of behavior which teachers regard as the most "problematical" among their pupils gives results consistent with our expectations.[6] The most serious problems, from the standpoint of the teacher, are those children who are restless and unruly, who fidget and squirm, who annoy and distract, who create "discipline" problems. The "good" children are the studious, the obedient, the docile. It is precisely the working-class children who are most likely to be "problems" because of their relative lack of training in order and discipline, their lack of interest in intellectual achievement and their lack of reinforcement by the home in conformity to the requirements of the school. Both in terms of "conduct" and in terms of academic achievement, the failures in the classroom are drawn disproportionately from the lower social class levels. The child has little or no choice in selecting the group within which he shall compete for status and, in the words of Troyer,

6. The best study is E. Koster Wickman, *Children's Behavior and Teachers' Attitudes,* New York: The Commonwealth Fund, 1928. The findings of later studies are consistent with Wickman's. See Harold H. Anderson, "The Construction of a Mental Hygiene Scale for Teachers," *American Journal of Orthopsychiatry,* X, April 1940, pp. 253–63, and Grace B. Cox and Harold H. Anderson, "A Study of Teachers' Responses to Problem Situations As Reported by Teachers and Students," *American Journal of Orthopsychiatry,* XIV, July 1944, pp. 528–44.

he is "evaluated against the total range of the ability distribution."

It is here that, day after day, most of the children in the
lower fourth of the distribution have their sense of worth
destroyed, develop feelings of insecurity, become frustrated
and lose confidence in their ability to learn even that which
they are capable of learning.[7]

In settlement houses and other adult-sponsored and managed recreational agencies similar conflicts may often be seen
between the middle-class values of the adults in charge and the
working-class values of the children for whose benefit the institutions ostensibly exist. Such organizations smile upon neat,
orderly, polite, personable, mannerly children who "want to
make something of themselves." The sponsors, directors and
group work leaders find it a pleasure to work with such children, whose values are so like their own, and make them feel
welcome and respected. They do indeed feel a special responsibility toward the boy whose family and neighborhood culture
have not equipped him with those values, the "rough" boy,
the "dirty" boy, the "bum" who just "hangs around" with the
gang on the corner, in the pool hall or in the candy store. But
the responsibility they feel toward him is to encourage him to
engage in more "worthwhile" activities, to join and to be a
"responsible" member of some "wholesome" adult-supervised
club or other group, to expurgate his language and, in general,
to participate in the "constructive" program of the institution.
Indeed, like the school, it functions to select potentially upwardly mobile working-class children and to help and encourage them in the upward climb. It is a common experience of
such organizations that they "are very successful and do a lot
of good but don't seem to get the children who need them
most." The reason is that here, as in the school, it is almost
impossible to reward one kind of behavior without at the same
time, by implication or quite openly, punishing its absence or

7. Maurice E. Troyer, "Squaring Evaluation Processes with Democratic Values," *American Council of Education Studies,* Series I, 34, January 1949, p. 42..

its opposite. The corner boy, as Whyte[8] has shown vividly and in detail, quickly senses that he is under the critical or at best condescending surveillance of people who are "foreigners" to his community and who appraise him in terms of values which he does not share. He is aware that he is being invidiously compared to others; he is uncomfortable; he finds it hard to accommodate himself to the rules of the organization. To win the favor of the people in charge he must change his habits, his values, his ambitions, his speech and his associates. Even were these things possible, the game might not be worth the candle. So, having sampled what they have to offer, he returns to the street or to his "clubhouse" in a cellar where "facilities" are meager but human relations more satisfying.

Not only in terms of standards of middle-class adults but in terms of their children's standards as well, the working-class boy of working-class culture is likely to be a "failure." Despite the existence among middle-class children of a "youth culture" which may differ in significant ways from the culture of their parents, the standards these children apply are likely to relegate to an inferior status their working-class peers. Coyle quotes from a fieldworker's report:

Gradually the group became more critical of prospective members. A process somewhat evident from the beginning became more obvious. In general only boys who measured up to the group's unwritten, unspoken and largely unconscious standards were ever considered. These standards, characteristic of their middle-class homes, required the suppression of impulsive disorderly behavior and put a high value on controlled cooperative attitudes. Hence even these normally healthy and boisterous boys were capable of rejecting schoolmates they considered too wild and boisterous. Coincident with this was an emphasis on intellectual capacity and achievement. They preferred "smart" as contrasted with "dumb" prospects. The

8. See William F. Whyte, *Street Corner Society*, Chicago: University of Chicago Press, 1943, *passim*, but especially pp. 98–104. See also E. L. Johnstone, "What Do Boys Think of Us—And Why?" *Proceedings of the American Prison Association*, 1944, New York: The American Prison Association, 1944, pp. 143–4.

boys seemed to use their club unconsciously to express and reinforce the standards learned in their homes and the community.[9]

Havighurst and Taba point out that not only teachers but schoolmates, in evaluating the character of other children, tend to give the highest ratings to the children of the higher social levels, although the correlation between social class and character reputation is far from perfect.[10] Positive correlations between various indices of social class status of the home and social status in the school as measured by pupils' choices have been found by Bonney and others.[11] Hollingshead has shown how social class and the behavior and personality associated with social class membership operate to determine prestige and clique and date patterns among high school boys and girls. "This process operates in all classes, but it is especially noticeable in contacts with class V [lower-lower]. This class is so repugnant socially that adolescents in the higher classes avoid clique and dating ties with its members."[12] Furthermore, working-class children are less likely to participate, and if they participate are less likely to achieve prominence, in extra-curricular activities, which are an important arena for the competition for status in the eyes of the students themselves. In the area of organized athletics the working-class boy is perhaps least unfitted for successful competition. Even here, however, he is likely to be at a disadvantage. Adherence to a training regimen and a schedule does not come to him as easily as to the middle-class boy and, unless he chooses to loosen his ties

9. Grace L. Coyle, *Group Work with American Youth, A Guide to the Practice of Leadership,* New York: Harper, 1948, p. 49.

10. Robert J. Havighurst and Hilda Taba, *Adolescent Character and Personality,* New York: Wiley, 1949, pp. 52–5.

11. Merl E. Bonney, "A Study of Social Status on the Second-Grade Level," *Journal of Genetic Psychology,* LX, June 1942, 271–305. See also Henry P. Smith, "A Study in the Selective Character of American Secondary Education: Participation in School Activities As Conditioned by Socio-Economic Status and Other Factors," *Journal of Educational Psychology,* XXXVI, April 1945, 229–46, and August B. Hollingshead, *Elmtown's Youth,* New York: Wiley, 1949, pp. 192–203.

12. Hollingshead, *op. cit.,* p. 241.

to his working-class friends, he is likely to find some conflict between the claims of the gang and those of his athletic career. Finally, although we must not minimize the importance of athletic achievement as a status-ladder, it is, after all, granted to relatively few, of whatever social class background, to achieve conspicuously in this area.[13]

In summary, it may confidently be said that the working-class boy, particularly if his training and values be those we have here defined as working-class, is more likely than his middle-class peers to find himself at the bottom of the status hierarchy whenever he moves in a middle-class world, whether it be of adults or of children. To the degree to which he values middle-class status, either because he values the good opinion of middle-class persons or because he has to some degree internalized middle-class standards himself, he faces a problem of adjustment and is in the market for a "solution."

13. There is tangible research evidence that, at least in the school area, low status is accompanied by maladjustment. Joel B. Montague, "Social Status and Adjustment in School," *Clearing House*, XXVII, September, 1952, 19–24, investigates the relationship between the adjustment of students and the students' own estimates of the status of their parents in the community. The lowest status group, in contrast to the middle and upper status groups, strikingly more often, in response to an attitude questionnaire, indicate that school is not interesting, the studies are too hard, they don't like their courses, they are not popular, they are left out of things, it is hard to make friends, they are unable to express themselves well, they can't seem to concentrate, there is not enough time to study. Onas Scandrette, "School—Through the Eyes of the Underchosen," in the same issue of *Clearing House*, pp. 35–37, compares the attitudes of children who are frequently chosen and those who are underchosen by their classmates to be members of a classroom project committee. The underchosen are much more likely to feel that teachers have little personal interest in their students, teachers are unfair, teachers are unkind, teachers are unfriendly, other students are unkind, association with the opposite sex is not enjoyable, school work is too hard.

"Instead of giving us what we need, they try to make
us be like them."

THE POOR DON'T WANT TO BE
MIDDLE CLASS*
Robert Coles

This article reports the views of the poor themselves,
not only about their needs but more particularly
about their opinions of those who undertake to plan
for them. Often those in charge of special programs
for educating, retraining, and housing the poor are
the same people the poor have perceived as their
oppressors, or, at best, as members of a power structure long indifferent to their needs. The legislation
establishing poverty programs under the Office of
Economic Opportunity specifies that many of these
programs must include the poor themselves in their
planning and operation. Schools in urban slums
rarely have substantial representation of the poor
either on their faculties or in parents' groups.

*In the light of the disaffection and hostility sug-
gested in Coles' article, how might the poor be involved in the efforts of the school? What do the
expressed feelings and wishes of Coles' reports
suggest for curriculum planning and school community relations?*

* From Robert Coles, "The Poor Don't Want To Be Middle Class,"
The New York Times Magazine, December 19, 1965. Copyright © 1965 by
the New York Times Co. Reprinted by permission.

WARS have a way of spreading. Poverty is now our declared domestic enemy, and we are presumably fighting to save its victims, the poor. Yet some of the poor talk as if they themselves were being attacked, while many of their allies—professors, organizers and activists of one sort or another—say that the poverty program is pitifully inadequate for such a rich nation, and worse, a number of its efforts are insulting to the citizens it aims to help.

In a recent example, a Job Corps center at Camp Kilmer, New Jersey, was severely criticized by a group of consultants chosen to evaluate it. The private company running the center was accused of using harshly authoritarian procedures geared toward exacting excessive obedience and compliance. "At Kilmer," the report said, "it appears that a kind of middle-class colonialism is occurring, with the corpsmen subjected to the value system of the Kilmer staff."

This was by no means the first such complaint. Other centers have experienced disturbances, some of them the result of tensions among the recruits themselves, others rising out of angry encounters between the recruits and people from nearby towns. Certain communities have refused even to allow Job Corps camps in their midst, as if the unemployed were some devilish adversary whose mere presence guarantees specific crimes or a vaguely felt contamination. Where the camps have been established it has been claimed that such attitudes from "outside," that is from the middle-class culture, have worked their way through and through the atmosphere and practices of the various projects. As a result, men from the slums, in desperate need of work, have found themselves transported to camps where they face what one report called "a tendency to view corpsmen as culprits, and degrade them in their own estimation; a failure to understand the nature and 'life styles' of a poverty culture; secrecy and surveillance; and frustrated, angry teachers and group leaders."

Whether such allegations are excessive or even true, the poor and those who patrol their streets or teach them have a long history of barely tolerating one another. Testimony submitted to Congress in support of the National Teachers Corps documented the extremely inadequate quality of teaching in ghetto schools. The very purpose of the corps is that of attracting and training people who would want to work alongside the poor, understand them, and comprehend their assumptions and hopes, rather than compel their acquiescence to every possible middle-class notion or, failing that, ignore them as both hopeless and undeserving of hope.

In city after city while poor children complain about their schools and the teachers inside them, or ignore all education as irrelevant to the lives they know, their parents protest bitterly the urban-renewal programs that tear down the slums only to scatter the poor and give the rich yet another bonus of land. "Look what they do," a woman in Boston told me recently. "They push us around, then they build their office buildings. The one thing we had was land, and now they're taking it away and throwing us away. You can be sure we won't go anywhere good though—just be moved to suit what the planners want."

What makes that woman so incomprehensible to the urban renewal authorities who claim an earnest wish to advance her cause? Why does she see them as her enemy? Why do some recruits protest bitterly the "attitudes" shown them by their teachers in the Job Corps? Why have I heard Negroes in Southern towns or the tenement blocks of Boston shout their angry defiance at some of the efforts made to "help" them? "They come here to be nice," one mother recently told me "but all they want to do is talk at us, and talk at us, and make us into them."

In order to answer such vexing questions many observers have postulated the existence of a "culture of poverty," with a style of life very much its own. Like all categorizations in the social sciences, the value of such a concept depends upon the vision it supplies. If I find that lack of money eventually sets in motion a rather distinct way of looking at the world and living in it, so that everything from child-rearing to religious beliefs and sexual customs fall in line accordingly, then I am up against a situation not—at least immediately—responsive only to infusions of cash.

Conversely, there are and have been poor, even jobless, people in America who nonetheless retain the same outlook (read "attitude" or "culture") characteristic of the more comfortable. Like most who come upon this article, they worry about the future and about their position in the world. They also have the conviction that their worries, harnessed to their hard work, or quest for hard work, will some day be rewarded by what they want: property, security, comfort, gain, the respect of others; the advancement of their children even further, to more property, more security, more comfort, more success even to significant prestige and influence. If they are now poor, if they are barely getting by, they nevertheless try to keep themselves and their homes tidy, their children's faces scrubbed, their confidence in the likelihood of a better day high enough to avoid daily gloom, or the recklessness and apathy which may express it.

Some other Americans find life a different matter. Because of where they live, or how they look, or when their ancestors came here, they are but another generation in a long story of apartness, plunder, mean living and indignity. They number millions, every article on poverty talks about them, and supposedly they now worry us as a nation.

They are in the Appalachian Mountains, or the Mississippi Delta. They are migrant farmers who have no fixed home, city folk by the dense millions who never venture beyond a few slum blocks, or Indians whose "reservations" are a final territorial summation of our record of homespun colonialism. They are white, black and red; and it cannot be stated often enough that many of them have been here long before the rest of us.

While waves of immigrants came here, to know poverty, eventually to win against it, never to lose that critical feeling that it is possible to win, these others stood by, as slaves, as yeomen on small farms, as tribesmen under attack, as hard-pressed mountaineers hopelessly removed from the centers of commerce—ironically as a consequence of the courage possessed by their pioneer ancestors.

Slowly such people and their descendants got the point: that life is quick and painful; that what is counts more than what will be, because what will be can only be what is; and that hunger, crowded quarters, uncertainty, are inevitable, only to be offset by the precarious pleasures of the moment.

"They keep on telling us, those welfare ladies, to take better care of our money, and save it away, and buy what's the best in the stores, and do like them for dresses, and keep the children in school, and keep our husbands from leaving us. There isn't nothing they don't have a sermon on. They'll tell you it's bad to spend your money on a smoke or a drink; and it's bad to have your kids sleep alongside you in the bed; and you're not supposed to want television because you should be serious with your dollar, and it's wrong for the kids, too; and it's bad for you to let them stay out after dark, and they should study their lessons hard and they'll get way ahead and up there.

"Well, I'll tell you, they sure don't know what it's about, and they can't, not if they come knocking on my door every week until the Lord takes all of us. They have their nice leather shoes, and their smart coats, and they speak the right order of words all right, so I know how many schools they been to. But us? Do they have any idea of what us is about? And let them start at zero the way we do, and see how many big numbers they can become themselves. I mean, if you have got nothing when you're born, and you know you can't get a thing no matter how you tries—well, then you dies with nothing. And no one can deny that arithmetic."

I have connected together several hours of tape-recorded conversation with this woman, a tough, shrewd, fiercely angry, occasionally humorous mother of seven children. Nor does she want to be anything but warm and kind to her children, even when she isn't. "I tries to give them what I can when they're little, so when they gets older and leaves they'll have a few good times to look back on."

While some of us marvel at such "folk wisdom"—in songs, stories and spirituals—those who daily pay the terrible price of its acquisition have other things to do. Life is an unending struggle for survival, and each day's shaky victory in that struggle a mere prelude to further hardship.

"They just don't understand"—I hear words like that almost daily in my work. They usually are followed by other words:

"They just don't understand what it's like. You are born in a
building where it's cold, and the rats keep you company all
day and you're lucky if they don't eat you at night, because
they're as hungary as you. Then the food, it's not always
around when you want it, and you don't have money to buy
what you *do* want. Then you go to those schools, and the
teachers, they looks down on you, and makes you think you
has done something wrong for being born. They shout and
make faces, and they treat you like dirt and then tell you to
be a doctor or a lawyer; if you just go to the library and stay
in school and be neat, that's all it takes. Once in a while lately
they want to take you on a trip crosstown, and show you a
museum or something. They tell you that you haven't got any
pictures at home, so there, take a look and now you own them,
and, man, you're rich.

"My father, he tried, and he tried. My mother, she tried,
too. My father, he would put his head on the kitchen table
and he would cry, all six foot three of him would cry. And my
mother would tell him to stop, and say it wasn't his fault; and
we would stay alive somehow. But my brothers and I, we knew
she wasn't so sure. She tried to make it easy for us by lying,
but we knew. Now they all tell us to level with them, and
work hard and we'll get ours, what we always deserved."

It is unfair to deny that youth, and his parents, their
strength and determination. It is also unfair to overlook how
eroded their lives have become—by illness and idleness, by
fearfulness and insulting dependency upon the slimmest kind
of relief checks.

It is a hard job, trying to do justice to such lives. Those
of us who try come from another land. We have gained literacy,
work, an ongoing sense of usefulness and purpose, a professional
life. No matter how hard we strive to observe and learn how
those "others" live we have our own past, our own experiences
to fall back upon, even when we try to forget them.

Moreover, we can always leave; whether in days or months
or years, somehow we know we can always leave, that we belong,
if only out of our past, elsewhere. That past—I am speaking of
time spent in the "middle-class" world, that elusive miscellan-

eous yet somehow quite real abstraction—has given us hope
and a number of opportunities. Now, whether in Mississippi,
Appalachia or Harlem, the same past gives us coherence, and
yet, ironically, bewilderment too.

The signs of bewilderment vary. We flee into romantic no-
tions of one sort or another: the poor are the only virtuous or
truly strong left; the poor are everything that is weak and destroyed; the poor see the diseases at work in our society, and
in fact by their very condition are immune to them; the poor
are the wretched, their existence a total judgment on the rest
of us.

"You have to watch your step. You have to be nice, but
you can't be friendly. You have to be serious, but you can't
have a sour face." I heard those words from a Negro mother
in New Orleans. She was telling me what she had to tell her
children as they left "home" to walk on white streets, shop in
white stores, and eventually seek jobs in white companies.

Those who are involved in both the civil-rights struggle
and the poverty program also walk a tightrope. Not only may
they themselves make unfair generalizations of one sort or another; but from various directions their every move and word
will be scrutinized and quite possibly misunderstood, perhaps
less by the poor themselves than any of their many appointed
and self-appointed "voices." I recently heard one youth in a
Boston slum say at a meeting, "Everybody says they speak for
us, and they want to speak for us, and they all argue about
what we want, but all I know is I don't want to speak for the
poor people, I want to get out of it and not be poor. That's
what I want and that's what I want to say."

What in fact does happen to those of us who now find ourselves—in a poverty program, a civil-rights project, a ghetto
school—face to face with other Americans sure or not sure about
what they want, but usually at least sure that they have cause
to feel afraid, suspicious, bitter and skeptical? Cannot our very
presence, our earnest, honest, generous presence undo the distrust of others? Our lives, after all, are gaining meaning from
the work we do. Soon—we hope—those we want to help will see

that, and then begin to forgo what we find to be their sullen inertia, or their resentful unwillingness to abide by our rules, or customs.

Often enough it is we who become confused, and afterwards candidates for weariness and straightlaced flight. Our strict sense of justice having met up with ungracious, even scornful rebuff, we can no longer give any quarter to the improvident. Yet, such disastrous results are by no means inevitable. To a large extent what happens will depend upon the manner of the meeting, the purpose of the encounter between those in need and those wanting to be of help.

The critical element may be the uncanny sensitivity possessed by people with empty stomachs. They are on their guard, or else they have surrendered totally to one form of oblivion or another, even then retaining a disordered wariness. I have spent a number of years now getting to know Negro and white families in the rural and urban South, in migrant labor camps, and in Northern slums. It is not that these people have inherited some special sociological genius that allows them to see the hard facts of money and power as they operate in the world. It is that the very nature of their lives compels in them a daily confrontation with those facts, even as our lives are shielded in countless ways from the same facts. The more money you have, the more possible it is for you to forget money, turn your attention elsewhere, to "higher" matters.

Perhaps it is better to let a man I have known several years say it. His name is Jim, and he is my age. Jim has no property, no bank account, no car. He works where he can find work, any work. He works hard. He draws relief when he can't find work. He wants his children to have a better life, but all his children can see is his life, the lives of others like him. Why should they think it will ever be better for them?

The school they know is not like the one my children will attend. The teachers in that school—I have visited the classrooms—were once dutiful and eager, then became tired and angry; now, finally, they are indifferent. The school building, like the crumbling walls Jim's children call "home," is a standing reminder to everyone—teacher, children, parents—in the neighborhood that what goes on elsewhere in the America they see on television bears little resemblance to that area's life.

"People say they want to wipe out poverty"—he began with a derisive tone that already anticipated his views. "That's what you hear, but it's a lot of talk, a lot of show, and maybe a little shake of salt here and there. They tell us they want to retrain us. 'That's right,' they say, 'come on along and we'll get you retrained.'

"But I know how to do all kinds of things already, and I still can't get a job. They don't take but a few colored, trained or untrained. I'm as good a carpenter and electrician as anyone is, but can I get a job? No, sir. No union wants me, and no one will hire me on my own. What is all this poverty thing but plugging up a lot of holes, when you need a new dam?

"They should say: 'O.K. man, we're so rich we don't know what to do with it. We're even flying over to visit the moon and into heaven, we got so much money. So here's what we'll do for you cats. We'll say every one of your children can have food, we have so much of it; and we'll give you a good apartment and a real nice school, and enough money so you won't be crawling on your belly for that relief check business. Then we have some work for you to do. Now you, Jim, we want you to help us build that hospital, or that school building for your kids and your brother's kids. You're a good builder, Jim; so help us build.' Then I'd have my head up and there wouldn't be anyone who would make me bow it and feel ashamed for sitting around or raking in them leaves.

"Isn't that the way to beat old man poverty, instead of taking some of our kids to a camp and trying to get them to learn something, when they figures after they learn it there still won't be the number of jobs we need? And what about that surplus food you have to beg to get, and saying only when you are older than 65 you can get a doctor for free? Who around here lives that long? They know right well all along that we need more than they're going to give. I see those kids on the block growing up, and they starts giving up around 10, I'd say. They just gives up. And it's because they knows the score, and no man can fool them, I don't care how clever he be.

"They try to, though. Instead of giving us what we need, they try to make us be like them. Why don't they give us what we deserve? We been working for them since the beginning, and for free most of the time. Now it's our turn to get our rights as Americans, and they should let us be as we finds it in our hearts to."

What Jim says many others like him have said, or feel like saying. He wants money and he badly needs money. For his family he wants a home, a good school, medical care. He is not sure that he wants to talk and dress like others in the suburbs do, and he resents any suggestion that he make a change in his speech, his appearance or his style of life as the price for food and cash. He does not see any glory in his condition, but he also can spot in a flash a new attempt to humiliate him. Or, as a tenant farmer in Mississippi once put it for me: "If they really mean to help us, we've been ready so long I can't count the years; but if they're kidding as usual, they won't find me buying an extra tie to go beg."

Is it not time for this nation to guarantee every one of its families an adequate yearly income? Then, at least, we will no longer have hungry and needy people in this land of surfeit. What we will continue to have is the presence of people who are still largely outside our middle-class world, with its widespread emphasis on competition, innovation, individual achievement and constantly increasing consumption. Many of the poor have never found such goals, as well as the cautions and restraints of suburban living, possible or rewarding. They have learned to be open and direct with one another, painfully so to many of us, but from another point of view, honestly.

The warmth they often give to their young children is not part of a romantic myth. Side by side with the cruelty, impulsivity, deviousness and futility of ghetto life are its fresh and poignant moments, its searing vision—such as I heard from one old woman when I asked her how old she was: "No older now than when I was 15. You're the same age here once you're old enough to know what it's like in the world. Every year is the same thing. I don't think you get older unless you have something different happen to you, or something better."

One by one, at crucial times in our history various immigrant groups have come, to lend a diversity and richness to our culture. Nevertheless, that same culture has plenty of rot in it—cheap abundance, anxious conformity, smug carelessness. Money and work are what the poor people I know demand and need, but I am not so sure that some of the qualities they already have are not in turn needed by the rest of us—the unmasking humor, the caustic distrust of fake morality, hypocritical authority, and dishonest piety. If most of the poor have been terribly crushed by our society, then in other ways so have many from our nervous, acquisitive middle-class.

Perhaps it is impossible for any large group of people to resist the powerful tug of our middle-class society once it decides to extend its welcome. Certainly I know many poor families who want without question what that society offers. They show no interest in rejecting any of it, even those qualities that reformers themselves have spurned, and indeed work with the poor to avoid.

Still, were poverty no longer a rallying ground for behavior, a few of those now in its clutches might resist the worst blandishments of our culture. Once comfortable in the flesh, they would hunger for other things, for vision and coherence, in ways that called upon their distinctive past experiences, and in so doing make us all pricelessly, truly richer. Presumably—though I am not sure—we are striving to have that choice, that kind of possibility for every American child.

STREET LIFE OF
THE INNER CITY
Mark Feldstein

The following photographs by Mark Feldstein illustrate an important aspect of the environment described in many of the pieces that follow. These were taken in New York, but they are typical of poverty-stricken urban neighborhoods in most United States cities.

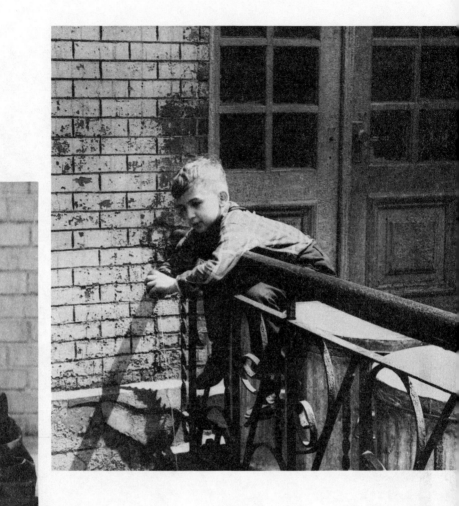

213

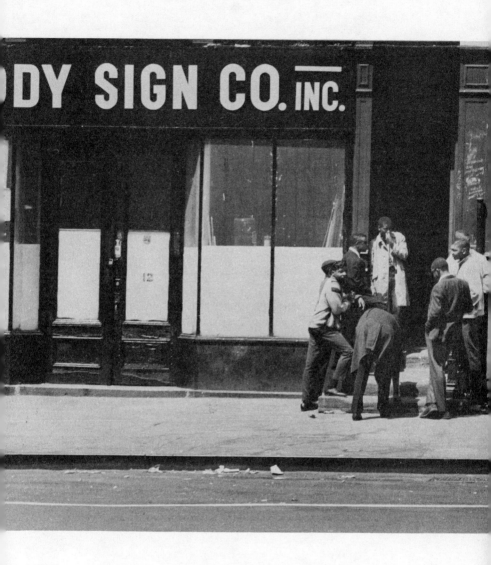

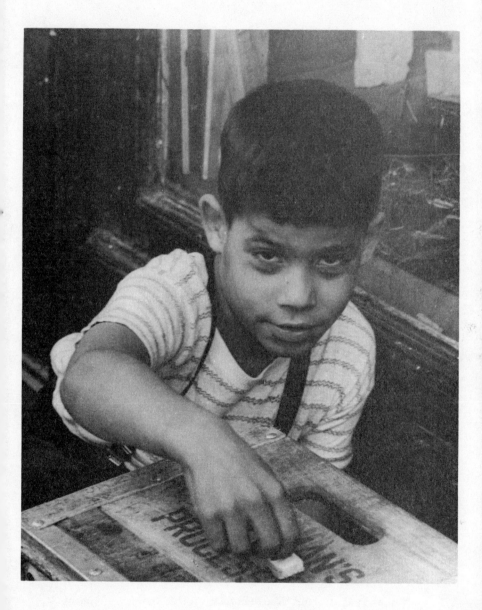

"I would like my neighborhood to be real nice, and not a whole lot of people be around there and fighting, fussing, police be always running around there."

A CHILD'S EYE VIEW
OF HIS WORLD*

Paul A. Fine

The following views of their own environment by a group of Negro boys are excerpted from a substantial report of an interview study conducted in Washington, D.C. The report is called *Neighbors of the President* because the interview sample was selected from Washington's Second Precinct, the area north of the White House. It is based on thirty depth interviews of considerable complexity and ingenuity, supplemented by data on fifty other youngsters. About two thirds of the boys interviewed had records of delinquency. Purely aside from its content, the material suggests how useful it can be to *listen* when children

* From Paul A. Fine, *Neighborhood of the President* (mimeo). Reprinted by permission of the author.

who are puzzling or difficult talk, and it suggests a
number of interesting questions:

> *One of Fine's major points is that lower-class
> children, far from being indifferent to surroundings
> to which they have been accustomed all their lives,
> take essentially a middle-class view of the squalor
> in which they live. How are they likely to have ac-
> quired such a view? How can one explain why they
> do not then see the school as a clean and orderly
> escape from their detested environments? The
> author makes a considerable issue of the boys' need
> for respect. To what extent can we attribute the
> fact that they do not get it in school to attitudes and
> feelings of teachers?*

WHAT does the slum child see? How does his world look to him? What does it mean to him?

Does it shine with excitement and wonder as the sentimentalists would say? Is it the "beautiful city" of the New York judge, or James Agee's rotten depths?

Or perhaps it is, as the sociologists tell us, a world the child learns to see—a world perceived through the screen of values and symbols of the slum culture?

If it is the latter, the child raised in the world of the slum should not see dirt as "filth," disrepair as "degradation," since these are *evaluations* of reality seen by the eyes of the middle-class suburbanite, only because his cultural symbols select them out. Even if such facts as grime, broken stairways, trash-cluttered streets are seen, they would not be evaluated as "bad" nor cathected as "unpleasant" as they are for the middle-class man who sees them through the screen of his cultural definitions. Clearly the "dissolute" behavior which the middle-class eyes would see, could not be so perceived by such children, for "dissoluteness" is a purely moral term, not an aspect of reality at all.

All this is widely accepted *theory*. The question remains: What *do* such children see?

To the eyes of the casual taxicab rider, passing through Washington, D.C.'s second precinct, it is far from a brooding slum in the Harlem style. Wide streets, trees, two-story brick buildings apparently in no worse disrepair than ten thousand neglected neighborhoods across a land of neglected cities dominated by legislatures that hate and fear the city.

This is to the casual eye. And to those who live there? Surely even less should they see poverty and squalor, for their eyes are "socialized" to these familiar sights.

We asked the children being interviewed to begin by pretending that they were guides for a man from the television station and they were to show him the things that would make all the people see "how it really is" in his neighborhood. (The complete rationale for this approach is discussed elsewhere in this report.) Here is what the children told us.

Elwood, age fourteen: "I would like them to know how dirty

the street look sometime. . . . *Wentworth, age sixteen:* ". . . some
live in bad houses. Some need to be taken down, some need to
be rebuilt. . . ." *Oscar, age fourteen:* ". . . and the yard ain't
right. Bottles broke in the yard, plastic [plaster], bricks, baby
carriages all broken up, whole lot of stuff in people's yards. . . ."
Wendell, age fourteen: "Some of them seventy-five to one hundred years old. A lot together, built right close to each other.
They hot in the summer. They crowded. Cold in the weather.
About to fall down, and the window panes about to come out,
and the houses are poor . . . Oh it's just dirty. All that dust
comes in. . . ."

The dirt and the neglect it bespeaks *is* seen—quite obviously.
And not only in the area around one's home. Everywhere the
child turns, this fact confronts him, and is seen and hated.

Albert, age sixteen: "Well, the neighborhood is pretty bad,
you know. Trash around the street, stuff like that and the movies
got trash all in the bathroom—dirty all over the floors. Places
you go in for recreation they aren't clean like they should be,
and some of the children that go to school wear clothes that
aren't clean as they should be. Some of them, you know, don't
take baths as often as they should (uh-huh). Well, my opinion
is of-of-of this neighborhood it's a nice neighborhood to live in,
but it's not clean as it should be (uh-huh) and-uh-if I had a
chance if my mother would, you know, move I would rather
move to another, to a better neighborhood. . . ."

The dirt is a symbol, and no minor one of the social dissolution that prevails about them.

A friend's parents become a public sideshow. *Thomas, age
thirteen:* ". . . this friend, and his mother and father, most of
the time they have fights around there and everybody come and
look. They be having a fight down the street. They get kinda
excited." And closer to home, "house across the street lady be
having fights." *Ellery, age fifteen:* "Sometimes, about every Friday or Saturday a fight occurs . . . these fights are not teenagers,
but grownups. Men and women. Maybe under influence of
alcohol, start arguing and then they start fighting. On the streets
mostly, sometime house. Some are real bad."

Norris, age fifteen: "Sometime where I live at people be

hitting each other, fighting next door. Then when they stop fighting then you can get some sleep. When they do fight you can't get no sleep. . . ."

The fighting erupts into violence.

Edward, age fourteen: ". . . drinking, cussing, fighting, shooting people, having policemen running all around on our street again." Summers are the worst time. ". . . drinking, cussing, stabbing people, having policemen running all around mostly every day in the summer time. In the winter time they can't come out because the whiskey store is closed, and then they can't have no argument, get drunk, and start fighting."

The killing reaches one of the boys from the adult world.

Jonathan, age sixteen: "Peoples shooting up everybody and things. Saturday after last we went to a death party. We stayed to dance at the end. We started to go home. This man come up to this boy. I don't know why—anyway he stabbed the boy in the back. . . ."

Such things can worry a boy, even if he is a delinquent. *Wendell, age fourteen:* "Well there's a lot of violence around. You see it and keep thinking about it. People get murdered in the back of your yard, where you have a backyard. People just get murdered—shot. We were watching television one night and —you see all this violence all around and you can't get it out of your mind. The more you try, the more it comes back. Eventually it wears away, but you keep thinking about it. It has a bad feeling on you. When I first started living around here it was really bad, but I have gotten used to it now. Been here two years. People getting shot and stuff. Lots of people getting hurt. People getting beat up. People getting shot. People getting hit with cars and murdered. Gee, there's a lot of violence around here. You see it all the time. . . ."

Of course there is gambling.

Carl, age fifteen: "Sometimes people be coming past late at night and making a lot of noise, and sometimes it be a man, he always have a card game or something in his house and people be down there makin' a lot of noise arguing over money . . .

_____ Street, that's where people fight at, shoot and cut, cut each other, and all that kind of stuff. . . ."

And bootlegging.

Andrew, age fourteen: ". . . and they can go in there and buy the wine even if the stores are closed, and the police comes to check up, keep selling it, but it ain't none my business, but they don't stop it, just check up, you known. . . ."

Wendell, age fourteen: "Theres a bootleg company right across from H____ Street. Policemen find out about it—it's peddling liquor and they don't do nothing about it. People just pay them off. You can't have a strong police force if two thirds of them are crooks. . . ."

"Wineheads" lie in filth in the back alleys.

Thomas, age thirteen: "There are a whole lot of winos who hang around, back in the alley there. Men who drink and lay around there dirty, smell bad. Cook stuff maybe. Chase you. Men who drink and when they get drunk they quit their job. They don't do nothing but hang around the alley and bust bottles and give 'em to a man named ____ ____, and collect papers and sell them to the junk shop."

In the eyes of a child it all blends together—is all of a piece: The drinking, the noise, the killing, the dirt, policemen swarming into the neighborhood. All come to symbolize much the same thing, appear with nearly equal weight in flow of thought and tone of voice. What does it symbolize? One would say "disorganization" but the term is too passive for this kind of disorganization which assaults the eye and the ear and the person.

Bill, age fourteen: (*What would you really want them to know, the good things, the bad things, the real truth about your neighborhood?* "The truth?" *Yes.*) "Well some of the people just drink wine and whiskey and stuff and go around cussing, they ought to try to be quiet. A man named Mr. D____, he takes and hustles up glass and stuff. And some of them that drink the wine drop the bottles in the barrel and the police comes through once in a while and check on Mr. D____. Some of the people want to act all right and some of them don't."

(*People that act all right. How do they act?*) "They act quiet and peaceful and don't never drink and aren't noisy. The people

that act all right you can tell, because they want their house
to be 'scrate.' " (*Straight?*) "Yes, sir, cleaned up, you don't see
no bottles on the floor or around the house. And some of them
don't clean their house, you always see bottles on the shelf and
stuff." (*Bottles?*) "Yes, sir, bottles." (*What kind of bottles?*)
"Wine bottles, whiskey bottles, and all kind of bottles."

"Course it ain't none of my business. The worst stuff that
goes and the worst wine drinkers in my neighborhood go back
in the alley called Bad Gal Hobo or something. Almost every
time I go through there men be sleeping in trucks and cars,
some of them are condemned cars and houses, don't hardly
take no baths, be dirty all the time. When they go git their
money they take and drink it up in wine."

Note in Bill's remarks the response to assaults that offend
the eye and ear in contrast to those assaults against "society."
There is no outrage, expressed at Mr. D's relations with the
police. "It ain't none of my business." But the drunks who go
around cussing. *They ought to be try to be quiet.* The *"worst
stuff"* is "men sleeping in trucks and cars, some of them are
condemned cars and houses, don't hardly take no baths be dirty
all the time." Note, however, the flow of thought from affront
to society, and back again to affront to personal sensibility.

BOYS VS. DOGS

Question: Does a boy, assaulted by filth, have a right to keep
the neighbor's dog from adding to the mess in his back yard?
The neighbor, and adult, has one view. Bill, the child, another.
Bill has a small victory to report. *Bill, age fourteen:* "Well,
some of the neighborhood is all right, but half of it ain't. Like
this old lady lives over next to me, she lets her dogs come out
there and go in my yard and mess up in it and then go back
over in her yard and in the old dog house and go to sleep. So
when she caught me running the dog out of my yard when he
was messing in there, she talking about you better leave that
dog 'lone or she'd call the police on me. That dog ain't got no
right to come over here messing in my yard and she say the
dog got freedom to go anywhere he wants to mess at. Then I

took and packed the hole up that he couldn't get out no more. Now he got to mess in her yard. Somewhere, I don't know which apartment, they sell wine and stuff around there, bootleggers, whatever it is." (*Tell me about that.*) "See, the wineheads back in the alley want something when the whiskey store be closed, they go in somebody's house, I don't know whose house it is 'cause that ain't none of my business, they go up there and get some fifths of brandy or 'Thunderbird' or something and come back out in the alley and drink it. Sometimes people get in fights around there." (*Tell me about the fights.*) "Some times they git all drunk and start fighting each other talking about who the best man and all this. Sometimes people get too drunk around there and they start raising sand and cussing all night and you can't hardly get no sleep. The lady up over top us always come down when she be passing thru and be talking to us and then she'll go on back up stairs."

Note how *without questioning by the interviewer* the flow of Bill's thought moves from his victory over the dog to talk about the local bootlegger and the affairs that again he calls "none of my business." Somehow the thought that *he* has forced the dog to mess in "her yard," by closing the hole in the fence leads to thoughts of the open hole in the fence that constitutes the bootleggers apartment.

Note, at the close of the passage, the transition from adults in the alley below "raising sand" all night to the lady above him "passing thru" and "talking at us." Here another theme of importance appears. It looks to the child as if all policemen, dogs, adults, winos, are on one side, the children on the other.

Keith tells much the same story in a very different way.

Keith, age fourteen: "Well, some people around here are nice and some of them don't get along too well . . ." (*Probe.*) ". . . No, Ma'am, some don't get along with the other children . . . and some of them help the children . . . they like to see the children friendly and not get into trouble. One time we were sitting in the alley this lady said we were messing with her dog and she called the police and told the police we were the ones but we were just sitting in the alley and a boy named J_____ knew a couple of the boys . . . and she told the police later that we not the boys and so our mother and my friend's mother had to come get us out . . . (*from where*) . . . from down number two" (*the precinct police station*). (*Probe*) "It was about the same number of boys and one of us had on a white 'T' shirt and one of the boys that was throwing at the dog had on a white 'T' shirt and . . . well . . . Sometimes when we want to play ball we can't play it cause they lock the school yard up and when we play ball sometimes when we knock the ball over the fence and it hits the person's porch, well they get mad . . ." (*Probe,*) "Well they come out yelling at you and when one time we were playing and a boy hit the ball into a lady's house and broke her vase . . . then when she asked us did we want to pay for the vase and get the ball back or she call the police so we had to pay for the vase . . . That's all the good things and some of the bad things I can think of except for some of the people. . . ."

Note the flow of imagery: "Truth about the neighborhood" —adults vs. children—sitting in the alley—lady calls police claiming children disturbing her dog—arrest—locked school yard— playing ball in the streets—adults call police because ball breaks a vase . . .

One affront becomes very like another. Assault by filth, by the disgrace of policemen swarming over the neighborhood, by the fights of noisy adults who keep you awake, should "socialize" the child to assault—blind him to insult. But it does not.

Bill is a delinquent who has served one and one half of his fourteen years in prison. Keith has no record, and in the interview reports no acts of delinquency. Still *both* could be psychopathic liars. Is the environment really so hostile to children?

Edward, also a nondelinquent, has something to say on this score. He reports the same sense of outrage—not in words, but in flow of thought. Note carefully his transition in thought (and quite spontaneously) from wish for flower boxes on *his* street to the homosexuals in the alley at Q street. (The, by now, familiar themes will also be noted.)

Edward, age fourteen: "I would like my neighborhood to be real nice, and not a whole lot of people be around there and fighting, fussing, police be always running around there. If they were making a movie around here, I would gather all the people up around on our street and tell them that 'I would like to see y'all best manners when the studio came and film our street.' So they come and we have our best manners and they film the picture and then show it. They'll say, that's a nice neighborhood. Then after that they'll forget all of their manners. All of the people will forget. They'll go back to drinking, cussing, fighting, shooting people, having policemen running all around on our street again. And then we have—throw a little block party for our street, and we'll have punch and cake and stuff, and no policemen will be around that day. And get all the people together and get em to paint our houses, clean up the street, grow some grass around the sidewalk over by the playground, and get swings, see-saws and everything and put in the playground. And then all the neighborhood children come in there and play." (*Example of some of these same old things people in his neighborhood do.*) "Drinking, cussing, stabbing people, having policemen running all around, mostly because the whiskey store be closed, and then they can't have no argument get drunk and start fighting, and all." (*How do you feel, I asked.*) "It don't seem right, people be fighting, killing people and everything, drinking, going around the street arguing at somebody all the time, nagging them." (*What are some good things?*) "People help people shovel snow, bring groceries home, and help paint their houses and everything, and put flower boxes up to the window and everything. In the alley at Q Street all those sissies and punks be running around there chasing after us and everything." (*Chasing after you?*) "A whole lot of children, they be back in the alley playing, and they be back in there having all their fun, and we be back there playing making noise, and then they start chasing after us." (*Why?*) "I don't know, but it is some reason—some kind of grudge they have against all children."

Note here how the presence of policemen symbolizes the fact of lawlessness rather than the presence of law and order. Note, too, how the problem assumes, again, personal focus in the way that it *invades* ones world. "Police be always running around there" and "don't seem right people be . . . arguing at somebody all the time nagging them." Again we see how all of it is of a piece: dirt, cussing, fighting, drinking, killing, being chased out of the alley by punks and sissies, and people "nagging at you." Too much impinges. Nothing bespeaks respect. The perceived attitudes of the punks and sissies serve to summarize the perception of the whole situation: "Some kind of a grudge against all children . . ."

There is good reason to believe that these are perceptions of reality. Edward, for example, seems to have an unusual sense of maturity as he talks to the adults in imagination, "I would like to see y'all best manners when the studio come and film our street." And he appears soundly close to reality when he says, "all of the people will forget. They'll go back to drinking, cussing, fighting, shooting people, having policemen running all around on our street again."

Nor does he anywhere express hostility himself. The tone, rather, is one of sorrow. "It don't seem right, people be fighting, killing people and everything, drinking, going around the street arguing at somebody all the time, nagging them." He does not want to punish or destroy. He wants flower boxes and paint.

The fact that Edward, another nondelinquent, sees what Bill the delinquent sees, also suggests that what he is telling us is fact. But the obvious intelligence here may raise doubts. Let us look, therefore, through the eyes of Norris, who is called "crazy" by his friends.

Norris, age fifteen: "The neighborhood where I live at, ain't too much to say. Some people round there are nice, some people aren't. Sometimes where I live at, people sometime be hitting each other, fighting next door. Then when they stop fighting then you get some sleep. And right around the corner from us is these people they shoot dice in the house all day long. When they loose their money they make so much noise that the police come round. Knock on *your* door and question *you.* Did you see who was fighting? Who bust who in the head? And all the wine drinkers be hanging out in the alley down the street from where ya live, and police come past there and see them drinking wine and don't say nothing. Some of them have fifths of wine in their car when they are driving and when *you* walk in the street and the police stops *you*. Sometimes he ask you where are you going and you tell him and they swear that you are lying and then he takes you home and your mother tells him that you wasn't lying and *then* he'll probably take you down, cause if'n you made him mad he probably keep me down there until my mother come."

It is of some importance to keep in mind that these images are on "top of the mind" so to speak. This is the first spontaneous answer to the question, "What would you show him so that the people could see the real truth about your neighborhood?" Again, as before, the flow of thought gives us: adult fighting—no sleep—cops bother *you*. But the real culprits are left alone. Just as noise invades sleep, so the cop invades the privacy of the house, and the problem is to contain outrage so as not to anger the policeman.

Insult may come from the neighbors, from the neighbor's dog, from the policemen. It may merely disturb sleep. Of, if one is not careful, it may lead to arrest. Norris is outraged by direct personal affront, but beyond the personal affront is repressed outrage at adults who act without concern or responsibility; symbols of law and propriety who expect respect but accord none; who ignore impropriety of adults, but expect cooperation from children.

Oscar, age thirteen, is also offended by the violations of standards, of decency by those who should uphold them.

"*. . . one special thing I don't like about it.* Our yard! The people just take trash and throw it out there in front of the yard and see ——! They put the trash cans out there so people can come out in the back yard and put it in there. And if they don't want to put it in there, they can burn it. People don't burn it. They don't put it in there. They just throw it all down in the alley way and in the yard, and it can blow any old place. And they just get up in the windows and drop it on down . . ."

Such a dissolute world threatens dissolution, becomes a fearful place. With no order to hold things together it threatens constantly to fall in upon the child.

And so, Oscar tells us, "I don't like the way those houses built. They curve. Like they go straight up there, they just

curve over like that. Curve over. They all built wrong. And I
don't like the way they look. (*Why?*) Make that street look
wrong. Street don't look right with all those crooked houses and
all that on the street. Down at the bottom they straight. But at
the top is all crooked over. I don't like the way they built. They
make the street look bad . . ."

There is here a terrible need for order, but for the order that
flows from respect. This world looks to this child as if it were
about to fall on him—as indeed it is.

Disrespect can come from any direction—literally with the
wind. Dirt and trash is free to go where it pleases, children have
no place to go. Notice the linking of these themes in this:

Wendell, age fourteen: "It's a lot of dirt around there, and
ain't enough playgrounds around for boys to play . . . I think
the government should put more playgrounds up and more
provisions like more clean trash disposals. Get rid of this garbage disposal. They burn this trash and smoke goes up and goes
all over the place. You can't hang your clothes up." Even the
trash disposal assaults!

Where can a child turn in this situation?

He can go for a walk. He can leave the neighborhood and
pay a visit to that other world two blocks away, that world of
fine shops, fine cars, well-groomed people. Donald takes us for
such a walk.

Donald, age fifteen: (*Tell me about your neighborhood.*) "I
feel pretty good about it. Well, the neighborhood—sometimes
people come up and they ask you why you're out so late and try
to run you home. Then you go through alleys and see wineheads and stuff laying up all in the alleys and standing by the
fire cooking chickens and stuff on the little pots and stuff on the
trash cans. (*What else?*) Just like you go in the store and pick
up something to see how much it cost and they try to say you're
stealing something. They go back in the back and call the police
on you. Then the police come pick you up and ask you if you're
trying to steal anything and take you down. Then the people
come back and say 'Oh, I'm sorry, I didn't know you were
looking at the stuff.' And everytime you walk up in our street if

you step on somebody's toe, they try to say you meant to step on their toe, but you tell them you don't mean to step on their toe then they try to hit you. (*Have you ever had that happen to you?*) Yes sir. (*Tell me about it.*) One day I came from _____ market and I slipped and the lady was coming by and I stepped on her toe and she hit me side the head with her umbrella. (*Do you like the neighborhood?*) Yes sir. (*Why?*) Well, I was born and raised up here. That's why I like it so much."

If you are fifteen and a child of the Second Precinct, you are the enemy. Wherever you go—you are the enemy.

Walk in the street—"people try to run you home."

Go into a store—"You are stealing . . . go into the back and call the police, and you get taken to the station."

Walk down the street and accidently step on someone's toe —and you again are looking for trouble and there's a fight.

Go over to the market—and a lady hits you "side the head" with her umbrella.

There is here a war in progress, a war between society and children. War in the most real sense. It is fought with guns and knives and clubs and attack and counterattack, and if you are captured you are a prisoner of war. Under such combat conditions you are never really out from under fire. Here is one way you get caught up in the eddy of a skirmish that swirls by where you sit.

Andrew, age sixteen; ". . . Me and four of my friends was sitting in this alley. I had just bought a box of doughnuts and each one of us bought a soda and we were sitting in the alley drinking soda and eatin' a doughnut. Well these boys ran through the alley—was throwing at this lady's dog. And the lady has a sick person in the house. And the lady she called the police, but the boys didn't know it. And anywell (sic) they ran, and when the police came were still in the alley sittin, you know, just talking and playing around. And, well, the lady she run out, she was excited and she said, 'those are the boys. Those are the ones.' But we hadn't did anything so the police took us down to number two and we couldn't leave till our parents came and got us . . ."

We have met this sort of situation before. It is interesting to note that this boy is not without understanding of the viewpoint of the lady who caused the trouble for him and his friends, "This lady has a sick person in the house." And the other boys *were* throwing rocks at the dog. When you are assaulted you assault back. The boys are not mere bystanders in this war. There is little chance of escaping your tour of combat if you are on the line. And you cannot get off the line.

If you are a child of the Second Precinct, you stay in the Second Precinct, because you are dangerous; you are a threat to society; you are "up to no good."

Louis, age seventeen; "I went out to Maryland with two of my friends. So, you know, we had just rode the bus to the end of the line, cause wasn't nothing else to do. So we started walkin' around. Well we walked pass these stores just lookin'; and so, uh, we had cut across this lady—this white lady's lawn. And they had a sign 'no trespassing' there. No one of us saw the sign. Then, you know, they call the police. And they came and looked down there and they saw us, and drove up. The other two friends of mine ran I kept walkin'; and so one of 'em hop out of the car, and say 'get in!' and I go get the other two. You know, the reason I didn't run was cause we hadn't done nothin' anyway. Like my grandmother, she always told me if you hadn't done anything no sense a running. So I still walked on. And he say 'come 'ere!' and he grabbed handcuffs on this thing and slapped them on over to a fence and he want to put me on to it. I hadn't done nothin! And I ain't gonna get handcuffs on, cause I ain't never been handcuffed before. So I just turned around and ran. And this one, he pulled out a gun, you know, he told us to stop. So I didn't want to be shot so I just stopped. One friend of mine stopped. Other boy, he had ducked somewhere. And they took us down to the car, and after awhile he came down there. So they took us down to the precinct . . ."

Where do you go? Where can you play? We have heard from Wentworth, age sixteen, before. Let us look at his whole description of the neighborhood from the first words of the interview, just as it come from the tape.

Wentworth, age sixteen; "Well, that there ain't no recrea-

tion around. There was a big recreation right across the street
and they tore it down. There's only one playground, and there's
poor houses around there for people to live in. People ain't got
the things they need. Ain't got enough money to buy the stuff,
and the high prices. Some of 'em seventy-five to one hundred
years old houses. A lot together, built right close to each other.
They hot in the summer. They crowded. Cold in the weather.
About to fall down, and the window panes about to come out
and the houses are poor. There ain't enough playgrounds, and
if you go down to the railroad station, there is a big yard down
there, play football down there. The cops come and chase us
off, and it's only big enough for one, for two teams to play football, baseball. It's got a basketball court, and the government
don't support it—they support it, but they don't put money into
it to buy new stuff. Most people think that people around there
are hardly any good because the way they live. It's not their fault
it's not the right stuff around there for them to live right. Like
when they working up there now—Oh, it's just dirty. All that
dust comes in. It's cold in the winter and hot in the summer. It's
a lot of dirt around there, and ain't enough playground for boys
to play. Their fathers and mothers don't make enough money
to support them. I don't think they have enough money to give
to them to spend. They get mad and they go out and they do
something to get money. And when they got it they go out and
get more until they get caught, I guess. Well, I think the government should put more playgrounds up and more provisions
like more clean disposals. This garbage disposal. They burn
this trash and smoke goes up and goes all over the place. You
can't hang your clothes up." (*I asked if government had this
disposal!*) "I don't know who has, but the government really
should do something if they want boys to stop getting in trouble.
Like they should try to get more playground and more recreation, and more camps the boys can go to. Some of the camps get
crowded around the summer. I only live a couple of streets up
from here. And it's crowded." (*I asked where kids played mostly
during summer.*) "In the streets. They usually go up to old
hospital or morgue—Sibley. They go there and play on the
grounds, and the police come and chase them away. It's private

property. And they go to the playground. It's too crowded up there. See they don't mostly play anything up there. We get ten or twelve boys and go out in Maryland and do something, like that." (?) "Yea, ain't nothing to do around Washington, and the police always after them. Cause one time we were playing around the railroad station and the police come and say we can't be around there. So Johnny got mad and kinda cussed, sweared at the policeman and the policeman locked him up, he chased us off the place. We don't have any place to play around there. You play on the streets you get in trouble. You play any place else you get in trouble too." (*Recreation building torn down?*) "Yes, sir, it was a good recreation building, and they tore it down. They wanted to build a road. And they tore it down just to build a road. I don't think the government—you know America, think as much about teenagers as they should, from nine up to seventeen or nineteen, because they get into trouble it's their own fault, but it's not their own faults, because they don't have no place to play and it's their fathers and mothers don't have good jobs, and the high prices of living, and stuff like that." (*I asked more about the recreation center that was torn down.*) "Basketball. Lots of youngsters went there. Tore it down last year—they just closed it up—instead of building a road they put up a parking lot."

Wentworth, age sixteen, one seventh of his life in detention. And the astonishing thing is the lack of bitterness, the amount of understanding. No playgrounds, "there *was* a big recreation right across the street, but they tore it down." Poor housing; "people ain't got the things they need, ain't got enough money and high prices. Crowded, cold, dirty housing. Go to play by the railroad station and get chased away." Poverty: "Most people think that people around there are hardly any good because of the way they live. It's not their fault. It's not the right stuff around there for them to live right."

". . . this was the white man's education, taught the way the white man wanted it taught, without giving it any meaning for us."

REPORT FROM A
SPANISH HARLEM "FORTRESS"*

Richard Hammer

Here is another insider view, from another city and a different kind of ghetto. The boy is more sophisticated than the Washington boys interviewed, but he might be speaking for them. Particularly so, perhaps, as he talks about his schooling. Because Hiram is so articulate, this article is useful as a test for the theoretical materials in the section preceding this on social class values:

> *What values is Hiram expressing about his environment? About education? About the world of the middle class? About those Gans calls the "caretakers"?*

* From Richard Hammer, "Report From a Spanish Harlem 'Fortress,'" *The New York Times Magazine* (July 5, 1964). Copyright © 1964 by the New York Times Co. Reprinted by permission.

THE PEOPLE will tell you that this block is a fortress. Its walls are invisible; they are inside the mind, built by the people who live on the block and by society outside. But the walls are as real as if they were made of mortar and stone; they keep 3,000 people locked up inside, afraid, and they keep most outsiders away, afraid.

The block is in the middle of Spanish Harlem, a section of New York that runs roughly from 96th Street to 118th Street between Fifth Avenue and Park Avenue. As events constantly make clear, the area is seething. To the outsider, it is a strange and unfamiliar and often frightening world—one he can never know on his own and one he can understand only partially even with the most expert help.

Recently I met a young man, eighteen years old, for whom Spanish Harlem is home. He was born on the block on which he lives and has spent his entire life on it, in the same small apartment he now shares with his mother, widowed for ten years, three brothers, three sisters and three other relatives. From all outward signs, Hiram Gonzales (this is not his name) could be a typical eighteen-year old from his block. He has grown up in its poverty and faced discrimination all his life because his skin is dark and he is recognizably of Puerto Rican descent. Twice he has dropped out of high school, once from vocational high school in Brooklyn and later from an academic high school in Manhattan.

But Hiram is articulate beyond his education and background, made so by self-education and by an innate brightness and intelligence, and he has thought long and hard about what it is like to grow up and live in Spanish Harlem. He also has a goal and the talent and determination to realize it: he wants to be a professional photographer and he is driven by a desire to return to school and then go on to college. And he has the sensitivity to see into and beneath the sights and sounds and texture of the life around him.

For several nights, we sat together and talked. At first, he was hesitant and wary, looking for something in the interviews other than interest in him and his problems. "To tell you the truth, man," he said later, "I dislike white men because I feel all the injustice that I, my family, my mother, my friends . . . you know, that all of us have gone through." Later, as respect and trust grew, Hiram led me through his world.

"When you walk through my block," he said, "probably the first thing you realize is that there are a lot of people on the streets all the time, from early in the morning to late at night. You'll see that the buildings are old, almost falling apart, but a lot of people have hung curtains in the windows.

"If you are an observing person, you'll notice prostitutes waiting for guys with money, most of them white men from downtown. You'll see drug addicts just moving nowhere; you'll see dope peddlers practically passing the stuff right out in the open. You'll see incidents of theft, you'll just walk along and see them. You'll see a lot of things that are wrong by moral standards and by the moral laws of the rest of society.

"But, man, ever since I was a little kid, this was my block, the block of the fellows who live in it. It was our property and we govern it and we make our own laws and no outsider or no people who don't live in the block can tell us what to do. There are a lot of people who come up and they try to tell us. But, man, they don't understand, they're living in some kind of dream.

"Their standards and ideas don't belong on this block. Because we've been made to feel like we're different, like we don't fit, like we don't belong any place but on our own crummy little block. And there's nobody up here who's going to listen until the white man lets us become a part of his society outside, and I don't mean just a couple of guys who are really exceptional, who've got a lot of brains, but I mean everybody who can make it."

One of the things the rest of society has to understand, Hiram thought, was that the people on his block are not different or strange. "To live on my block," he said, "is to live anywhere where there are a lot of people who are poor and who don't have any place else to go. There's a lot of pain and a lot of sorrow, but underneath there's also a lot of glory and happiness and love. Sure, there are a lot of problems on my block, and maybe more problems than a lot of other places. And everybody on the block knows that you think we brought all the problems with us. Well, man, we didn't. The problems were all here before the people came, or anyway, the things that made the problems. For every unjust act done by the people in my neighborhood, there was an unjust act, directly or indirectly done to these people by society."

By indirect, Hiram meant the often unthinking attitudes of whites. "There was this white woman from downtown," he said, "who sometimes came into the neighborhood to help my mother when she was sick. One day, this woman said to me, 'Now, I don't have anything against the Irish or the Italians, but I just don't like most Negroes and I don't like most Puerto Ricans.'

"Now, man, even though she was helping us when we needed help, I got damn mad. 'Now just a minute,' I said to her, 'how many Puerto Ricans or Negroes do you know? How many do you associate with? Where do you come off saying something like that?'

" 'Well,' she told me, 'I see lots of Negro and Puerto Rican boys hanging on the street corners who look tough, and I'm afraid of them.'

" 'You go out to Bedford-Stuyvesant and you'll see plenty of white boys hanging on the street corners who are just as tough; you go anywhere where people have to live in this kind of filth and you'll see the same damn thing. When you and your kind first came here, you weren't any better.' "

Later, Hiram said, "You know, I'd like to move all the people from Scarsdale, New York, right into my block, into the same apartments where some of them have to pay maybe seventy dollar for a couple of crummy little rooms for ten or eleven people and have to share a bathroom in the hall with the door falling off. Let them live in a place where somebody throws a tire in the furnace and stinks out the place and then the cops come along and tell you that it's nothing and laugh when they're telling you.

"I'll tell you, I think they'd make just as much of a mess

as we do, maybe more, because we're used to it, we're used to dodging those weak spots in the floors and not leaning on the wall because it will fall in.

"I don't think those people from Scarsdale could take it. In Scarsdale, the first things the kids learn are how to read and write; that's taken for granted. In my neighborhood, the first things the kids learn are how to fight and steal and not take any crap from anyone. We grow up knowing about narcotics, I mean we don't even remember when we didn't know about them, and everybody just takes that for granted.

"In my block, there are five places where you can buy marijuana cigarettes and I know, even though he's never said anything, that my little brother who's fourteen knows where most of them are, that he's known for a long time."

I suggested that nobody forces the kids to use narcotics. "Of course nobody comes up to us and says, 'Man, here's some pot, you *got* to take a drag; man, here's some horse, you *got* to shoot.' But, man, these little kids look at the teen-agers who are using, and they *look* bigger, and, man, they can laugh and forget everything that's around. So, the little kids think, 'That's a tough man; he's great.' And then they see the pushers and racketeers in their $50 shoes and $100 suits, driving a big car, and they think, 'Man, he's tough; he's into some money and he's doing good.' So, when the pusher talks, they listen."

Hiram told me that by the time the boys on the block get to be twenty probably 95 per cent of them have tried some kinds of drugs and about 40 per cent of them are hooked.

"We aren't fooling ourselves," he said, "when we try drugs. We know what can happen. When I was thirteen, I saw somebody die of heroin. I went up to the roof of the house next door . . . I think it was to fly my kite . . . anyway, when I came out the door I nearly fell over these addicts who were sort of sitting around in the hallway next to the door. They saw I was only a kid, so they kept right on shooting.

"All of a sudden, I heard of lot of rumbling and this one guy leaped out through the door and started running and turning and jumping all over the roof. Man, he still had the needle sticking in his arm. His friends, and they were still half asleep, sort of staggered out and grabbed him and held him down until he was quiet; they they started walking him back and forth to keep him awake. After a while, they sent me downstairs to get some milk, and more people began coming up to try to help. But nobody could do nothing, and by the time the ambulance got there, he was dead."

Most of the young people in Spanish Harlem are bitter and disillusioned. They sit on the stoops because there isn't anything else most of them can do, and they play cards and they joke. "Our goal is to have a good time, to keep having fun so we don't have to think," said Hiram. "You know what we're doing? We think we're sending the world on its own way while we go on ours. But we know, and, man, that's the trouble, we know that we can't send the world away, that we're part of the world and the world is looking down at us and snarling and laughing at us."

Isn't there, I asked, a desire to get out of the block and into that world to stop that sneering?

"Man, when I was a kid, I used to have dreams that maybe I'd be a scientist and discover all kinds of things. But they were only dreams; when I woke up, there wasn't anything real about them, there couldn't be anything real about them. I've never seen a scientist; I don't understand anything about them; there aren't any scientists, or anybody else who has a big job, on my block so I haven't got the least idea of what they're like. It's hard to even picture them mentally. These things are so far above us they aren't real. They're like a cloud that looks solid until you grab into it and find it falls apart in your hands."

The boys on the block feel that even with an education they have no hope of realizing any dreams. "I know guys with a diploma who start looking for jobs. You know what they can get? A stockboy or a delivery boy or something like that, but not something where they feel they can move ahead.

"I've got a friend who wants to be a mathematician and he's a real smart guy. But when he graduated from high school, an academic one, too, not a lousy vocational one like most of us dropped out of, he went looking for a job so he could make the money to go to college. Nobody had nothing for him.

Finally, he answered an ad for a lousy busboy's job at a crummy cafeteria.

"You know what they told him? They told him that he had too much education, that they were afraid he would quit. Now this kid would have worked like hell because he needed the money; but he couldn't even get that crummy job, a job any fink who didn't even know how to read could handle."

So most of the boys just sit. They are convinced that if they went back to school, it would not assure them of a decent job; besides, they are disenchanted with the schools themselves. "When I reached sixth grade, I couldn't read," said Hiram. "The teachers, most of them, didn't give a damn."

The school, instead of revealing the world, merely mirrored the world the young people from the block already knew. "But when I was in seventh grade, I went to a Catholic school for a year. They put a kind of wrench in my mind and opened it a crack and I began to see that there was a world outside my block. Man, that school cared, about me and about everybody, and they wanted to teach and they wanted me to learn.

"Then I went back to public school because, man, the work just got too hard and I wasn't ready for it. In public school, the only thing the teachers wanted was quiet. If they thought we didn't want to learn, they'd sit there smoking and reading and if you got out of line, sometimes they'd curse at you: "You little spic, sit down.' "

But in that school Hiram's horizons were broadened by one teacher of a subject he hated, English. "One day, the teacher came in and played us 'The Three Penny Opera,' and there was something about this 'Mack the Knife' character that really hit us. We asked him to play it over and over, and the next day he brought in 'West Side Story,' and every day he played us records for a while. Then he began to read to us. He read 'The Old Man and the Sea,' 'The Most Dangerous Game,' and a lot of others.

"Now, man, we weren't angels after that; we still carried on, maybe even more because we were getting some freedom, but when that man asked for silence, he got it, and when he began to suggest things, they began to move."

While there were some who managed to get an education, Hiram explained that they paid a terrible price for it. They had to be the teacher's pet, and this put them at the mercy of their fellows, who were not slow to deal out fitting punishment. For most, however, "this was the white man's education, taught the way the white man wanted it taught, without giving it any meaning for us. It was routine, do this and do that, and today we try to escape routine all the time. And it was using things from the white man's world which didn't mean anything to us or things that were so completely against everything we knew that we laughed at them. They even had books telling us what great guys the cops are.

"Now look, man, I know that most cops are just doing their jobs and trying to protect people most of the time. But I've grown up admiring people, I mean *admiring,* who would fight back at cops; to some extent, I still admire them. Why, I think that if right now, right this minute, a cop walked into this room and told me to do something, I don't think I'd do it, just because he was a cop."

This is the way Hiram and his friends see the law. "In my neighborhood, the cops feel that they're superior to the people, and man, they let us know they think they're better than us. They walk into our homes and look around and tell us to open up, and we're afraid, and I mean afraid, to do anything or say anything. We just do what the cops say.

"And they'll come walking down the street and see us sitting on the stoop, and you know what they do? They come up to us, asking us who we're going to rape next and what job we're planning to pull, and then they tell us to get moving. Man, it can be our stoop, right in front of our house, with our mothers watching out the windows, and the cops are cursing and, man, even demanding that we show them identification."

Another group of "outsiders," youth board and social workers, also rank low in the opinion of the block, Hiram said. "They're all around the neighborhood and most of them are rat fink types. They act like they think that we're not human. They think they've got all there is and all they've got to do is convert us to think and do what they think and do. Then, everything will be just great. But, man, these jerks pop up in the morning with their little briefcases and they cut out for their homes a hell of a way around five or six at night, and that's it. If you ever are nuts enough to go to one of them, they hand you the old crap, 'Now, son, you shouldn't feel that way.'

"Now, look, I don't think these guys mean any harm. I think the least thing they want is to do any harm. But harm comes in many forms."

So Hiram and the people on the block have come to distrust those who arrive with good words and offers of help. They feel that they have only themselves to depend on, that only within their group is there reliability.

"As bad as things are here," Hiram said, "in my lifetime I have seen more good things on this block than I have seen bad. On my block, people help each other and most of them do the right things, for themselves and for everybody. Man, I have seen thieves help thieves; I have seen thieves help other guys; I have seen guys who have to rob for a living, and I mean really rob because they don't have any other way, I have seen them give their money to make another guy a little happier.

"I have seen an addict—and this guy was nearly crying for a fix and practically running across the street to get one—stop and shove his last three in the shirt pocket of another guy who was married and had a lot of kids but who couldn't find a job and didn't have any money. And this junkie went walking away, kicking himself and cursing, 'Now, why the hell did I do that?'

"Now, man, this may not sound like much, but that one incident, for me, could equal fifty unjust things, because it shows that these people do have concern about each other, even though it may be hard for them to show it or express it or maybe even to understand it."

The people on the block are not unconscious of the horror and the filth and destitution around them. They know that it is bad and, at times, they talk of leaving it, though few ever do. But now, today, most of them are afraid. They are afraid because their block is going; all around, new housing projects have risen and this is almost the last block to remain unchanged.

It will not remain so for long, and the people know it. Hiram said that most of them would not be able to get into the new projects; some because they wouldn't be able to afford the rents, some because they have an addict or a criminal in the family and the rules forbid such tenants.

"The people are going to have to move, like up to the Bronx, and the landlords know that these people are going to need houses, so instead of fifty they'll make it seventy or one hundred an apartment; they're already doing it.

"Man, this is the end of my block," said Hiram. "This is something that we all evade; like, this has been going on for five years. All the other blocks have been going, and this has been in my mind, in everybody's mind, but I haven't really given it any thought, but it scares me, I fear it. But wherever, any place, there is poverty and minorities like us, you will find another block like this one, with all the same problems and the same horrors that we have. Maybe that's where we will have to go. Forget it, man, let me live in this rathole that I have now, that I know, instead of some other new rathole that I don't know."

"... A national effort toward the problems of Negro Americans must be directed towards the question of family structure."

THE NEGRO FAMILY*

The report from which this selection is taken was written by Daniel Moynihan and presented as a working paper at a conference of professionals and civil rights workers. It aroused a storm of controversy. The issue of national and local policy that it dramatically raised is where one can most effectively intervene in the circle of prejudice, economic and social discrimination, social pathology, leading to further prejudice. Moynihan argues that massive effort must be directed toward the establishment of a stable Negro family structure. His critics retort that he is, by implication, blaming the Negroes themselves for a condition directly caused by the society's discrimination; they urge that the major effort of

* From *The Negro Family, The Case for National Action,* Office of Policy Planning and Research, United States Department of Labor, March, 1965. The extensive footnotes in this report have been eliminated, as have the many tables and charts, in the interests of readability. The reader interested in sources should consult the original report.

society should be to provide Negroes with equal access to jobs and other opportunities.

Assuming that his picture of the pathology resulting from Negro family structure is correct, is Moynihan's solution the best one? What are the possible consequences of a concentration on rebuilding the family structure, assuming that we know how to do it?

THAT the Negro American has survived at all is extraordinary —a lesser people might simply have died out, as indeed others have. That the Negro community has not only survived, but in this political generation has entered national affairs as a moderate, humane, and constructive national force is the highest testament to the healing powers of the democratic ideal and the creative vitality of the Negro people.

But it may not be supposed that the Negro American community has not paid a fearful price for the incredible mistreatment to which it has been subjected over the past three centuries.

In essence, the Negro community has been forced into a matriarchal structure which, because it is so out of line with the rest of the American society, seriously retards the progress of the group as a whole, and imposes a crushing burden on the Negro male and, in consequence, on a great many Negro women as well.

There is, presumably, no special reason why a society in which males are dominant in family relationships is to be preferred to a matriarchal arrangement. However, it is clearly a disadvantage for a minority group to be operating on one principle, while the great majority of the population, and the one with the most advantages to begin with, is operating on another. This is the present situation of the Negro. Ours is a society which presumes male leadership in private and public affairs. The arrangements of society facilitate such leadership and reward it. A subculture, such as that of the Negro American, in which this is not the pattern, is placed at a distinct disadvantage.

Here an earlier word of caution should be repeated. There is much evidence that a considerable number of Negro families have managed to break out of the tangle of pathology and to establish themselves as stable, effective units, living according to patterns of American society in general. E. Franklin Frazier has suggested that the middle-class Negro American family is, if anything, more patriarchal and protective of its children than the general run of such families. Given equal opportunities,

251

the children of these families will perform as well or better than their white peers. They need no help from anyone, and ask none.

While this phenomenon is not easily measured, one index is that middle-class Negroes have even fewer children than middle-class whites, indicating a desire to conserve the advances they have made and to insure that their children do as well or better. Negro women who marry early to uneducated laborers have more children than white women in the same situation; Negro women who marry at the common age for the middle class to educated men doing technical or professional work have only four-fifths as many children as their white counterparts.

It might be estimated that as much as half of the Negro community falls into the middle class. However, the remaining half is in desperate and deteriorating circumstances. Moreover, because of housing segregation it is immensely difficult for the stable half to escape from the cultural influences of the unstable one. The children of middle-class Negroes often as not must grow up in, or next to the slums, an experience almost unknown to white middle-class children. They are therefore constantly exposed to the pathology of the disturbed group and constantly in danger of being drawn into it. It is for this reason that the propositions put forth in this study may be thought of as having a more or less general application.

In a word, most Negro youth are in *danger* of being caught up in the tangle of pathology that affects their world, and probably a majority are so entrapped. Many of those who escape do so for one generation only: as things now are, their children may have to run the gauntlet all over again. That is not the least vicious aspect of the world that white America has made for the Negro.

Obviously, not every instance of social pathology afflicting the Negro community can be traced to the weakness of family structure. If, for example, organized crime in the Negro community were not largely controlled by whites, there would be more capital accumulation among Negroes, and therefore probably more Negro enterprises. If it were not for the hostility and fear many whites exhibit toward Negroes, they in turn would be less afflicted by hostility and fear and so on. There is no one Negro community. There is no one Negro problem. There is no one solution. Nonetheless, at the center of the tangle of pathology is the weakness of the family structure. Once or twice removed, it will be found to be the principal source of most of the aberrant, inadequate, or antisocial behavior that did not establish, but now serves to perpetuate the cycle of poverty and deprivation.

It was by destroying the Negro family under slavery that white America broke the will of the Negro people. Although that will has reasserted itself in our time, it is a resurgence doomed to frustration unless the viability of the Negro family is restored.

MATRIARCHY

A fundamental fact of Negro American family life is the often reversed roles of husband and wife.

Robert O. Blood, Jr. and Donald M. Wolfe, in a study of Detroit families, note that "Negro husbands have unusually low power," and while this is characteristic of all low income families, the pattern pervades the Negro social structure: "the cumulative result of discrimination in jobs . . . , the segregated housing, and the poor schooling of Negro men." In 44 per cent of the Negro families studied, the wife was dominant, as against 20 per cent of white wives. "Whereas the majority of white families are equalitarian, the largest percentage of Negro families are dominated by the wife."

The matriarchal pattern of so many Negro families reinforces itself over the generations. This process begins with education. Although the gap appears to be closing at the moment, for a long while, Negro females were better educated than Negro males, and this remains true today for the Negro population as a whole.

The difference in educational attainment between nonwhite men and women in the labor force is even greater; men lag 1.1 years behind women.

The disparity in educational attainment of male and female

youth age sixteen to twenty-one who were out of school in February 1963, is striking. Among the nonwhite males, 66.3 per cent were not high-school graduates, compared with 55.0 per cent of the females. A similar difference existed at the college level, with 4.5 per cent of the males having completed one to three years of college compared with 7.3 per cent of the females.

The poorer performance of the male in school exists from the very beginning, and the magnitude of the difference was documented by the 1960 Census in statistics on the number of children who have fallen one or more grades below the typical grade for children of the same age. The boys have more frequently fallen behind at every age level. (White boys also lag behind white girls, but at a differential of 1 to 6 percentage points.)

In 1960, 39 per cent of all white persons twenty-five years of age and over who had completed four or more years of college were women. Fifty-three per cent of the nonwhites who had attained this level were women.

However, the gap is closing. By October, 1963, there were slightly more Negro men in college than women. Among whites there were almost twice as many men as women enrolled.

There is much evidence that Negro females are better students than their male counterparts.

Daniel Thompson of Dillard University, in a private communication on January 9, 1965, writes:

> As low as is the aspirational level among lower-class Negro girls, it is considerably higher than among the boys. For example, I have examined the honor rolls in Negro high schools for about ten years. As a rule, from 75 to 90 per cent of all Negro honor students are girls.

Dr. Thompson reports that 70 per cent of all applications for the National Achievement Scholarship Program financed by the Ford Foundation for outstanding Negro high-school graduates are girls, despite special efforts by high school principals to submit the names of boys.

The finalists for this new program for outstanding Negro

students were recently announced. Based on an inspection of the names, only about 43 per cent of all the 639 finalists were male. (However, in the regular National Merit Scholarship program, males received 67 per cent of the 1964 scholarship awards.)

Inevitably, these disparities have carried over to the area of employment and income.

In one out of four Negro families where the husband is present, is an earner, and someone else in the family works, the husband is not the principal earner. The comparable figure for whites is 18 per cent.

More important, it is clear that Negro females have established a strong position for themselves in white-collar and professional employment, precisely the areas of the economy which are growing most rapidly, and to which the highest prestige is accorded.

The President's Committee on Equal Employment Opportunity, making a preliminary report on employment in 1964 of over 16,000 companies with nearly five million employees, revealed this pattern with dramatic emphasis.

> In this work force, Negro males outnumber Negro females by a ratio of 4 to 1. Yet Negro males represent only 1.2 per cent of all males in white collar occupations, while Negro females represent 3.1 per cent of the total female white collar work force. Negro males represent 1.1 per cent of all male professionals, whereas Negro females represent roughly 6 per cent of all female professionals. Again, in technician occupations, Negro males represent 2.1 per cent of all male technicians while Negro females represent roughly 10 per cent of all female technicians. It would appear therefore that there are proportionately four times as many Negro females in significant white-collar jobs than Negro males.
>
> Although it is evident that office and clerical jobs account for approximately 50 per cent of all Negro female white-collar workers, it is significant that six out of every 100 Negro females are in professional jobs. This is substantially similar to the rate of all females in such jobs. Approximately seven out of every 100 Negro females are in technician jobs. This exceeds the proportion of all females in technician jobs—approximately five out of every 100.

Negro females in skilled jobs are almost the same as that of all females in such jobs. Nine out of every 100 Negro males are in skilled occupations while 21 out of 100 of all males are in such jobs.

This pattern is to be seen in the Federal government, where special efforts have been made recently to insure equal employment opportunity for Negroes. These efforts have been notably successful in Departments such as Labor, where some 19 per cent of employees are now Negro. (A not disproportionate percentage, given the composition of the work force in the areas where the main Department offices are located.) However, it may well be that these efforts have redounded mostly to the benefit of Negro women, and may even have accentuated the comparative disadvantage of Negro men. Seventy percent of the Negro employees of the Department of Labor are women, as contrasted with only 42 per cent of the white employees.

Among nonprofessional Labor Department employees— where the most employment opportunities exist for all groups —Negro women outnumber Negro men 4 to 1, and average almost one grade higher in classification.

The testimony to the effects of these patterns in Negro family structure is widespread, and hardly to be doubted.

Whitney Young

Historically, in the matriarchal Negro society, mothers made sure that if one of their children had a chance for higher education the daughter was the one to pursue it.

The effect on family functioning and role performance of this historical experience [economic deprivation] is what you might predict. Both as a husband and as a father the Negro male is made to feel inadequate, not because he is unlovable or unaffectionate, lacks intelligence or even a gray flannel suit. But in a society that measures a man by the size of his pay check, he doesn't stand very tall in a comparison with his white counterpart. To this situation he may react with withdrawal, bitterness toward society, aggression both within the family and racial group, self-hatred, or crime. Or he may escape through a number of avenues that help him to lose himself in fantasy or to compensate for his low status through a variety of exploits.

Thomas Pettigrew

The Negro wife in this situation can easily become disgusted with her financially dependent husband, and her rejection of him further alienates the male from family life. Embittered by their experiences with men, many Negro mothers often act to perpetuate the mother-centered pattern by taking a greater interest in their daughters than their sons.

Deton Brooks

In a matriarchal structure, the women are transmitting the culture.

Dorothy Height

If the Negro woman has a major underlying concern, it is the status of the Negro man and his position in the community and his need for feeling himself an important person, free and able to make his contribution in the whole society in order that he may strengthen his home.

Duncan M. MacIntyre

The Negro illegitimacy rate always has been high—about eight times the white rate in 1940 and somewhat higher today even though the white illegitimacy rate also is climbing. The Negro statistics are symtomatic of some old socioeconomic problems, not the least of which are underemployment among Negro men and compensating higher labor force propensity among Negro women. Both operate to enlarge the mother's role, undercutting the status of the male and making many Negro families essentially matriarchal. The Negro man's uncertain employment prospects, matriarchy, and the high cost of divorces combine to encourage desertion (the poor man's divorce), increases the number of couples not married, and thereby also increases the Negro illegitimacy rate. In the meantime, higher Negro birth rates are increasing the nonwhite population, while migration into cities like Detroit, New York, Philadelphia, and Washington, D.C. is making the public assistance rolls in such cities heavily, even predominantly, **Negro**.

Robin M. Williams, Jr.
(in a study of Elmira, New York)

Only 57 per cent of Negro adults reported themselves as married—spouse present, as compared with 78 per cent of native white American gentiles, 91 per cent of Italian-American, and 96 per cent of Jewish informants. Of the 93 unmarried Negro youths interviewed, 22 per cent did not have their mother living in the home with them, and 42 per cent reported that their father was not living in their home. One third of the youths did not know their father's present occupation, and two thirds of a sample of 150 Negro adults did not know what the occupation of their father's father had been. Forty per cent of the youths said that they had brothers and sisters living in other communities: another 40 per cent reported relatives living in their home who were not parents, siblings, or grandparents.

THE FAILURE OF YOUTH

Williams' account of Negro youth growing up with little knowledge of their fathers, less of their fathers' occupations, still less of family occupational traditions, is in sharp contrast to the experience of the white child. The white family, despite many variants, remains a powerful agency not only for transmitting property from one generation to the next, but also for transmitting no less valuable contacts with the world of education and work. In an earlier age, the Carpenters, Wainwrights, Weavers, Mercers, Farmers, Smiths, acquired their names as well as their trades from their fathers and grandfathers. Children today still learn the patterns of work from their fathers even though they may no longer go into the same jobs.

White children without fathers at least perceive all about them the pattern of men working.

Negro children without fathers flounder—and fail.

Not always, to be sure. The Negro community, produces its share, very possibly more than its share, of young people who have the something extra that carries them over the worst obstacles. But such persons are always a minority. The common run of young people in a group facing serious obstacles to success do not succeed.

A prime index of the disadvantage of Negro youth in the United States is their consistently poor performance on the mental tests that are a standard means of measuring ability and performance in the present generation.

There is absolutely no question of any genetic differential: Intelligence potential is distributed among Negro infants in the same proportion and pattern as among Icelanders or Chinese or any other group. American society, however, impairs the Negro potential. The statement of the HARYOU report that "there is no basic disagreement over the fact that central Harlem students are performing poorly in school" may be taken as true of Negro slum children throughout the United States.

Eighth-grade children in central Harlem have a median IQ of 87.7, which means that perhaps a third of the children are scoring at levels perilously near to those of retardation. IQ *declines* in the first decade of life, rising only slightly thereafter.

The effect of broken families on the performance of Negro youth has not been extensively measured, but studies that have been made show an unmistakable influence.

Martin Deutch and Bert Brown, investigating intelligence test differences between Negro and white first and fifth graders of different social classes, found that there is a direct relationship between social class and IQ. As the one rises so does the other: but more for whites than Negroes. This is surely a result of housing segregation, referred to earlier, which makes it difficult for middle-class Negro families to escape the slums.

The authors explain that "it is much more difficult for the Negro to attain identical middle- or upper-middle-class status with whites, and the social class gradations are less marked for Negroes because Negro life in a caste society is considerably more homogeneous than is life for the majority group."

Therefore, the authors look for background variables other than social class which might explain the difference: "One of the most striking differences between the Negro and white groups is the consistently higher frequency of broken homes and resulting family disorganization in the Negro group."

Father Absent from the Home

LOWEST SOCIAL CLASS LEVEL		MIDDLE SOCIAL CLASS LEVEL		HIGHEST SOCIAL CLASS LEVEL	
Per cent of		Per cent of		Per cent of	
White	Negro	White	Negro	White	Negro
15.4	43.9	10.3	27.9	0.0	13.7

(Adapted from authors' table)

Further, they found that children from homes where fathers are present have significantly higher scores than children in homes without fathers.

	Mean Intelligence Scores
Father Present	97.83
Father Absent	90.79

The influence of the father's presence was then tested *within* the social classes and school grades for Negroes alone. They found that "a consistent trend within both grades at the lower SES [social class] level appears, and in no case is there a reversal of this trend: for males, females, and the combined group, the IQ's of children with fathers in the home are always higher than those who have no father in the home."

The authors say that broken homes "may also account for some of the differences between Negro and white intelligence scores."

The scores of fifth graders with fathers absent were lower than the scores of first graders with fathers absent, and while the authors point out that it is cross sectional data and does not reveal the duration of the fathers' absence, "What we might be tapping is the cumulative effect of fatherless years."

This difference in ability to perform has its counterpart in statistics on actual school performance. Nonwhite boys from families with both parents present are more likely to be going to school than boys with only one parent present, and enrollment rates are even lower when neither parent is present.

When the boys from broken homes are in school, they do

not do as well as the boys from whole families. Grade retardation is higher when only one parent is present, and highest when neither parent is present.

The loneliness of the Negro youth in making fundamental decisions about education is shown in a 1959 study of Negro and white dropouts in Connecticut high schools.

Only 29 per cent of the Negro male dropouts discussed their decision to drop out of school with their fathers, compared with 65 per cent of the white males (38 per cent of the Negro males were from broken homes). In fact, 26 per cent of the Negro males did not discuss this major decision in their lives with anyone at all, compared with only 8 per cent of white males.

A study of Negro apprenticeship by the New York State Commission Against Discrimination in 1960 concluded:

Negro youth are seldom exposed to influences which can lead to apprenticeship. Negroes are not apt to have relatives, friends, or neighbors in skilled occupations. Nor are they likely to be in secondary schools where they receive encouragement and direction from alternate role models. Within the minority community, skilled Negro 'models' after whom the Negro youth might pattern himself are rare, while substitute sources which could provide the direction, encouragement, resources, and information needed to achieve skilled craft standing are nonexistent.

DELINQUENCY AND CRIME

The combined impact of poverty, failure, and isolation among Negro youth has had the predictable outcome in a disastrous delinquency and crime rate.

In a typical pattern of discrimination, Negro children in all public and private orphanages are a smaller proportion of all children than their proportion of the population although their needs are clearly greater.

On the other hand Negroes represent a third of all youth in training schools for juvenile delinquents.

It is probable that at present, a majority of the crimes

against the person, such as rape, murder, and aggravated assault are committed by Negroes. There is, of course, no absolute evidence; inference can only be made from arrest and prison population statistics. The data that follow unquestionably are biased against Negroes, who are arraigned much more casually than are whites, but it may be doubted that the bias is great enough to affect the general proportions.

Again on the urban frontier the ratio is worse: three out of every five arrests for these crimes were of Negroes.

In Chicago in 1963, three quarters of the persons arrested for such crimes were Negro; in Detroit, the same proportions held.

In 1960, 37 per cent of all persons in Federal and state prisons were Negro. In that year, 56 per cent of the homicide and 57 per cent of the assault offenders committed to state institutions were Negro.

The overwhelming number of offenses committed by Negroes are directed toward other Negroes: the cost of crime to the Negro community is a combination of that to the criminal and to the victim.

Some of the research on the effects of broken homes on delinquent behavior recently surveyed by Thomas F. Pettigrew in *A Profile of the Negro American* is summarized below, along with several other studies of the question.

Mary Diggs found that three fourths—twice the expected ratio—of Philadelphia's Negro delinquents who came before the law during 1948 did not live with both their natural parents.

In predicting juvenile crime, Eleanor and Sheldon Glueck also found that a higher proportion of delinquent than non-delinquent boys came from broken homes. They identified five critical factors in the home environment that made a difference in whether boys would become delinquents: discipline of boy by father, supervision of boy by mother, affection of father for boy, affection of mother for boy, and cohesiveness of family.

In 1952, when the New York City Youth Board set out to test the validity of these five factors as predictors of delinquency, a problem quickly emerged. The Glueck sample consisted of white boys of mainly Irish, Lithuanian, and English descent.

However, the Youth Board group was 44 per cent Negro and
14 per cent Puerto Rican, and the frequency of broken homes
within these groups was out of proportion to the total number
of delinquents in the population.

> In the majority of these cases, the father was usually never in
> the home at all, absent for the major proportion of the boy's
> life, or was present only on occasion.

(The final prediction table was reduced to three factors:
supervision of boy by mother, discipline of boy by mother, and
family cohesiveness within what family, in fact, existed, but
was, nonetheless, 85 per cent accurate in predicting delinquents
and 96 per cent accurate in predicting nondelinquents.)

Researchers who have focussed upon the "good" boy in high
delinquency neighborhoods noted that they typically come from
exceptionally stable, intact families.

Recent psychological research demonstrates the personality
effects of being reared in a disorganized home without a father.
One study showed that children from fatherless homes seek
immediate gratification of their desires far more than children
with fathers present. Others revealed that children who hunger
for immediate gratification are more prone to delinquency,
along with other less social behavior. Two psychologists, Pettigrew says, maintain that inability to delay gratification is a
critical factor in immature, criminal, and neurotic behavior.

Finally, Pettigrew discussed the evidence that a stable home
is a crucial factor in counteracting the effects of racism upon
Negro personality.

> A warm, supportive home can effectively compensate for many
> of the restrictions the Negro child faces outside of the ghetto;
> consequently, the type of home life a Negro enjoys as a child
> may be far more crucial for governing the influence of segre-
> gation upon his personality than the form the segregation takes
> —legal or informal, Southern or Northern.

A Yale University study of youth in the lowest socioeconomic class in New Haven in 1950 whose behavior was followed
through their eighteenth year revealed that among the delin-

quents in the group, 38 per cent came from broken homes, compared with 24 per cent of nondelinquents.

The President's Task Force on Manpower Conservation in 1963 found that of young men rejected for the draft for failure to pass the mental tests, 42 per cent of those with a court record came from broken homes, compared with 30 per cent of those without a court record. Half of all the nonwhite rejectees in the study with a court record came from broken homes.

An examination of the family background of 44,448 delinquency cases in Philadelphia between 1949 and 1954 documents the frequency of broken homes among delinquents. Sixty-two per cent of the Negro delinquents and 36 per cent of white delinquents were not living with both parents. In 1950, 33 per cent of nonwhite children and 7 per cent of white children in Philadelphia were living in homes without both parents. Repeaters were even more likely to be from broken homes than first offenders.

THE ARMED FORCES

The ultimate mark of inadequate preparation for life is the failure rate on the Armed Forces mental test. The Armed Forces Qualification Test is not quite a mental test, nor yet an education test. It is a test of ability to perform at an acceptable level of competence. It roughly measures ability that ought to be found in an average seventh- or eighth-grade student. A grown young man who cannot pass this test is in trouble.

Fifty-six per cent of Negroes fail it.

This is a rate almost four times that of the whites.

The Army, Navy, Air Force, and Marines conduct by far the largest and most important education and training activities of the Federal Government, as well as provide the largest single source of employment in the nation.

Military service is disruptive in some respects. For those comparatively few who are killed or wounded in combat, or otherwise, the personal sacrifice is inestimable. But on balance service in the Armed Forces over the past quarter-century has worked greatly to the advantage of those involved. The training and experience of military duty itself is unique; the advantages that have generally followed in the form of the G.I. Bill, mortgage guarantees, Federal life insurance, Civil Service preference, veterans hospitals, and veterans pensions are singular, to say the least.

Although service in the Armed Forces is at least nominally a duty of all male citizens coming of age, it is clear that the present system does not enable Negroes to serve in anything like their proportionate numbers. This is not a question of discrimination. Induction into the Armed Forces is based on a variety of objective tests and standards, but these tests nonetheless have the effect of keeping the number of Negroes disproportionately small.

In 1963, the United States Commission on Civil Rights reported that "A decade ago, Negroes constituted 8 per cent of the Armed Forces. Today . . . they continue to constitute 8 per cent of the Armed Forces."

In 1964, Negroes constituted 11.8 per cent of the population, but probably remain at 8 per cent of the Armed Forces.

The significance of Negro underrepresentation in the Armed Forces is greater than might at first be supposed. If Negroes were represented in the same proportions in the military as they are in the population, they would number 300,000 plus. This would be over 100,000 more than at present (using 1964 strength figures). If the more than 100,000 unemployed Negro men were to have gone into the military the Negro male unemployment rate would have been 7.0 per cent in 1964 instead of 9.1 per cent.

In 1963, the Civil Rights Commission commented on the occupational aspect of military service for Negroes. "Negro enlisted men enjoy relatively better opportunities in the Armed Forces than in the civilian economy in every clerical, technical, and skilled field for which the data permit comparison."

There is, however, an even more important issue involved in military service for Negroes. Service in the United States Armed Forces is the *only* experience open to the Negro American in which he is truly treated as an equal: not as a Negro equal to a white, but as one man equal to any other man in a world where the category "Negro" and "white" do not exist.

If this is a statement of the ideal rather than reality, it is an ideal that is close to realization. In food, dress, housing, pay, work—the Negro in the Armed Forces *is* equal and is treated that way.

There is another special quality about military service for Negro men: it is an utterly masculine world. Given the strains of the disorganized and matrifocal family life in which so many Negro youth come of age, the Armed Forces are a dramatic and desperately needed change: a world away from women, a world run by strong men of unquestioned authority, where discipline, if harsh, is nonetheless orderly and predictable, and where rewards, if limited, are granted on the basis of performance.

The theme of a current Army recruiting message states it as clearly as can be: "In the U.S. Army you get to know what it means to feel like a man."

At the recent Civil Rights Commission hearings in Mississippi a witness testified that his Army service was in fact "the only time I ever felt like a man."

Yet a majority of Negro youth (and probably three-quarters of Mississippi Negroes) fail the Selective Service education test and are rejected. Negro participation in the Armed Forces would be less than it is, were it not for a proportionately larger share of voluntary enlistments and reenlistments. (Thus 16.3 per cent of Army sergeants are Negro.)

ALIENATION

The term alienation may by now have been used in too many ways to retain a clear meaning, but it will serve to sum up the equally numerous ways in which large numbers of Negro youth appear to be withdrawing from American society.

One startling way in which this occurs is that the men are just not there when the Census enumerator comes around.

According to Bureau of Census population estimates for 1963, there are only 87 nonwhite males for every 100 females in the thirty-to-thirty-four-year age group. The ratio does not exceed 90 to 100 throughout the twenty-five-to-forty-four-year age bracket. In the urban Northeast, there are only 76 males per 100 females twenty-to-twenty-four-years of age, and males as a percent of females are below 90 per cent throughout all ages after fourteen.

There are not really fewer men than women in the twenty-to-forty age bracket. What obviously is involved is an error in counting: the surveyors simply do not find the Negro man. Donald J. Bogue and his associates, who have studied the the Federal count of the Negro man, place the error as high as 19.8 per cent at age twenty-eight; a typical error of around 15 per cent is estimated from age nineteen through forty-three. Preliminary research in the Bureau of the Census on the 1960 enumeration has resulted in similar conclusions, although not necessarily the same estimates of the extent of the error. The Negro male *can* be found at age seventeen and eighteen. On the basis of birth records and mortality records, the conclusion must be that he is there at age nineteen as well.

When the enumerators do find him, his answers to the standard questions asked in the monthly unemployment survey often result in counting him as "not in the labor force." In other words, Negro male unemployment may in truth be somewhat greater than reported.

The labor force participation rates of nonwhite men have been falling since the beginning of the century and for the past decade have been lower than the rates for white men. In 1964, the participation rates were 78.0 per cent for white men and 75.8 per cent for nonwhite men. Almost one percentage point of this difference was due to a higher proportion of nonwhite men unable to work because of long-term physical or mental illness; it seems reasonable to assume that the rest of the difference is due to discouragement about finding a job.

If nonwhite male labor force participation rates were as high as the white rates, there would have been 140,000 more nonwhite males in the labor force in 1964. If we further assume that the 140,000 would have been unemployed, the unemployment rate for nonwhite men would have been 11.5 per cent instead of the recorded rate of 9 per cent, and the ratio between the nonwhite rate and the white rate would have jumped from 2:1 to 2.4:1.

Understated or not, the official unemployment rates for Negroes are almost unbelievable.

The unemployment statistics for Negro teenagers—29 per cent in January, 1965—reflect lack of training and opportunity in the greatest measure, but it may not be doubted that they also reflect a certain failure of nerve.

"Are you looking for a job?" Secretary of Labor Wirtz asked a young man on a Harlem street corner. "Why?" was the reply.

Richard A. Cloward and Robert Ontell have commented on this withdrawal in a discussion of the Mobilization for Youth project on the lower East Side of New York.

> What contemporary slum and minority youth probably lack that similar children in earlier periods possessed is not motivation but some minimal sense of competence.
>
> We are plagued, in work with these youth, by what appears to be a low tolerance for frustration. They are not able to absorb setbacks. Minor irritants and rebuffs are magnified out of all proportion to reality. Perhaps they react as they do because they are not equal to the world that confronts them, and they know it. And it is the knowing that is devastating. Had the occupational structure remained intact, or had the education provided to them kept pace with occupational changes, the situation would be a different one. But it is not, and that is what we and they have to contend with.

Narcotic addiction is a characteristic form of withdrawal. In 1963, Negroes made up 54 per cent of the addict population of the United States. Although the Federal Bureau of Narcotics reports a decline in the Negro proportion of new addicts, HARYOU reports the addiction rate in central Harlem rose from 22.1 per 10,000 in 1955 to 40.4 in 1961.

There is a larger fact about the alienation of Negro youth than the tangle of pathology described by these statistics. It is a fact particularly difficult to grasp by white persons who have in recent years shown increasing awareness of Negro problems.

The present generation of Negro youth growing up in the urban ghettos has probably less personal contact with the white world than any generation in the history of the Negro American.

Until World War II, it could be said that in general the Negro and white worlds lived, if not together, at least side by side. Certainly they did, and do, in the South.

Since World War II, however, the two worlds have drawn physically apart. The symbol of this development was the construction in the 1940's and 1950's of the vast white, middle- and lower-middle class suburbs around all of the Nation's cities. Increasingly the inner cities have been left to Negroes—who now share almost no community life with whites.

In turn, because of this new housing pattern—most of which has been financially assisted by the Federal government—it is probable that the American school system has become *more,* rather than less segregated in the past two decades.

School integration has not occurred in the South, where a decade after *Brown v. Board of Education* only one Negro in nine is attending school with white children.

And in the North, despite strenuous official efforts, neighborhoods and therefore schools are becoming more and more of one class and one color.

In New York City, in the school year 1957–58 there were 64 schools that were 90 per cent of more Negro or Puerto Rican. Six years later there were 134 such schools.

Along with the diminution of white middle-class contacts for a large percentage of Negroes, observers report that the Negro churches have all but lost contact with men in the Northern cities as well. This may be a normal condition of urban life, but it is probably a changed condition for the Negro American and cannot be a socially desirable development.

The only religious movement that appears to have enlisted a considerable number of lower class Negro males in Northern cities of late is that of the Black Muslims: a movement based on total rejection of white society, even though it emulates whites more.

In a word: the tangle of pathology is tightening.

". . . for a long time I didn't go back very often. There was shame there."

YOU DON'T HAVE A DADDY*

Dick Gregory

A successful Negro comedian, Gregory has partici- pated very actively in the civil rights movement, both in the South and in the North. This brief excerpt from his autobiography, *Nigger,* illustrates heart- breakingly the impact on the child of Moynihan's sociological generalizations.

* From Dick Gregory (with Robert Lipsyte), *Nigger,* New York and London: E. P. Dutton and Co. and Allen and Unwin, Ltd., 1964, pp. 44–6. Copyright © 1964 by Dick Gregory Enterprises, Inc. Reprinted by permis- sion of the publishers.

IT WAS on a Thursday, the day before the Negro payday. The eagle always flew on Friday. The teacher was asking each student how much his father would give to the Community Chest. On Friday night, each kid would get the money from his father, and on Monday he would bring it to the school. I decided I was going to buy me a Daddy right then. I had money in my pocket from shining shoes and selling papers, and whatever Helene Tucker pledged for her Daddy I was going to top it. And I'd hand the money right in. I wasn't going to wait until Monday to buy me a Daddy.

I was shaking, scared to death. The teacher opened her book and started calling out names alphabetically.

"Helene Tucker?"

"My Daddy said he'd give two dollars and fifty cents."

"That's very nice, Helene. Very, very nice indeed."

That made me feel pretty good. It wouldn't take too much to top that. I had almost three dollars in dimes and quarters in my pocket. I stuck my hand in my pocket and held onto the money, waiting for her to call my name. But the teacher closed her book after she called everybody else in the class.

I stood up and raised my hand.

"What is it now?"

"You forgot me."

She turned toward the blackboard. "I don't have time to be playing with you, Richard."

"My Daddy said he'd . . ."

"Sit down, Richard, you're disturbing the class."

"My Daddy said he'd give . . . fifteen dollars."

She turned around and looked mad. "We are collecting this money for you and your kind, Richard Gregory. If your Daddy can give fifteen dollars you have no business being on relief."

"I got it right now, I got it right now, my Daddy gave it to me to turn in today, my Daddy said . . ."

"And furthermore," she said, looking right at me, her nostrils getting big and her lips getting thin and her eyes opening wide, "we know you don't have a Daddy."

Helene Tucker turned around, her eyes full of tears. She

felt sorry for me. Then I couldn't see her too well because I was crying, too.

"Sit down, Richard."

And I always thought the teacher kind of liked me. She always picked me to wash the blackboard on Friday, after school. That was a big thrill, it made me feel important. If I didn't wash it, come Monday the school might not function right.

"Where are you going, Richard?"

I walked out of school that day, and for a long time I didn't go back very often. There was shame there.

". . . Clearly these children have a profound initial handicap in the scholastic competition with middle class children."

THE SOCIAL WORLD OF
THE URBAN SLUM CHILD*

Suzanne Keller

The emphasis on the schooling problems of the Negro child, and the members of other ethnic minorities, often obscures the fact that many of the same difficulties are present among white children of lower social class levels. Chicago and Detroit, for example, have sizeable numbers of poor white families who migrate into the city from the mountain areas south and east of these cities. This article is valuable not only for its demonstration of similarities due to socio-economic level, but also for its carefully drawn distinction between Negro and white children at the same level. As a background piece, it supplements the data presented in other selections in this section, and adds to the sophistication with which one can approach the issues of inner city education generally.

* From Suzanne Keller, "The Social World of the Urban Slum Child," *American Journal of Orthopsychiatry*, XXXIII, 5, 1963, 824–21. Copyright © by The American Orthopsychiatric Association, Inc. Reproduced by permission.

THE CHILDREN studied are forty-six first- and fifth-grade children currently living and attending public school in the poorer sections of New York City. Both colored and white children are included, though in view of the incompleteness of the larger study from which they are drawn, they are not equally represented. By means of an Index of Social Class developed at the Institute, based on occupational and educational level of the main support of the family and on a Crowding Index, these children were all classified as Level IV on a ten-level stratification continuum, which might be considered as somewhere at the top of the lower-lower class stratum or at the bottom of the upper-lower class stratum. The children were seen in the schools for several hours, during which they took a number of tests tapping their verbal, intellectual and conceptual abilities. Their parents received questionnaires by mail and the children themselves gave accounts of their typical weekend activities and their life at home. It must be pointed out that the major purpose of the larger study was to compare test performances on various measures, and not to obtain full and comprehensive information on socioeconomic backgrounds. The background measures, in fact, permit at best only a rough classification of the socioeconomic levels of the children. But, although these measures are gross, they do depict some aspects of life in the slums of Harlem and in some of the poorer white sections in the changing neighborhoods of Brooklyn and Manhattan. One-fifth of the families were interviewed in their own homes.

The following summary is divided into two parts: an over-all comparison, and a comparison of Negroes and whites separately. Four areas are discussed: (1) social and economic characteristics of the families, such as size, available space, regional origins of the parents and educational and occupational attainments; (2) the children's after-school and weekend activities; (3) the children's self-perceptions; and (4) parental aspirations for the children.

SOCIAL AND ECONOMIC BACKGROUNDS

The children were selected so as to be roughly comparable in the educational and occupational attainments of the main support of the family and a Crowding Index. On all three of these they fell on the lower end of a socioeconomic continuum, although gross measures such as these hardly tap more than a fraction of the characteristics associated with lower-class life. The breadwinners in these families were employed as porters, short-order cooks, unskilled and semiskilled factory workers and maintenance and service workers. A few were bus or taxi drivers, clerks and self-employed. The somewhat higher occupational positions of the self-employed were offset by over-crowded living conditions and conspicuously low educational attainments. One out of six of the breadwinners was unemployed at the time of the study and these families were receiving welfare assistance. On the average, the parents of these children had not gone beyond the first year of high school, and the mothers had somewhat more schooling than the fathers.

Family size, nativity and family composition showed some important variations within the group. Less than three-fifths of these families conformed to the modal American type of two parents with between two and three children; more than two-fifths were large families with six to ten members. The average number of persons per room in the household was 1.2; this went as high as 1.5 persons per room for the larger families.

These families are not by and large the poor immigrant of half a century ago. These poor are Americanized, the majority born and raised on native ground. They also have been poor for a long time—two thirds have held their current low-level jobs for six years or more, one third for as long as ten years or more. Nor have they experienced extensive job mobility —one half have had no other job during the past ten years, and none more than three jobs during that time. If either rapid horizontal or vertical mobility is characteristic of workers at higher levels and at the lowest levels, it does not, apparently, characterize these.

These, then, are among the poorest elements of the population, they hold low-level jobs, they have had such jobs for a number of years, and they typically have not finished high school. Their actual chances for upward mobility are therefore objectively low. Thus their own subjective appraisals for such mobility are interesting. When asked to classify themselves in one of three groups, those going up, those going down in the world, and those doing neither, fully two thirds felt they were going up in the world, three tenths felt they were at a standstill, and only 2 per cent stated that they were going downhill: The ethic of success is very much in evidence.

LIFE OUTSIDE OF SCHOOL

All forty-six children live in homes that contain both radio and television sets and all utilize both media regularly and frequently. Three fourths had spent at least two hours (a sizable proportion as many as five) before their television sets the previous day watching a variety of entertainment programs—cartoons, the fights, Westerns, a few adult shows such as "I Love Lucy" and "Hitchcock Presents," and some of the better known comedians. The larger society seems to come to these children via entertainment and escapist stories on television. The children are familiar, even in the first grade, with the names of programs and of leading characters—a fact which might be used in school instruction.

This emphasis on peer-group entertainment also runs through their accounts of typical weekend activities. These children are between the ages of five and thirteen, years crucial for the acquisition of skills and information and the development of any talents they may possess. Life is not yet as serious as it will one day be, responsibilities are at a minimum, and the mind is receptive to new experiences and to the exploration of the natural and the social world. Yet hardly any of these children mention using their time to prepare themselves for something—they play, they watch television, they see films and they listen to music on the radio. Sometimes they visit relatives and go to Church on Sundays. They do not read, they do not study, they do not take lessons, they do not get instruction in any of the things that interest many children at these ages.

There is clearly a lack of sustained interaction with adult members of their families—a fact corroborating the findings of studies by Esther Milner, Walter B. Miller and others. Only about one half, for example, regularly eat one meal with one or both parents, the rest either eat alone or with brothers and sisters only. This robs them of one of the important socializing and intellectually stimulating experiences of childhood. According to Bossard and Boll,[1] the family meal is a focus for a number of important emotional, cultural and educational experiences. Participation and interaction with significant others in an organized way helps shape the personality and sensitizes the participants to each other's needs and inclinations. Organized conversation helps shape vocabulary, influences the development of verbal facility and subtlety and determines a whole set of complex attitudes and feelings about the use of language. The family meal also serves as an acculturating agency, for, in their interaction, the members teach each other and develop a way of seeing themselves and the world in which they live. The family meal has been described as a forum, as a clearing house for information, as a school for life and as an opportunity to act out deeper personality needs. Such experiences were absent in the lives of at least one-half of the lower-class children here discussed.

SELF-PERCEPTIONS

Compared to middle-class children these children are evidently handicapped, both in their objective living conditions and in their opportunities for learning outside of school, either from their parents and other family members through sustained relationships and contacts, or through organized activities other than play or passive response to the mass media. Presumably, this will affect their self-perceptions and their school performance.

The Self-Concept and Motivation Test of the Institute con-

1. J. H. S. Bossard and E. S. Boll, *The Sociology of Child Development,* New York: Harper, 1960, Chap. 13.

tains ten incompleted sentences, each relating to some wish, judgment or evaluation of the child. One in particular seems to tap the self-image of the child by comparison with other children: "When I look at other boys and girls, and then look at myself, I feel. . . ." In all, 28 of 46 responses (or 60 per cent) were unfavorable to the child, and only 14 of the 46 (30 per cent) were favorable. The favorable responses read: "I feel good, happy, the same." The unfavorable ones read: "I feel ashamed, sad, heartbroken." The proportion of unfavorable self-references, moreover, increases from 55 per cent in the first grade to 65 per cent in the fifth. These children, then, typically express a low self-esteem, drawing unfavorable comparisons between themselves and their school mates. If such self-deprecation is representative of the feelings of most young children from lower socioeconomic backgrounds, it suggests one potential source for early school failure.

PARENTAL ASPIRATIONS FOR THEIR CHILDREN

A number of studies have shown that parents may abandon their hopes for conspicuous achievements only to project them the more intensely onto their children.[2] These parents, too, conform to this pattern. When they were asked to indicate a first and a second choice of possible future occupations, although they could have nothing but vague hopes and expectations about the occupational future of their young children, their replies provide some insight into their ambitions and hopes. In their choices for the boys, fully two thirds of the parents currently engaged in unskilled and semiskilled labor or unemployed hoped that their sons would become professional men such as doctors, lawyers, engineers or business executives. Parents of girls most frequently mentioned such traditional feminine callings as nursing and teaching.

2. E. Chinoy, *Automobile Workers and the American Dream,* New York: Random House, 1955.

S. M. Lipset and R. Bendix, *Social Mobility in Industrial Society,* Berkeley and Los Angeles: University of California Press, 1962, Chap. IX.

F. Zweig, *The Worker in an Affluent Society,* New York: The Free Press, 1961, p. 21.

As to the amount of schooling they would like their children to obtain, here again, aspirations were high. Eight tenths of the parents wish their children to acquire a college degree. Only one tenth would be satisfied with a high school diploma.

These responses compare interestingly with those given in private interviews in the homes of the ten families who had not answered the mail questionnaire. When asked what they considered the best sort of job to have, security and steady work, rather than prestige, power or riches, received greatest emphasis. Ideally, then, on the fantasy level perhaps, these parents would like to see their sons get to the top. More realistically, they will be satisfied if their children manage to do what they themselves have failed to do—get a steady and secure job.

In sum, the children described in this paper come from large families living in relatively crowded quarters in the midst or on the edge of poverty. Only two out of three are being supported solely by their fathers' earnings in low-level jobs, and one out of six are currently exposed to the stings of their parents' unemployment and the mixed blessings of public assistance. The majority of the parents, most of whom are native born, have been in this relatively deprived status for a long time—two thirds for more than six years, one third for more then ten. Nor has there been the sort of rapid job mobility one has come to expect from the official statistics on national trends, for, most of these people had held at most two other jobs at similar levels during the previous ten years.

All of this might lead to a pervasive sense of discouragement among them—and well it may, for we have no data to tap these feelings directly. Such discouragement is not, however, translated into resignation or indifference toward upward mobility. For, fully two thirds of the group believe that they are on the way up in the world and a bare 2 per cent feel that things are going downhill. These great expectations are further reflected in the high hopes they have for their children, whom they would like to see graduating from college and entering one of the professions. Whether these desires reflect concrete plans or unrealistic fantasies about the future cannot be assessed.

What else do we know about these children, most of whom do poorly in school about which they care very little? Television seems to be a rather persistent influence. They like to play and they have friends. But they have little sustained contact with adults, they have few organized conversations with other adults the way middle-class children do, and few participate in shared family activities. Even at meal times, one half of these children are alone or in the company of their brothers and sisters. It is interesting that, although these children are poor, they are not starving—the foods typically eaten at breakfast and dinner include a considerable variety of nutritionally adequate foods although amounts were not indicated. Poverty, today, probably extends more to housing, to lack of spending money, to lack of comforts and to a constricted milieu for learning and exploring the world. A city, especially a metropolis, would seem to be a fascinating place in which to grow up, but one would not believe this from these accounts of restricted movement and the monotonous repetitiveness of activities— TV and more TV, play with other children, movies and, as the single organized activity besides school, Church on Sunday for one-half of the group. Their world seems to be small and monotonous, though not necessarily unhappy.

This constriction of experience and the poverty of spirit it engenders may account for the below normal IQ scores of this group of poor children by the time of the fifth grade (mean IQ is 88.57 on Lorge Thorndike nonverbal IQ test; in first grade, Lorge Thorndike IQ mean scores were 96.56), confirming countless other studies that have shown a similar scholastic and verbal inferiority for children from underprivileged environments. It may also account for the high degree of negative self-evaluations already discussed.

In recent years there has been talk of the existence of a lower-class culture that performs much the same function for its members as any culture does: It defines the world, structures perceptions and habitual reactions, sets goals and standards and permits people to evaluate and approve each other's conduct. This means that lower-class culture patterns, while substantially different from middle-class patterns, nevertheless provide a web of shared meanings for those subject to its rewards and penalties. Still, cultural relativism ignores the fact that schools and industry are middle-class in organization and outlook. If lower-class children conform to the "focal concerns"[3] of their milieu they will typically be misfits in the schools they attend. Short of adapting the public school to the cultural milieu of different groups, the children of this background will be at a disadvantage.

Clearly these children have a profound initial handicap in the scholastic competition with middle-class children. This initial disadvantage rarely turns to later advantage—instead, they become negativistic or bored and fail to learn the rudiments of the verbal and intellectual skills expected of adults in an industrial society.

The discrepancy in preschool orientation by social class is duplicated within the lower class by race. Using the same index of socioeconomic status, we find that even when gross socioeconomic factors are controlled, Negroes and whites do not live in comparable social environments.

For one thing, lower-class Negro (Level IV on the Index) children come from larger families than white children (nearly one half as compared to one third among the white children have at least three brothers or sisters). Thus an already low income must stretch farther for one group than for the other. More significantly, only one half the Negro children were supported solely by the earnings of their fathers, whereas fully nine tenths of the white children had fathers who could assume the traditional male role of chief breadwinner. In addition, three times as many Negro as white children at the same socioeconomic level live in families where the adults are currently unemployed and receiving welfare and other types of aid for the indigent. In educational attainment, too, the white families were somewhat at an advantage, the fathers of the white children having on the average one more year of schooling than the Negro fathers, and the white mothers having one half a year more. In each group, however, the mothers were somewhat better educated than the fathers.

3. W. B. Miller, "Lower Class Culture as a Generating Milieu of Gang Delinquency," *Journal of Social Issues,* 14: 5–19 (1958).

One of the striking differences occurs with regard to place of birth. Three fourths of the Negro parents were geographically mobile, two thirds having been born in the South and one tenth outside the United States. None of the white children came from mobile families—all had parents both of whom had been born in the North.

As regards occupational mobility, however, Negro families were more likely to have held their present low-level jobs for a long time. In fact, whereas more than half the white families were at this low level for less than six years, more than half the Negro families had been there for six years or more. Thus, whereas Negro families at this level were more mobile geographically, they were less mobile occupationally. This does not, apparently, diminish their belief in their own success. Fully three fourths of the Negro families, as against only one third of the white families, felt that they were going up in the world. Only one fifth of the Negro families felt that they were at a standstill, but three fifths of the white felt this way. Negro lower-class children are thus raised in objectively inferior homes in which subjective appraisals of life's chances are much higher than among a comparable group of white families. Without more extensive data it is impossible to account for this discrepancy, although two possibilities suggest themselves. One relates to the differential geographical mobility of Negro families, which may lead them to expect other types of mobility as well. That is, they may have migrated to New York in the hope of improving their standing. The other relates to the relative standing of two equally low-level socioeconomic groups in the larger world. Level IV has been described as somewhere at the top of the lowest and most underprivileged stratum, or at the bottom of the upper-lower stratum. But, while the two groups were objectively at the same socioeconomic level, their status relative to most others of their rate is quite different. The majority of white persons in this country are above the lower-class level but the same does not hold true for Negroes. This means, then, that the top of the lower-lower class is an exceedingly low status for most of the white families but perhaps a relatively high one for the Negro families. In other words, the white families may feel relatively deprived by comparison with others, whereas the Negro families may feel relatively favored. Further exploration on a larger sample should clarify this. It would be interesting, for example, to see whether this expressed optimism is also characteristic of the very lowest socioeconomic group among Negroes.

The most striking finding regarding the children themselves concerns the self-perceptions of the fifth graders. Negro children definitely exhibit more negative self-evaluations than do white children; 30 per cent of the white children but fully 80 per cent of the Negro children draw unfavorable self-other comparisons, paralleling findings from a number of other studies.[4]

These fifth-grade Negro children had also been evaluated by their teachers and some of their observations are relevant. More than half were judged to have little motivation for school work, to be typically sad or preoccupied, and to be working below capacity in school. The interplay between self-perception and school achievement must be explored further, particularly in view of the fact that the parents of the Negro children were very much concerned about their children's work, for, whereas nearly all the white families were satisfied with their children's school work, only one half of the Negro families were. This may be yet another indication of the greater ambitiousness of the Negro families already noted.

These preliminary results reveal rather striking differences between Negro and white school children at the same socio-economic level in their objective living conditions, parental aspirations, and their self-evaluations. Similarly, by inference, lower-class children, irrespective of race, differ sharply in their preparation for school from the ideal middle-class children with whom they must compete. Presumably, in both instances, this will exert a negative effect on intellectual interests and ambitions and may thus help account for the long-demonstrated correlation between socioeconomic deprivation and school failure.

4. For a summary of such studies, see R. M. Drager and K. S. Miller, "Comparative Psychological Studies of Negroes and Whites in the United States," *Psycholog. Bull.,* 57(5): 382–383 (1960).

". . . the learning environment of the culturally deprived child is both generally inferior and specifically inappropriate."

A TEACHING STRATEGY
FOR CULTURALLY
DEPRIVED PUPILS:
COGNITIVE AND MOTIVATIONAL CONSIDERATIONS*

David P. Ausubel

The linkages between family structure and its accompanying economic deprivation, as described by Moynihan, and the school achievement of the inner-city child, are treated from the point of view of the educator in this article by Ausubel, a psychologist experienced with the problem. Teachers and other school personnel have known for some time that the language and general cognitive development of the slum child suffered as a result of many elements of lower-lower class culture: relative absence of verbal

* From David P. Ausubel, "A Teaching Strategy for Culturally Deprived Pupils: Cognitive and Motivational Considerations," *The School Review*, LXXI, 4, Winter 1963, 454–63. Reprinted by permission of the publisher.

communication between adults and children, orientation to the concrete and distrust of the abstract, and
even the fact that the home has relatively few objects
for the child to learn and name in early linguistic
stages. Prenursery programs like Head Start are based
on differences between lower- and middle-class life
styles, as are many suggestions for programs of special
motivation. Ausubel agrees with many of these attempts, the Higher Horizons Program, for example,
but advocates a general strategy in regard to motivation that is at odds with much current thinking in
the field.

*How valid is his argument that the schools
should rely on a motivation that results from feelings of reward associated with the learning itself?
What demands does this view make on the kind
of teachers that one would have to develop for the
slum schools?*

THE POSSIBILITY of arresting and reversing the course of intellectual retardation in the culturally deprived pupil depends largely on providing him with an optimal learning environment as early as possible in the course of his educational career. If the limiting effects of prolonged cultural deprivation on the development of verbal intelligence and on the acquisition of verbal knowledge are to be at least partially overcome, better-than-average strategies of teaching are obviously necessary in terms of both general effectiveness and specific appropriateness for his particular learning situation. Yet precisely the opposite state of affairs typically prevails: the learning environment of the culturally deprived child is both generally inferior and specifically inappropriate. His cumulative intellectual deficit, therefore, almost invariably reflects, in part, the cumulative impact of a continuing and consistently deficient learning environment, as well as his emotional and motivational reaction to this environment. Thus, much of the lower-class child's alienation from the school is not so much a reflection of discriminatory or rejecting attitudes on the part of teachers and other school personnel—although the importance of this factor should not be underestimated; it is in greater measure a reflection of the cumulative effects of a curriculum that is too demanding of him, and of the resulting load of frustration, confusion, demoralization, resentment, and impaired self-confidence that he must bear.

An effective and appropriate teaching strategy for the culturally deprived child must therefore emphasize these three considerations: (*a*) the selection of initial learning material geared to the learner's existing state of readiness; (*b*) mastery and consolidation of all ongoing learning tasks before new tasks are introduced, so as to provide the necessary foundation for successful sequential learning and to prevent unreadiness for future learning tasks; and (*c*) the use of structured learning materials optimally organized to facilitate efficient sequential learning. Attention to these three factors can go a long way toward insuring effective learning for the first time, and toward restoring the child's educational morale and confidence in his ability to learn. Later possible consequences are partial restoration of both intrinsic and extrinsic motivation for academic achievement, diminution of anti-intellectualism, and decreased alienation from the school to the point where his studies make sense and he sees some purpose in learning. In my opinion, of all the available teaching strategies, programmed instruction, minus the teaching-machine format, has the greatest potentialities for meeting the aforementioned three criteria of an effective and appropriate approach to the teaching of culturally deprived pupils.

Readiness

A curriculum that takes the readiness of the culturally deprived child into account always takes as its starting point his existing knowledge and sophistication in the various subject-matter areas and intellectual skills, no matter how far down the scale this happens to be. This policy demands rigid elimination of all subject matter that he cannot economically assimilate on the basis of his current level of cognitive sophistication. It presupposes emphasis on his acquisition of the basic intellectual skills before any attempt is made to teach him algebra, geometry, literature, and foreign languages. However, in many urban high schools and junior high schools today, pupils who cannot read at a third-grade level and who cannot speak or write grammatically or perform simple arithmetical computations are subjected to irregular French verbs, Shakespearean drama, and geometrical theorems. Nothing more educationally futile or better calculated to destroy educational morale could be imagined!

In the terms of readiness for a given level of school work, a child is no less ready because of a history of cultural deprivation, chronic academic failure, and exposure to an unsuitable curriculum than because of deficient intellectual endowment. Hence, realistic recognition of this fact is not undemocratic, reactionary, or evidence of social class bias, of intellectual snobbery, of a "soft," patronizing approach, or a belief in the inherent uneducability of lower-class children. Neither is it indicative of a desire to surrender to the culturally deprived child's current intellectual level, to perpetuate the status quo, or to institute a double, class-oriented standard of education. It is merely a necessary first step in preparing him to cope with more advanced subject matter, and hence in eventually reducing existing social class differentials in aademic achievement. To set the same *initial* standards and expectations for the academically retarded culturally deprived child as for the nonretarded middle- or lower-class child is automatically to insure the former's failure and to widen prevailing discrepancies between social class groups.

Consolidation

By insisting on consolidation or mastery of ongoing lessons before new material is introduced, we make sure of continued readiness and success in sequentially organized learning. Abundant experimental research has confirmed the proposition that prior learnings are not transferable to new learning tasks unless they are first overlearned.[1] Overlearning, in turn, requires an adequate number of adequately spaced repetitions and reviews, sufficient intratask repetitiveness prior to intra- and intertask diversification,[2] and opportunity for differential practice of the more difficult components of a task. Frequent testing and provision of feedback, especially with test items demanding fine discrimination among alternatives varying in degrees of correctness, also enhance consolidation by confirming, clarifying, and correcting previous learnings. Lastly, in view of the fact that the culturally deprived child tends to learn more slowly

1. See R. W. Bruce, "Conditions of Transfer of Training," *Journal of Experimental Psychology*, XVI, 1933, 343–61; C. P. Duncan, "Transfer in Motor Learning as a Function of Degree of First-task Learning and Intertask Similarity," *Journal of Experimental Psychology*, XLV, 1953, 1–11, and his "Transfer after Training with Single versus Multiple Tasks," *Journal of Experimental Psychology*, LV, 1958, 63–72; L. Morrisett and C. I. Hovland, "A Comparison of Three Varieties of Training in Human Problem Solving," *Journal of Experimental Psychology*, LV 1958, 52–5; and J. M. Sassenrath, "Learning without Awareness and Transfer of Learning Sets," *Journal of Educational Psychology*, L, 1959, 202–12.

2. See Duncan, "Transfer after Training with Single versus Multiple Tasks," *op. cit.*; Morrisett and Hovland, *op. cit.*; and Sassenrath, *op. Cit.*

than his non-deprived peers, self-pacing helps to facilitate consolidation.

Structured, sequential materials

The principal advantage of programmed instruction, apart from the fact that it furthers consolidation, is its careful sequential arrangement and gradation of difficulty which insures that each attained increment in learning serves as an appropriate foundation and anchoring post for the learning and retention of subsequent items in the ordered sequence.[3] Adequate programming of materials also presupposes maximum attention to such matters as lucidity, organization, and the explanatory and integrative power of substantive content. It is helpful, for example, if sequential materials are so organized that they become progressively more differentiated in terms of generality and inclusiveness, and if similarities and differences between the current learning task and previous learnings are explicitly delineated.[4] Both of these aims can be accomplished by using an advance organizer or brief introductory passage before each new unit of material, which both makes available relevant explanatory principles at a high level of abstraction and increases discriminability. Programmed instruction can also be especially adapted to meet the greater needs of culturally deprived pupils for concrete-empirical props in learning relational propositions.

Although programmed instruction in general is particularly well suited to the needs of the culturally deprived child, I cannot recommend the small-frame format characteristic of

3. D. P. Ausubel and D. Fitzgerald, "Organizer, General Background, and Antecedent Learning Variables in Sequential Verbal Learning," *Journal of Educational Psychology,* LIII, 1962, 243–9.

4. D. P. Ausubel, "The Use of Advance Organizers in the Learning and Retention of Meaningful Verbal Learning," *Journal of Educational Psychology,* LI, 1960, 267–72; D. P. Ausubel and D. Fitzgerald, "The Role of Discriminability in Meaningful Verbal Learning and Retention," *Journal of Educational Psychology,* LII, 1961, 266–74, and their "Organizer, General Background, and Antecedent Learning Variables in Sequential Verbal Learning," *op. cit.*

teaching-machine programs and most programmed textbooks. In terms of both the logical requirements of meaningful learning and the actual size of the task that can be conveniently accommodated by the learner, the frame length typically used by teaching machines is artifically and unnecessarily abbreviated. It tends to fragment the ideas presented in the program so that their interrelationships are obscured and their logical structure is destroyed.[5] Hence it is relatively easy for less able students to master each granulated step of a given program without understanding the logical relationships and development of the concepts presented.[6] In my opinion, therefore, the traditional textbook format or oral didactic exposition that follows the programming principles outlined above, supplemented by frequent self-scoring and feedback-giving tests, is far superior to the teaching-machine approach for the actual presentation of subject-matter content.[7]

MOTIVATIONAL CONSIDERATIONS

Thus far I have considered various environmental factors that induce retardation in the culturally deprived child's intellectual growth, as well as different cognitive techniques of counteracting and reversing such retardation. These factors and techniques, however, do not operate in a motivational vacuum. Although it is possible separately to consider cognitive and motivational aspects of learning for purposes of theoretical analysis, they are nonetheless inseparably intertwined in any real-life learning situation. For example, school failure and loss of confidence resulting from an inappropriate curriculum further depress the culturally deprived pupil's motivation to learn and thereby increase his existing learning and intellectual

5. S. L. Pressey, "Basic Unresolved Teaching-Machine Problems," *Theory into Practice,* I, 1962, 30–7.

6. D. G. Beane, "A Comparison of Linear and Branching Techniques of Programed Instruction in Plane Geometry," *Technical Report, No. 1,* Urbana: Training Research Laboratory, University of Illinois, July 1962.

7. Pressey, *op. cit.*

deficit. Similarly, although a number of practice and task variables are potentially important for effective learning in a programmed instruction context, appropriate manipulation of these variables can, in the final analysis, only insure successful long-term learning of subject matter provided that the individual is adequately motivated.

Doing without being interested in what one is doing results in relatively little permanent learning, since it is reasonable to suppose that only those materials can be meaningfully incorporated on a long-term basis into an individual's structure of knowledge that are relevant to areas of concern in his psychological field. Learners who have little need to know and understand quite naturally expend little learning effort; manifest an insufficiently meaningful learning set; fail to develop precise meanings, to reconcile new ideas with existing concepts, and to formulate new propositions in their own words; and do not devote enough time and energy to practice and review. Material is therefore never sufficiently consolidated to form an adequate foundation for sequential learning.

The problem of reversibility exists in regard to the motivational as well as in regard to the cognitive status of the culturally deprived pupil, inasmuch as his environment typically stunts not only his intellectual development, but also the development of appropriate motivations for academic achievement. Motivations for learning, like cognitive abilities are only potential rather than inherent or endogenous capacities in human beings; their actual development is invariably dependent upon adequate environmental stimulation. Cognitive drive or intrinsic motivation to learn, for example, is probably derived in a very general sense from curiosity tendencies and from related predispositions to explore, manipulate, and cope with the environment; but these tendencies and predispositions are only actualized as a result of successful exercise and the anticipation of future satisfying consequences from further exercise and as a result of internalization of the values of those significant persons in the family and subcultural community with whom the child identifies.

Intrinsic motivation

The development of cognitive drive or of intrinsic motivation for learning, that is, the acquisition of knowledge as an end in itself or for its own sake, is, in my opinion, the most promising motivational strategy which we can adopt in relation to the culturally deprived child. It is true, of course, in view of the anti-intellectualism and pragmatic attitude toward education that is characteristic of lower-class ideology,[8] that a superficially better case can be made for the alternative strategy of appealing to the incentives to job acquisition, retention, and advancement that now apply so saliently to continuing education because of the rapid rate of technological change. Actually, however, intrinsic motivation for learning is more potent, relevant, durable, and easier to arouse than its extrinsic counterpart. Meaningful school learning, in contrast to most kinds of laboratory learning, requires relatively little effort or extrinsic incentive, and, when successful, furnishes its own reward. In most instances of school learning, cognitive drive is also the only immediately relevant motivation, since the greater part of school learning cannot be rationalized as necessary for meeting the demands of daily living. Furthermore, it does not lose its relevance or potency in later adult life when utilitarian and career advancement considerations are no longer applicable. Lastly, as we know from the high dropout rate among culturally deprived high-school youth, appeals to extrinsic motivation are not very effective. Among other reasons, the latter situation reflects a limited time perspective focused primarily on the present; a character structure that is oriented more to immediate than delayed gratification of needs; the lack of strong internalized needs for and anxiety about high academic and vocational achievement, as part of the prevailing family, peer group, and community ideology;[9] and the seeming

8. F. Riessman, *The Culturally Deprived Child,* New York: Harper & Bros., 1962.

9. A. Davis, "Child Training and Social Class," *Child Behavior and Development,* ed. R. G. Barker, J. S. Kounin, and H. F. Wright, New York: McGraw-Hill Book Co., 1963, pp. 607–20.

unreality and impossibility of attaining the rewards of prolonged striving and self-denial in view of current living conditions and family circumstances, previous lack of school success,
and the discriminatory attitudes of middle-class society.[10]

If we wish to develop the cognitive drive so that it remains
viable during the school years and in adult life, it is necessary
to move still further away from the educational doctrine of
gearing the curriculum to the spontaneously expressed interests,
current concerns, and life-adjustment problems of pupils. Although it is undoubtedly unrealistic and even undesirable in
our culture to eschew entirely the utilitarian, ego-enhancement,
and anxiety-reduction motivations for learning, we must place
increasingly greater emphasis upon the value of knowing and
understanding as goals in their own right, quite apart from
any practical benefits they may confer. Instead of denigrating
subject-matter knowledge, we must discover more efficient
methods of fostering the long-term acquisition or meaningful
and usable bodies of knowledge, and of developing appropriate
intrinsic motivations for such learning.

It must be conceded at the outset that culturally deprived
children typically manifest little intrinsic motivation to learn.
They come from family and cultural environments in which
the veneration of learning for its own sake is not a conspicuous
value, and in which there is little or no tradition of scholarship.
Moreover, they have not been notably successful in their previous learning efforts in school. Nevertheless we need not
necessarily despair of motivating them to learn for intrinsic
reasons. Psychologists have been emphasizing the motivation-
learning and the interest-activity sequences of cause and effect
for so long that they tend to overlook their reciprocal aspects. Since motivation is not an indispensable condition for
short-term and limited-quantity learning, it is not necessary
to postpone learning activities until appropriate interests and
motivations have been developed. Frequently the best way of
motivating an unmotivated pupil is to ignore his motivational
state for the time being and concentrate on teaching him as

10. *Ibid.*

effectively as possible. Much to his surprise and to his teacher's, he will learn despite his lack of motivation; and from the satisfaction of learning he will characteristically develop the motivation to learn more.

Paradoxically, therefore, we may discover that the most effective method of developing intrinsic motivation to learn is to focus on the cognitive rather than on the motivational aspects of learning, and to rely on the motivation that is developed retroactively from successful educational achievement. This is particularly true when a teacher is able to generate contagious excitement and enthusiasm about the subject he teaches, and when he is the kind of person with whom culturally deprived children can identify. Recruiting more men teachers and dramatizing the lives and exploits of cultural, intellectual, and scientific heroes can also enhance the process of identification. At the same time, of course, we can attempt to combat the anti-intellectualism and lack of cultural tradition in the home through programs of adult education and cultural enrichment.

Extrinsic motivation

The emphasis I have placed on intrinsic motivation for learning should not be interpreted to mean that I deny the importance of developing extrinsic motivations. The need for ego enhancement, status, and prestige through achievement, the internalization of long-term vocational aspirations, and the development of such implementing traits as responsibility, initiative, self-denial, frustration tolerance, impulse control, and the ability to postpone immediate hedonistic gratification are, after all, traditional hallmarks of personality maturation in our culture; and educational aspirations and achievement are both necessary prerequisites for, and way-station prototypes of, their vocational counterparts. Hence, in addition to encouraging intrinsic motivation for learning, it is also necessary to foster ego-enhancement and career-advancement motivations for academic achievement.

As previously pointed out, however, the current situation with respect to developing adequate motivations for higher academic and vocational achievement among culturally deprived children is not very encouraging. But just as in the case of cognitive drive, much extrinsic motivation for academic success can be generated retroactively from the experience of current success in schoolwork. Intensive counseling can also compensate greatly for the absence of appropriate home, community, and peer-group support and expectations for the development of long-term vocational ambitions. In a sense counselors must be prepared to act *in loco parentis* in this situation. By identifying with a mature, stable, striving, and successful male adult figure, culturally deprived boys can be encouraged to internalize long-term and realistic aspirations, as well as to develop the mature personality traits necessary for their implementation. Hence, as a result of achieving current ego enhancement in the school setting, obtaining positive encouragement and practical guidance in the counseling relationship, and experiencing less rejection and discrimination at the hands of school personnel, higher vocational aspirations appear to lie more realistically within their grasp. Further encouragement to strive for more ambitious academic and vocational goals can be provided by making available abundant scholarship aid to universities, to community colleges, and to technical institues; by eliminating the color, ethnic, and class bar in housing, education, and employment; by acquainting culturally deprived youth with examples of successful professional persons originating from their own racial, ethnic, and class backgrounds; and by involving parents sympathetically in the newly fostered ambitions of their children. The success of the Higher Horizons project indicates that an energetic program organized along the lines outlined above can do much to reverse the effects of cultural deprivation on the development of extrinsic motivations for academic and vocational achievement.